THE WHOLESALE-BY-MAIL CATALOG

By THE PRINT PROJECT

LOWELL MILLER, Executive Producer PRUDENCE McCULLOUGH, Editor

St. Martin's Press / New York

Copyright © 1979 by Lowell Miller
All rights reserved. For information, write:
St. Martin's Press, Inc., 175 Fifth Avenue, New York, N.Y. 10010.
Manufactured in the United States of America
Library of Congress Catalog Card Number:

Library of Congress Cataloging in Publication Data

The Print Project.
  The wholesale-by-mail catalog.

  1. Catalogs, Commercial. 2. Advertising, Direct-
mail—United States. 3. Wholesale trade—United States
—Directories. I. Miller, Lowell. II. McCullough,
Prudence. III. Title.
HF5861.P72 1979   659.13′3   78-21204
ISBN 0-312-87762-5
ISBN 0-312-87763-3 pbk.

The WHOLESALE-BY-MAIL CATALOG is a resource for the general public. Companies in this catalog are listed at the sole discretion of the editors, and no advertising fees are solicited or accepted.

CONTENTS

INTRODUCTION

This catalog is a door. Behind the door, which you have just opened, are bargains.

In our competitive economy, you seldom need to pay the full "retail" price ordinarily charged in stores. Somewhere there is someone who will sell almost any product cheaper. Yet it often takes days, even weeks, of sidewalk pounding to uncover genuine bargains—the search is not always worth the savings. And if you live away from the major commercial centers, really low prices may be simply unavailable.

There is a solution to the problems of quest and/or unavailability. It is mail order business.

You can purchase almost anything by mail. And, because mail order suppliers have low overhead and often skip a middleman or two, you can buy things much cheaper. Starting from that premise we asked ourselves, "Just how much cheaper is it to shop by mail? Can you get prices so low you are actually buying at, or close to, the wholesale price?"

The answer is yes. You can avoid the retailer's mark-up, even if you are an individual desiring only one item, through mail order purchasing from selected suppliers. If you want to "get it wholesale," this catalog will show you where and how. Whether it's worms, stereos, craft supplies, sweaters, magnets, tropical fish, Tibetan boots, burglar alarms, solar panels, hearing aids, gems, jewelry, watches, cameras, antiques, or pulsating shower heads, you can buy whatever you need for anywhere from 30% to a full 90% off the retail price you would have to pay in a store.

And *that's* wholesale. Though the retail mark-up varies on different products, the most common figure is about 30%; so we drew our cut-off line at that point. In other words, if a product sells for $10 in a store, the store owner paid about $7 for it; maybe a little more, maybe a little less, depending upon what the item is. Using THE WHOLESALE-BY-MAIL CATALOG you'll pay what the retailer does, *before* he adds on his profit. Even "sale" prices will rarely be as low as the prices to be found from sources in this book.

Just one more note: *please* read our explanations of the listings and our simple codes before you begin. You'll find it much easier to understand what you're reading. Happy bargain hunting, then, and look for our address on the Feedback Page if you feel like contacting us.

The Print Project

Lowell Miller
Executive Producer

Prudence McCullough
Editor

1

LISTINGS EXPLANATION

In choosing companies for the listings in this catalog, we followed two guidelines.

1) Either they must sell brand names at a minimum of 30% off list, or

2) They must sell an equivalent to a brand name whose price is 30% less than that of the brand name. There are some rare cases in which the discount may be not quite this high. These listings are for products that absolutely cannot be purchased by individuals at any lower price.

Where specific discounts are not listed, you should assume that the discount on at least several items is 30% or more below retail. To establish retail prices we used manufacturers suggested list or typical selling prices in New York City retail stores. We tried to cover as broad a range as possible. Some brands or kinds of products simply are not available by mail and/or at significant discounts.

IMPORTANT: In some cases our sources would not ordinarily offer acceptable discounts to meet the 30% guideline, but said they would offer special discounts to readers of THE WHOLE-SALE-BY-MAIL CATALOG. Be alert for an indication of a special WBMC reader discount, listed in the margin between the left and right hand information columns. You MUST mention WBMC to receive the special price. (We cannot guarantee how long these companies will keep the special offer open—policies and prices are, of course, always subject to change.) In general, mention WBMC when ordering—sellers often like to know the source of their customers.

ORGANIZATION OF LISTINGS

The listings are organized according to general product categories. A company receives a full listing in its main category, and a less complete listing for additional products it may sell in other categories. For example, Icemart sells beautiful sweaters as their main product, so their main listing will be found in CLOTHING, FURS, AND ACCESSORIES. However, Icemart also sells a knitting kit which is found in CRAFTS AND HOBBIES, gourmet food which is found in FOOD AND DRINK, fur rugs and pillows which are located in HOME, silver jewelry listed in JEWELRY, GEMS, AND WATCHES, and volcanic pottery in HANDICRAFTS AND NATIVE PRODUCTS.

In Icemart's main listing you will be referred to the other categories in which Icemart appears, and in Icemart's minor listings you will be sent to the main listing for further information. In each chapter the listings are placed alphabetically.

It's important to look at the cross references if you plan to write a company for its catalog, since some companies put out separate catalogs for each line of products and you might as well get all of their catalogs in one mailing.

Since companies are constantly revising their catalogs and printing new ones, you will sometimes have to be patient. Whenever we were able to determine when new catalogs are issued, we have included this information in the listings. Some products, you should note, like tulip bulbs, can only be ordered at certain times of the year.

Some companies do not issue catalogs at all. These operate under a price-quote system: you must tell them the exact make and model number of the item you want and they will give you a price, either by mail or by phone. Businesses that operate this way are clearly marked in the listings. Often these price-quote businesses have the lowest prices, selling well below both the formal manufacturers suggested list prices and below the less formal minimum prices that some manufacturers try to enforce.

In a few cases the very best prices are to be found from companies who require a minimum dollar order, though most listings in this book have no such minimum. Don't be put off by a minimum requirement. If you want something that's a real bargain, chances are you'll have friends or work associates who'll want it too. Ask around. Even if you can't find someone to go in with you, remember that a great buy can also be a great gift, and you can stock up on a supply of that special product. This will also keep you one small step ahead of inflation.

A NOTE ABOUT SPECIFIC PRICES: Our criterion for selecting companies centers on percentage discounts; 30% off today ought to be 30% off tomorrow, or next year, even if prices change, unless profit margins become squeezed. Ordinarily most sellers set their prices in relation to the rest of the market. When you do see specific prices, though, please keep in mind that we live in a time of nasty inflation. Prices are liable to change by the time this catalog reaches you.

A CAVEAT: THE WHOLESALE-BY-MAIL CATALOG is intended as a resource, pointing you to the bargains available by mail. You *should not* simply pick a company and send your money. Always write first and get a catalog and up-to-date price quotes, and be sure to follow each company's ordering and payment instructions.

THE LISTING CODE

To save time and space, and avoid excessive repetition, you will find that some of the information is presented in a *simple* coded form. The inside column of each page includes comments and remarks when such are called for, and there are no code abbreviations in this area. The outside column includes all the "hard" factual information, encoded as follows:

Left Hand Column

1) **Company name, address, and phone**

2) **Catalog and cost for it; price quote; SASE—send stamped self-addressed envelope**

3) **Discount level—stated in main listing**

4) **Kind of goods sold—name brand or house brand**

5) **Minimum order, if any**

6) **Shipping costs and method of payment**

   a) **FOB—you pay freight and postage, usually from a designated city, as in "FOB Chicago."**

   b) **Prepaid—Company pays freight**

   c) **Included—Company pays freight**

   d) **UPS—United Parcel Service**

   e) **PP—Parcel Post**

   f) **REA—Railway Express**

   g) **Surface—surface mail**

   h) **Air—air mail**

7) **Sales Tax or Duty, where applicable—if the company is in your state, you will have to add sales tax**

8) **Return Policy—guarantees and warranties; who is responsible and for how long**

9) **Payment**

   a) **Check—personal check**

   b) **MO—money order (virtually always accepted)**

   c) **IMO—international money order**

   d) **Bank Draft—certified or cashier's check**

   e) **MC—Mastercharge**

   f) **BA and VISA—Visa is the new name of Bankamericard, but sellers have been slow to change to the new name in their catalogs and advertising.**

   g) **DC—Diner's Club**

   h) **AE—American Express**

   i) **C.O.D.—cash on delivery**

   j) **L/C—Letter of credit**

10) **Resale/Tax Exemption Number or Business Letterhead—see the special section on these topics in the Process Introduction.**

THE DOLLAR CODE: The dollar code represents our opinion of the overall "worth" of the listing for the average bargain hunter. That is, we take into account the quality of the products, their availability, ease of ordering, completeness and range of catalog, and, of course, price. The final judgment is somewhat subjective, but after you've analyzed as many companies as we have, certain ones simply stand out and others fade away.

Four "dollar signs" is the top rating; 1 dollar sign is the lowest rating. *But* a low rating may mean no more than that a company only has one or two worthwhile products at low prices—not necessarily that it's a poor source for these products. There has to be some way of separating the thrilling bargain suppliers from the merely good ones.

A few companies lack a dollar sign rating. One problem or another caused us to feel it would not be fair to give a rating. For example, price-quote businesses were hard to check up on without actually buying a tremendous amount of merchandise, and where would we put fifty-two color TVs? The lack of a dollar code rating should not be considered a poor rating of a business. All it means is that we did not feel, for whatever reason, qualified to make a judgment. Companies to whom we were able to give a clear "poor" rating were *eliminated* from the catalog.

All prices and percentage discounts are based on our research as of February 1, 1979.

THE COMPLETE GUIDE TO BUY-ING BY MAIL

If you don't know UPS from PP, or what FOB factory means, this section will prove an invaluable tool in untangling the confusion that can sometimes occur when you buy by mail order. Armed with knowledge and patience, you will be prepared to conquer the world of mail order bargains and emerge victorious—a satisfied customer reaping huge savings.

Read this section before you order a catalog or do anything else. It will save you time, and it may save you even more money.

CATALOGS, PRICE QUOTES, and INFORMATION

CATALOGS: Most mail order firms issue catalogs, which can range in volume and sophistication from mimeographed one-sheet price lists to lavish books with hundreds of color photographs and detailed descriptions. Many are free, and none here are higher than $5 (usually for huge furniture catalogs). If the catalog's price is listed as refundable, this means that the company will credit the price of the catalog to your first order.

When you write for a catalog, write a complete letter stating which catalog you want (some firms have several), and *always include your return address in the letter.* Please refer to WBMC as your source, as it may qualify you for discounts with several of the firms listed here. You should make a point of mentioning any enclosures of coin or checks, so they won't be overlooked. Date the letter and make a carbon or xerox. You'll find that getting into the habit of keeping complete records of all mail order correspondence will prove helpful later.

If the catalog costs under $1.00, send coins taped securely between thick pieces of cardboard. For catalogs costing $1.00 or more, send a money order, since personal checks will take 2 weeks to clear. Never send stamps to any company, unless they request them. When ordering a catalog from a foreign firm, use an International Money Order (IMO), or International Reply Coupons (IRCs). IRCs cost 42¢, and equal 18¢ in value. IMOs cost 90¢ for orders up to $10, $1.10 for orders of $11 to $50, and $1.40 for orders of $51 to $400. Use IRCs when they are requested or the catalog costs 35¢ or less; if it costs more, it's cheaper to use an IMO. If you must send a personal check, add $1.00 for the foreign bank charges the shop will have to pay on clearing your check, and allow extra time.

Sometimes the company specifies an SASE instead of a catalog charge. This is a stamped, self-addressed envelope, and it saves the company the cost of postage. When you send an SASE, use a long business envelope, address it to yourself clearly, *stamp* it, and include with it a letter requesting the catalog.

When a foreign firm offers a catalog at air mail and surface mail rates, spend a little more and get it sent by air; surface mail can take a long, long time—sometimes two months or more.

PRICE QUOTES: Many companies dealing in cameras, appliances, electronics, audio equipment, clothing, auto parts, and leather goods use price quotes exclusively when selling by mail. They almost always carry name brand goods, and request that you send them model or style numbers of the products you want so that they can make the price quotes. Most of the companies will make quotes over the phone, but a letter is cheaper, unless the firm has a WATS line. To get the model numbers, style numbers, colors, sizes, etc., you must first find the item in a store or in a catalog. Copy down all the information about the items or items that you can find, and write it all out clearly. Leave space on the letter so the company can enter the price—they often don't have the time to write out another letter. If you do decide to phone for price quote, be sure to have all this information in front of you. *Don't* make collect calls.

REQUESTING INFORMATION: There are a very few firms that are small, or do custom orders, to whom you must write with your specific requests in order to find out what they have or whether they can get something for you. Whether it's a handmade quilt or a 16th-century Japanese print that you're interested in, you must be sure to be very descriptive and include all the information that could possibly help the company serve you. Send pictures, drawings, or photos of what you need. Since whoever you're writing to may have to answer many letters like yours, be patient and allow extra time.

HOW TO ORDER

ORDERING: The first thing you should do upon receipt of your catalog is note the date on which you received it, and see how long it took the company to reply. In many cases this is the amount of time it will take for mailed packages to reach you (especially from Europe).

When selecting merchandise, take note of the units; that is, whether the items are sold individually or in dozens, lots of 50, etc. Make sure you're aware of the minimum orders, if there are any.

If a firm offers quantity discounts, they may apply only to specific items or there may be a minimum number or dollar amount you must buy to get the discount. Read the catalog carefully. Check THE WHOLESALE-BY-MAIL CATALOG entry for the company to see whether they might offer a special WBMC reader discount. If they do, figure the discount on the company's regular catalog price—they usually can't afford *both* a quantity discount and the WBMC discount. See the listings for specific cases.

When the firm advises it, give second choices; and if you want them to make substitutions, you must authorize the company on the order form to make them.

INSURANCE, PACKING, HANDLING, AND SALES TAX: The charges for insurance, packing, and handling are usually nominal, and are often figured into the transportation costs. *Always ask whether insurance is included, and request it if it isn't.* The small cost is worth it—something you know if you've ever had an uninsured shipment damaged or ruined in transit. Add sales tax if applicable: you add it if they request it, or if you live in the state where the firm or any of its branches is located.

SHIPPING: Orders from U.S. companies are delivered either by the Postal Service (Parcel Post), the United Parcel Service (UPS), or by truckers. Orders that weigh up to 50 pounds can go by PP or UPS, but there are also some restrictions on the size of the package (consult UPS for these).

• UPS: The amount of postage you are charged on packages sent by UPS is determined by where you live, where the company that is sending your goods is located, and the dimensions and weight of the package.

UPS has divided the country into 63 sections. Each section has a zoning chart that breaks down the rest of the country into seven zones (which run from "zone 2" to "zone 8") according to distance, via the first three digits of the zip code.

The system works like this: a firm located in New York City uses a zone chart that lists New York City zip codes (prefix 100—) as the #2, or closest zone, and California zip codes (prefix 900—) as the #8, or farthest zone. In California, 900— prefix zip codes are in zone 2, while New York zip code prefixes are in zone 8.

To translate these zone numbers into shipping costs, you must consult the Common Carrier Rate Chart (see sample chart on p. 16). This chart lists rates for packages weighing up to 50 lbs., from zone 2 to zone 8. Naturally, the lowest charge is on a shipment of 1 lb. to zone 2, and the highest is on a shipment of 50 lbs. to zone 8.

Some firms will include all the rate charts you need to figure postage, while others will state at the bottom of their order forms "Add enough for postage and insurance. We will refund overpayment." When a firm leaves it up to you, you should call your local UPS office to find out what zone you are in in relation to the company, and request a rate chart so you can figure costs down to the penny. We have included UPS rate charts on pp. 16-17 to give you an idea of the costs, but be sure to check with your local UPS office for the most up-to-date rates.

● PARCEL POST (PP): The costs for PP are somewhat higher than those for UPS, but there is one distinct advantage: *only packages sent by Parcel Post can be delivered to a pot office box.* (UPS must have a street address to deliver goods to.) If you are having a package delivered to a post office box, in order to avoid delays and the possibility that the package will be returned to the company if sent by UPS, write DELIVERY BY PARCEL POST ONLY; UPS NOT ACCEPTABLE in bold red letters on the order form. On the check, write GOODS TO BE DELIVERED BY PARCEL POST ONLY. When the company endorses or cashes the check, they are implicitly agreeing to this and must send the order by Parcel Post.

Some companies determine postage on a flat rate, which saves you the trouble of estimating costs. The goods will still be delivered by either UPS or PP, and will be subject to the same limitations.

Consult your local post office for Parcel Post rates, as these are generally more subject to change than UPS.

● TRUCKERS: When the company specifies that goods must be sent by truck, or if you have a combined order with goods that are both mailable (under 50 lbs., in general) and nonmailable, the entire order will go by truck. Truck charges are always collected upon delivery. Since truck charges are based on weight and distance, the additional expense is a real factor to consider when ordering very heavy items from a firm located far from you. A typical minimum charge for orders up to 100 pounds is $20, with an additional charge of $7 or more for home delivery. If you can pick up your order at the truck terminal, you will save that much. There is also a fee for delivery notification. For exact fees, you should consult your local carrier.

The term "FOB factory" stands for "free on board," and the location listed after it (for instance, FOB Chicago) is the place from which the goods are shipped, either by mail or truck, depending on which is cheaper.

For very heavy shipments, up to a maximum of 500 pounds, you can contact the REA Express instead of a trucker and have the goods delivered by their trucks or by air freight. If you live close to an airport and near the company shipping the goods, REA Express can be cheaper than local carriers, and most goods will take only one to three days to arrive.

When the carrier arrives, you must pay the charges with cash or a certified check—no personal checks.

FOREIGN ORDERS: When placing an order with a company in Europe, India, or another corner of the earth, remember that there are fundamental differences in foreign sizing systems, measurements, and color descriptions (see the chart on p. 21 for equivalent sizings). Always measure yourself before you order clothing, and use metric tables to convert inches into centimeters. If you are unsure of the European measurement, give the exact body measurements and the company will determine what size it is. When ordering shoes and gloves, send tracings of your hands or feet. If you are ordering clothing or home furnishings and want to get an exact color match, ask for swatches, or send a swatch to be matched.

A few European shops list prices in their own currency. You must obtain a conversion table in order to price the goods and order, or write to the firm and ask for prices, shipping, and insurance costs in dollars. We have included a conversion chart on pp. 20-21 to give you a rough idea of foreign currency values. You can get up-to-date conversion tables from Perera, 636 Fifth Avenue, New York, New York 10020; or get the current rate of exchange from a bank.

Foreign orders get away without state sales taxes, but make up for it with duty charges. Duty is usually charged on the *wholesale* value of the goods (the invoice accompanying the goods shipped into the U.S. states this value), and you should write for booklets listing common rates of duty before you order so you can get at least an approximation of the cost. There are some items such as perfumes, cameras, and watches that can't be brought into this country unless their trademarks are removed. There are also some products from certain developing countries that can come into the country free of duty. For booklets with all the information you'll need, write to the Office of Information and Publication, Bureau of Customs, Dept. of the Treasury, Washington, DC 20226. Ask for "Rates of Duty For Popular Tourist Items," and "Know Before You Go," for duty rates and import information; "U.S. Customs Trademark Information" for details on trademarks; and "GSP and the Traveler" for information on duty-free products from developing countries. You can't import things like narcotics, fireworks, and pornography; certain other items require permits for importation. If you are interested in importing fruits, vegetables, or plants, you should write to Quarantines, Dept. of Agriculture, Federal Center Bld., Hyattsville, MD 20782, for an application for an import permit.

Request all the forms and information you need before you order. Remember that duty is payable only at customs by you or someone acting as your agent, so *don't* pay it to the firm you're ordering from.

PAYMENT: Each company lists its preferred methods of payment. A few companies accept only certified checks, but most will take your personal check or money order, and many accept interbank charge cards (Mastercharge, Visa, American Express, etc.). Each method of payment has its own advantages and drawbacks, and can affect how long it takes to receive your goods.

Most firms accept *personal checks*, but often require that you allow two weeks for the check to clear before they send out the order. This is the cheapest means of payment for you, and should be used for goods ordered in the U.S. only, as there are more efficient methods for paying foreign companies.

Money orders from banks or the post office are also good for paying U.S. orders and, since they are equivalent to cash, don't take any time to clear. A typical *bank* money order costs 50¢ for any amount up to $1,000, and, like a check, can be stopped if you have to cancel the order (time to stop is the same as for a check). *Postal* money orders are comparable in price and also convenient.

Stamps and *currency* should never be sent through the mails, except in small amounts for catalog costs.

The Post Office sells *International Money Orders (IMOs)* which are accepted almost anywhere and are good for paying for orders in foreign countries. They cost from 90¢ to $1.40 for amounts up to $400. When a foreign firm specifies money orders, this is the only kind to send.

Sending a *bank draft* (or transfer or certified check) is the closest you can come to sending cash by mail. To get a draft, you pay the amount you want to send plus a mailing charge and a service fee to your bank in the U.S. You send a copy of the draft form to the firm's bank overseas and to the firm itself. The company will take their form to their bank, match it with the other form, and collect the funds. The fees start at about $2.25, and the money will reach the foreign bank as quickly as a letter does— anywhere from one to two weeks.

If you are in a big hurry, you can *cable* money to your firm's bank, and straight into their account if you know the number. You pay your bank the amount you want sent plus a service fee (about $3.50 and up), and they transfer the money from their bank into the one overseas, which takes two days at most. Then the bank notifies the firm of the payment, and they can ship your goods.

Paying for anything *C.O.D.* is not recommended because it incurs more costs; but if you want to have goods delivered this way, remember that most firms require a deposit of 10% to 50%

on C.O.D. orders before they will ship them, and you must have cash or a certified check ready when the goods are delivered.

When you are sending any kind of payment to India, send it via *registered mail.* Every firm we corresponded with in India indicated that mail is frequently tampered with there, and money in any form is likely to be stolen if sent unregistered.

Charge cards are very convenient methods of payment, but can also be very expensive. Unless you pay the charge card bill quickly, the finance charges can cancel out half of your discounts, and so the cards are not recommended if you want to hold down expenses. If you do use a charge card, include the full account number as it appears on your card, the expiration date, bank numbers (appearing on Master Charge), and your signature as it appears on the card itself. Note that there may be a minimum dollar order for use of charge cards.

RESALE NUMBERS AND LETTERHEAD: In order to get really low discounts from some firms, you are sometimes required to write to them on stationery with a business letterhead and/or to state your resale or tax exemption number.

To be eligible for a resale number you must have a business, using the number to buy goods for resale and "not for personal use." Usually you must post bond anywhere from $50 to $150, against the taxes you are supposed to collect and turn over to the state. By forming a cooperative, you could legitimately hold a resale number, buy and sell goods to members, collect taxes, and still get tremendous discounts even after the taxes. To get a resale number, call or write to your local department of licensing and ask them to send you the forms and requirements.

You can also obtain from your department of licensing a license to do business as a firm. You can then "do business as" a given name—i.e., John and Mary Smith might get a license to do business as "MaryJo Interiors." The license enables you to use a business letterhead legitimately, but you aren't required to actually *do* any business (check the regulations in your area concerning this).

If you want to place an order with a firm that requires resale numbers or a letterhead and you have neither, ask them if you can place a *sample order.* This is a small order not subject to the minimums that businesses usually have to meet when buying from wholesalers. U.S. firms will often fill sample orders in the hopes of developing new dealers, while European firms and Asian firms often play a little game in which they *want* you to request a sample order so that they can sell retail at wholesale prices without risking the wrath of their regular dealer accounts. In many cases you will only be able to place a sample order once, but you may be able to get just what you need in that order, and at tremendous discounts.

If you *do* establish some kind of business (and it can be very, very small), you will be able to go *beyond* this catalog and buy things direct from the many wholesalers in your area who do not sell by mail to the public. Again, a cooperative as a business with a resale number can be extremely useful.

RECEIVING YOUR ORDER

DELAYED ORDERS: Keeping careful records of your orders will come in handy if your order is delayed. Be aware that the (U.S.) company *must* respond to your order within 30 days by either sending it, explaining any delays, or returning your payment. Call or write the company if you haven't heard within 30 days, give them the order number and the items you requested and ask for an explanation.

When you receive your order, open it carefully. Save all the wrappers and cartons, and report any damages, short shipments, and other problems to the shippers immediately. See the section titled *Refunds, Returns, and Defective Merchandise* for further information.

DELIVERY OF FOREIGN SHIPMENTS: Anything sent by mail from a foreign country passes through customs. Duty-free packages are passed from customs to the Postal Service and are then forwarded to you with no additional charges incurred. If the package contains dutiable items, however, the customs officer will attach a form to the package stating how much duty is due, and then pass the package to the Postal Service. Your postman will collect the duty, plus a postal handling fee.

Freight shipments have to clear customs at the first port of arrival, or you can have the merchandise forwarded in customs custody (bond) from the port of arrival to another customs port of entry for customs clearance. You must make all the arrangements for forwarding, or have a freight forwarder do it. This will entail freight forwarding charges, inland transportation costs, broker's fees, insurance, and delivery charges. Larger, freight-shipped items from overseas can get tricky. If the shipment is valued at $250 or more, you should use a customs broker. Typical fees for the broker's services are $85 to $90, but you can get discount rates of $50 to $75 from the Bruce Duncan Co., Inc., 1 World Trade Center, Suite 1453, New York, New York 10048; telephone: (212) 432-0037.

When you hire a broker to handle the shipment, be sure to write to the "Officer in Charge of Customs" at the port of arrival with authorization for the broker to act as your agent. The foreign firm will send you a bill of lading and an invoice when they are ready to ship your goods. You should send copies to your broker, who will send you a bill for his fee, transportation costs, duty, etc. You *must* pay this before your shipment reaches port. If the broker has not been paid and your shipment arrives with no one to pick it up, it will be put into storage after five days at your expense. So as soon as the invoices arrive from the company, send them to the broker and pay him by certified check to avoid delays.

REFUNDS, RETURNS, and DEFECTIVE MERCHANDISE

CANCELING YOUR ORDER: If you decide to cancel your order, the FTC requires that your refund be sent to you within seven days. See section on *Complaints*, below, for information on what to do if you don't receive the refund.

RETURNS: Return policies vary from company to company. Some give you thirty day trial periods with no-questions-asked refunds; some require that returns be authorized (which means writing a letter detailing the reason for the returns and getting permission from the company to send the merchandise back); and some firms don't allow any returns at all. *Read their policy before ordering, and save the original boxes an wrappings*—some firms accept returns only when packed in the boxes in which they were sent. Anything you send back will be at your own expense.

COMPLAINTS: If you have a complaint about the goods or the firm, the first thing to do is write the firm a letter stating the problem and what you would like done about it. If you don't get any action, write again. If, after the second complaint, you get no response, write to the U.S. Postal Service, the Federal Trade Commission (FTC), or the Direct Mail/Marketing Association. The Postal Service investigates *every* complaint, and resolves about 85% of the problems, partly because they have the power to withold mail delivery to a company if it doesn't cooperate.

The FTC investigates companies with profiles of bad service and frauds, but probably won't offer immediate action. To lodge a complaint with the FTC, write to the Bureau of Consumer Protection, Federal Trade Commission, Washington, DC 20580.

The Direct Mail/Marketing Association is a trade organization whose members make up about 70% of major U.S. mail order businesses. DMMA will help by referring complaints to appropriate agencies and by putting pressure on the offending firm. Write to them at Mail Order Action Line, DMMA, 6 East 43rd St., New York, New York 10017.

REORDERING: If you want to order from a company again, you should request the current catalog if yours is over a year old or if the dollar has devalued, and especially if the dollar is worth more—the prices will then be lower in other countries.

GUARANTEES AND WARRANTIES: The simplest guarantee, and one offered by many stores, is "satisfaction guaranteed or your money back." This means that if you are not pleased with the product, you can return it for a refund, exchange, or credit. Sometimes the guarantee is conditional or limited to very specific uses or functions of the product; and sometimes it's a no-questions-asked policy. To prepare for the possibility that you might want to return something you have ordered by mail, you should be famiiar with the company's rules regarding guarantees and returns. Most returns must be authorized; that is, you must write to the company and receive permission to return the goods. Sometimes you will have to pay a "restocking" charge, and almost always you have to pay the return postage and insurance. Remembering to keep all the wrapping and the original carton and invoices will make returns much easier.

Warranties are basically the same as guarantees, but usually cover the life and function of a particular item rather than all the goods a manufacturer produces. (In this catalog, we refer to guarantee or warranty based on the term the seller has chosen to use.) Warranty information is included with products that are covered by them, and detail the limits of use of the product, its ideal operating conditions, and conditions that would invalidate the warranty. For instance, immersing many electrical appliances in water will immediately void the guarantee. Warranties usually run from ninety days on goods with a high rate of failure after that point, to five and even ten years for goods that have proven durability records. Products covered by a warranty are usually accompanied by a postcard which you then fill out and send to the manufacturer or head service station. A warranty is not valid unless the manufacturer has received the completed postcard.

The most important thing to remember when you are buying a warrantied item is to read the details of the warranty very carefully and try to discern the real value in terms of time covered, percentage of the item's parts covered, and how difficult it will be to have it honored.

United Parcel Service

COMMON CARRIER RATE CHART

ANY FRACTION OF A POUND OVER THE WEIGHT SHOWN TAKES THE NEXT HIGHER RATE

WEIGHT NOT TO EXCEED	RATES TO							WEIGHT NOT TO EXCEED	RATES TO						
	ZONE 2	ZONE 3	ZONE 4	ZONE 5	ZONE 6	ZONE 7	ZONE 8		ZONE 2	ZONE 3	ZONE 4	ZONE 5	ZONE 6	ZONE 7	ZONE 8
1 lb.	$.82	$.84	$.87	$.90	$.94	$.99	$1.04	26 lb.	$2.67	$3.14	$3.89	$4.70	$5.87	$7.06	$8.49
2 "	.89	.93	.99	1.05	1.14	1.23	1.34	27 "	2.74	3.23	4.01	4.85	6.06	7.31	8.79
3 "	.97	1.02	1.11	1.20	1.34	1.47	1.64	28 "	2.82	3.32	4.13	5.00	6.26	7.55	9.09
4 "	1.04	1.11	1.23	1.35	1.53	1.72	1.94	29 "	2.89	3.41	4.25	5.15	6.46	7.79	9.39
5 "	1.11	1.20	1.35	1.50	1.73	1.96	2.23	30 "	2.96	3.50	4.37	5.30	6.65	8.03	9.68
6 "	1.19	1.30	1.47	1.66	1.93	2.20	2.53	31 "	3.04	3.60	4.50	5.46	6.85	8.28	9.98
7 "	1.26	1.39	1.59	1.81	2.12	2.45	2.83	32 "	3.11	3.69	4.62	5.61	7.05	8.52	10.28
8 "	1.34	1.48	1.71	1.96	2.32	2.69	3.13	33 "	3.19	3.78	4.74	5.76	7.25	8.76	10.58
9 "	1.41	1.57	1.83	2.11	2.52	2.93	3.43	34 "	3.26	3.87	4.86	5.91	7.44	9.01	10.88
10 "	1.48	1.66	1.95	2.26	2.71	3.17	3.72	35 "	3.33	3.96	4.98	6.06	7.64	9.25	11.17
11 "	1.56	1.76	2.08	2.42	2.91	3.42	4.02	36 "	3.41	4.06	5.10	6.22	7.84	9.49	11.47
12 "	1.63	1.85	2.20	2.57	3.11	3.66	4.32	37 "	3.48	4.15	5.22	6.37	8.03	9.74	11.77
13 "	1.71	1.94	2.32	2.72	3.31	3.90	4.62	38 "	3.56	4.24	5.34	6.52	8.23	9.98	12.07
14 "	1.78	2.03	2.44	2.87	3.50	4.15	4.92	39 "	3.63	4.33	5.46	6.67	8.43	10.22	12.37
15 "	1.85	2.12	2.56	3.02	3.70	4.39	5.21	40 "	3.70	4.42	5.58	6.82	8.62	10.46	12.66
16 "	1.93	2.22	2.68	3.18	3.90	4.63	5.51	41 "	3.78	4.52	5.71	6.98	8.82	10.71	12.96
17 "	2.00	2.31	2.80	3.33	4.09	4.88	5.81	42 "	3.85	4.61	5.83	7.13	9.02	10.95	13.26
18 "	2.08	2.40	2.92	3.48	4.29	5.12	6.11	43 "	3.93	4.70	5.95	7.28	9.22	11.19	13.56
19 "	2.15	2.49	3.04	3.63	4.49	5.36	6.41	44 "	4.00	4.79	6.07	7.43	9.41	11.44	13.86
20 "	2.22	2.58	3.16	3.78	4.68	5.60	6.70	45 "	4.07	4.88	6.19	7.58	9.61	11.68	14.15
21 "	2.30	2.68	3.29	3.94	4.88	5.85	7.00	46 "	4.15	4.98	6.31	7.74	9.81	11.92	14.45
22 "	2.37	2.77	3.41	4.09	5.08	6.09	7.30	47 "	4.22	5.07	6.43	7.89	10.00	12.17	14.75
23 "	2.45	2.86	3.53	4.24	5.28	6.33	7.60	48 "	4.30	5.16	6.55	8.04	10.20	12.41	15.05
24 "	2.52	2.95	3.65	4.39	5.47	6.58	7.90	49 "	4.37	5.25	6.67	8.19	10.40	12.65	15.35
25 "	2.59	3.04	3.77	4.54	5.67	6.82	8.19	50 "	4.44	5.34	6.79	8.34	10.59	12.89	15.64

ADDITIONAL CHARGES:
For each COD received for collection — 85 cents.
For each Address Correction — 85 cents.
For each Acknowledgment of Delivery (AOD) — 20 cents.
For each package with a declared value over $100 — 25 cents for each additional $100 or fraction thereof.

WEIGHT AND SIZE LIMITS:
Maximum Weight per package — 50 POUNDS.
Maximum Weight of all packages from one shipper to one consignee in one day — 100 pounds.
Maximum Size per package — 108 INCHES IN LENGTH AND GIRTH COMBINED.
Minimum charge for a package measuring over 84 inches in length and girth combined will be equal
  to charge for a package weighing 25 pounds.

UPS ZONE CHART FOR NEW YORK CITY AREA

UPS United Parcel Service

ZONE CHART — For Shippers With Zip Codes 100-01 to 108-99

TERRITORY SERVED — 48 CONTINENTAL UNITED STATES

TO DETERMINE ZONE TAKE FIRST THREE DIGITS OF ZIP CODE TO WHICH PARCEL IS ADDRESSED AND REFER TO CHART BELOW

ZIP CODE PREFIXES	UPS ZONE	ZIP CODE PREFIXES	UPS ZONE	ZIP CODE PREFIXES	UPS ZONE	ZIP CODE PREFIXES	UPS ZONE	ZIP CODE PREFIXES	UPS ZONE	ZIP CODE PREFIXES	UPS ZONE
010-013	2	100-127	2	200-218	3	335-338	5	410-418	4	654-655	5
014	3	128-136	3	219	2	339	6	420-427	5	656-676	6
015-018	2	137-139	2	220-238	3	350-364	5	430-458	4	677-679	7
019	3	140-149	3	239-253	4	365-366	6	460-466	5	680-692	6
020-024	2	150-154	4	254	3	367-374	5	467-468	4	693	7
025-026	3	155	3	255-266	4	376	4	469	5	700-722	6
027-029	2	156	4	267	3	377-386	5	470	4	723-724	5
030-033	3	157-159	4	268-288	4	387	6	471-472	5	725-738	7
034	3	160-162	4	289	5	388-389	4	473	4	739	7
035-043	3	163	3	290-293	4	390-392	6	474-479	5	740-762	6
044	4	164-165	4	294	5	393	5	480-489	4	763-770	7
045	3	166-169	3	295-297	4	394-396	6	490-491	5	773	6
046-049	4	170-171	2	298-299	5	397	5	492	4	774-775	7
050-051	3	172-174	3	300-324	5	400-402	5	493-499	5	776-777	6
052-053	2	175-176	2	325	6	403-406	4	500-503	6	778-797	7
054-059	3	177	3	326-329	5	407-409	5	504	5	798-799	8
060-089	2	178-199	2	330-334	6			505	6	800-812	7
								506-507	5	813	8
								508-516	6	814	7
								520-539	5	815	8
								540	6	816-820	7
								541-549	5	821	8
								550-554	5	829-874	7
								556-559	5	875-877	7
								560-576	6	878-880	8
								577	7	881-884	7
								580-585	6	890-898	8
								586-593	7	900-961	8
								594-599	8	970-986	6
										988-994	8

UPS ZONE CHART FOR LOS ANGELES AREA

UPS United Parcel Service

ZONE CHART — For Shippers With Zip Codes 900-01 to 900-99

TO DETERMINE ZONE TAKE FIRST THREE DIGITS OF ZIP CODE TO WHICH PARCEL IS ADDRESSED AND REFER TO CHART BELOW

ZIP CODE PREFIXES	UPS ZONE	ZIP CODE PREFIXES	UPS ZONE	ZIP CODE PREFIXES	UPS ZONE
010-089	8	506-507	7	778-789	6
100-199	8	508-516	6	790-791	5
200-299	8	520-560	7	792	6
300-339	8	561	6	793-794	5
350-359	7	562-567	7	795-796	6
360-364	8	570-581	6	797-799	5
365-367	7	582	7	800-838	5
368	8	583-588	6	840-863	4
369-372	7	590-591	5	864	3
373-379	8	592-593	6	865	4
380-384	7	594	5	870-871	5
385	8	595	6	873-874	4
386-397	7	596-599	5	875-884	5
400-402	7	600-639	7	890-891	3
403-418	8	640-648	6	893-898	4
420-424	7	650-652	7	900-935	2
425-426	7	653	6	936-939	3
427	7	654-655	7	940-949	6
430-458	8	656-676	6	950-953	3
460-466	7	677	5	954-961	4
467-468	8	678	6	970-974	5
469	7	679	5	975-976	4
470	8	680-692	6	977-986	5
471-472	8	693	5	988-994	5
473	8	700-708	7		
474-479	7	710-711	7		
480-497	8	712-717	7		
498-499	7	718-719	6		
500-504	7	720-725	7		
505	6	726-738	6		
		739	5		
		740-775	6		
		776-777	7		

LOCAL ZONE

See separate list for Points in Los Angeles Local Zone

U.S. POSTAL RATES

FIRST CLASS

Letter Rates
1st ounce .... 15¢
Each add'l ounce .... 13¢

Over 12 ounces .... Priority mail (heavy pieces) rates apply.

Single postal cards sold by the post office .... 10¢ each.

Double postal cards sold by the post office .... 10¢ each half.

Single post cards .... 10¢ each.

Double post cards (reply half of double post card does not have to bear postage when originally mailed) ..... 10¢ each half.

Presort rate .... Consult Postmaster

Business reply mail .... Consult Postmaster

SECOND CLASS

(Newspapers and periodicals with second-class mail privileges).

Copies mailed by public: 10¢ for first 2 ounces, 6¢ each additional ounce or fraction thereof, or the applicable fourth-class rate, whichever is lower.

THIRD CLASS

Circulars, books, catalogs, and other printed matter; merchandise, seeds, cuttings, bulbs, roots, scions, and plants, weighing less than 16 ounces.

SINGLE PIECE RATE*

0 to 2 ozs.	$0.20	Over 8 to 10 ozs.	$0.79
Over 2 to 4 ozs.	0.40	Over 10 to 12 ozs.	0.92
Over 4 to 6 ozs.	0.53	Over 12 to 14 ozs.	1.05
Over 6 to 8 ozs.	0.66	Over 14 to 15.99 ozs.	1.18

BULK RATE
CONSULT POSTMASTER

*Over 14 ounces, use the 4th class zone rate if lower.

MONEY ORDERS

Amount of money order	Amount of fee Domestic
$0.01 to $10	$0.55
$10.01 to $50	0.80
$50.01 to $400.00	1.10

INSURANCE

For Coverage Against Loss or Damage

Fees (in addition to postage)

LIABILITY	FEE
$0.01 to $15	$0.50
15.01 to 50	0.85
50.01 to 100	1.10
100.01 to 150	1.40
150.01 to 200	1.75
200.01 to 300	2.25
300.01 to 400	2.75

COD Consult postmaster for fees and conditions of mailing

CERTIFIED MAIL For proof of mailing and delivery

Fee (in addition to postage) $0.80
Restricted delivery 0.80
Return receipts:
Requested at time of mailing:
  Showing to whom and when delivered 0.45
  Showing to whom, when and address where delivered .. 0.55
Requested after mailing:
  Showing to whom and when delivered 2.10

REGISTRY For maximum protection and security

Value	FEES (in addition to postage)	
	For articles not covered by commercial or other insurance	For articles also covered by commercial or other insurance
$0.00 to $100	$3.00	$3.00
$100.01 to $200	3.30	3.30
$200.01 to $400	3.70	3.70
$400.01 to $600	4.10	4.10
$600.01 to $800	4.50	4.50
$800.01 to $1,000	4.90	4.90
$1,000.01 to $2,000	$5.30	$4.90 plus handling charge of 35¢ per $1,000 or fraction over first $1,000

For higher values—Consult Postmaster

U.S. POSTAL RATES

FOURTH CLASS
(Parcel Post) Zone Rates
Consult Postmaster for weight and size

Weight 1 pound and not exceeding (pounds)	Local	Zones 1 & 2	Zone 3	Zone 4	Zone 5	Zone 6	Zone 7	Zone 8
2	$1.15	$1.35	$1.39	$1.56	$1.72	$1.84	$1.98	$2.22
3	1.23	1.45	1.53	1.73	1.86	2.04	2.24	2.61
4	1.29	1.56	1.65	1.82	2.00	2.23	2.50	3.00
5	1.36	1.66	1.77	1.92	2.14	2.43	2.77	3.39
6	1.42	1.71	1.84	2.01	2.28	2.62	3.03	3.78
7	1.47	1.76	1.90	2.11	2.41	2.82	3.29	4.17
8	1.51	1.80	1.97	2.20	2.55	3.02	3.56	4.56
9	1.54	1.85	2.03	2.29	2.69	3.21	3.82	4.95
10	1.57	1.89	2.10	2.39	2.83	3.41	4.08	5.34
11	1.60	1.94	2.17	2.50	3.00	3.65	4.42	5.73
12	1.64	1.98	2.22	2.56	3.09	3.77	4.57	6.12
13	1.67	2.02	2.27	2.63	3.17	3.89	4.72	6.41
14	1.70	2.05	2.32	2.69	3.25	3.99	4.86	6.62
15	1.73	2.09	2.36	2.74	3.33	4.09	4.99	6.80
16	1.76	2.13	2.41	2.80	3.40	4.19	5.11	6.98
17	1.79	2.16	2.45	2.85	3.47	4.28	5.23	7.15
18	1.82	2.20	2.49	2.91	3.54	4.37	5.34	7.31
19	1.86	2.23	2.53	2.96	3.61	4.46	5.45	7.47
20	1.89	2.27	2.58	3.01	3.67	4.54	5.55	7.62
21	1.92	2.30	2.62	3.06	3.74	4.62	5.66	7.76
22	1.95	2.34	2.66	3.14	3.85	4.78	5.80	7.90
23	1.98	2.37	2.72	3.25	3.99	4.96	6.02	8.03
24	2.01	2.44	2.80	3.35	4.12	5.13	6.24	8.16
25	2.04	2.51	2.89	3.46	4.26	5.31	6.46	8.28
26	2.07	2.58	2.97	3.56	4.39	5.48	6.68	8.40
27	2.11	2.65	3.06	3.67	4.53	5.66	6.90	8.52
28	2.14	2.72	3.14	3.77	4.66	5.83	7.12	8.63
29	2.17	2.79	3.23	3.88	4.80	6.01	7.34	8.75
30	2.20	2.86	3.31	3.98	4.93	6.18	7.56	8.85
31	2.68	3.09	3.46	4.09	5.07	6.36	7.78	9.41
32	2.71	3.12	3.49	4.19	5.20	6.53	8.00	9.51
33	2.74	3.16	3.57	4.30	5.34	6.71	8.22	9.61
34	2.77	3.19	3.65	4.40	5.47	6.88	8.44	9.80
35	2.80	3.22	3.74	4.51	5.61	7.06	8.66	10.06
36	2.83	3.28	3.82	4.61	5.74	7.23	8.88	10.32
37	2.86	3.35	3.91	4.72	5.88	7.41	9.10	10.58
38	2.89	3.42	3.99	4.82	6.01	7.58	9.32	10.84
39	2.93	3.49	4.08	4.93	6.15	7.76	9.54	11.10
40	2.96	3.56	4.16	5.03	6.28	7.93	9.76	11.36
41	2.99	3.63	4.25	5.14	6.42	8.11	9.98	11.62
42	3.02	3.70	4.33	5.24	6.55	8.28	10.20	11.88
43	3.05	3.77	4.42	5.35	6.69	8.46	10.42	12.14
44	3.08	3.84	4.50	5.45	6.82	8.63	10.64	12.40
45	3.11	3.91	4.59	5.56	6.96	8.81	10.86	12.66
46	3.14	3.98	4.67	5.66	7.09	8.98	11.08	12.92
47	3.17	4.05	4.76	5.77	7.23	9.16	11.30	13.18
48	3.20	4.12	4.84	5.87	7.36	9.33	11.52	13.44
49	3.23	4.19	4.93	5.98	7.50	9.51	11.74	13.70
50	3.27	4.26	5.01	6.08	7.63	9.68	11.96	13.96
51	3.30	4.33	5.10	6.19	7.77	9.86	12.18	14.22
52	3.33	4.40	5.18	6.29	7.90	10.03	12.40	14.48
53	3.36	4.47	5.27	6.40	8.04	10.21	12.62	14.74
54	3.39	4.54	5.35	6.50	8.17	10.38	12.84	15.00
55	3.42	4.61	5.44	6.61	8.31	10.56	13.06	15.26
56	3.45	4.68	5.52	6.71	8.44	10.73	13.28	15.52
57	3.48	4.75	5.61	6.82	8.58	10.91	13.50	15.78
58	3.51	4.82	5.69	6.92	8.71	11.08	13.72	16.04
59	3.54	4.89	5.78	7.03	8.85	11.26	13.94	16.30
60	3.57	4.96	5.86	7.13	8.98	11.43	14.16	16.56
61	3.60	5.03	5.95	7.24	9.12	11.61	14.38	16.82
62	3.64	5.10	6.03	7.34	9.25	11.78	14.60	17.08
63	3.67	5.17	6.12	7.45	9.39	11.96	14.82	17.34
64	3.70	5.24	6.20	7.55	9.52	12.13	15.04	17.60
65	3.73	5.31	6.29	7.66	9.66	12.31	15.26	17.86
66	3.76	5.38	6.37	7.76	9.79	12.48	15.48	18.12
67	3.79	5.45	6.46	7.87	9.93	12.66	15.70	18.38
68	3.82	5.52	6.54	7.97	10.06	12.83	15.92	18.64
69	3.85	5.59	6.63	8.08	10.20	13.01	16.14	18.90
70	3.88	5.66	6.71	8.18	10.33	13.18	16.36	19.16

Exception: Parcels weighing less than 15 pounds. and measuring over 84 inches but not exceeding 100 inches in length and girth combined. are chargeable with a minimum rate equal to that for a 15 pound parcel for the zone to which addressed. See Postal Service Manual section 135.3 for size and weight restrictions.

Consult postmaster for rates on bound printed matter and other exceptions.

PRIORITY MAIL (HEAVY PIECES)

Weight over 12 oz. but not exceeding (pounds)	Local 1, 2 & 3	Zone 4	Zone 5	Zone 6	Zone 7	Zone 8
1.0	$1.71	$1.81	$1.88	$1.97	$2.06	$2.25
1.5	1.86	1.96	2.07	2.21	2.34	2.50
2.0	1.99	2.12	2.27	2.44	2.61	2.83
2.5	2.11	2.27	2.46	2.68	2.89	3.16
3.0	2.23	2.42	2.65	2.91	3.17	3.50
3.5	2.35	2.58	2.84	3.15	3.45	3.83
4.0	2.47	2.73	3.03	3.38	3.73	4.16
4.5	2.59	2.89	3.22	3.62	4.01	4.50
5	2.72	3.04	3.42	3.85	4.29	4.83
6	2.96	3.35	3.80	4.32	4.84	5.50
7	3.20	3.66	4.18	4.79	5.40	6.16
8	3.44	3.96	4.56	5.26	5.96	6.83
9	3.69	4.27	4.95	5.73	6.51	7.49
10	3.93	4.58	5.33	6.20	7.07	8.16
11	4.17	4.89	5.71	6.67	7.63	8.83
12	4.42	5.20	6.10	7.14	8.18	9.49
13	4.66	5.50	6.48	7.61	8.74	10.16
14	4.90	5.81	6.86	8.08	9.30	10.82
15	5.15	6.12	7.25	8.55	9.86	11.49
16	5.39	6.43	7.63	9.02	10.41	12.16
17	5.63	6.74	8.01	9.49	10.97	12.82
18	5.87	7.04	8.39	9.96	11.53	13.49
19	6.12	7.35	8.78	10.43	12.08	14.15
20	6.36	7.66	9.16	10.90	12.64	14.82
21	6.60	7.97	9.54	11.37	13.20	15.49
22	6.85	8.28	9.93	11.84	13.75	16.15
23	7.09	8.58	10.31	12.31	14.31	16.82
24	7.33	8.89	10.69	12.78	14.87	17.48
25	7.58	9.20	11.08	13.25	15.43	18.15
26	7.82	9.51	11.46	13.72	15.98	18.82
27	8.06	9.82	11.84	14.19	16.54	19.48
28	8.30	10.12	12.22	14.66	17.10	20.15
29	8.55	10.43	12.61	15.13	17.65	20.81
30	8.79	10.74	12.99	15.60	18.21	21.48
31	9.03	11.05	13.37	16.07	18.77	22.15
32	9.28	11.36	13.76	16.54	19.32	22.81
33	9.52	11.66	14.14	17.01	19.88	23.48
34	9.76	11.97	14.52	17.48	20.44	24.14
35	10.01	12.28	14.91	17.95	21.00	24.81
36	10.25	12.59	15.29	18.42	21.55	25.48
37	10.49	12.90	15.67	18.89	22.11	26.14
38	10.73	13.20	16.05	19.36	22.67	26.81
39	10.98	13.51	16.44	19.83	23.22	27.47
40	11.22	13.82	16.82	20.30	23.78	28.14
41	11.46	14.13	17.20	20.77	24.34	28.81
42	11.71	14.44	17.59	21.24	24.89	29.47
43	11.95	14.74	17.97	21.71	25.45	30.14
44	12.19	15.05	18.35	22.18	26.01	30.80
45	12.44	15.36	18.74	22.65	26.57	31.47
46	12.68	15.67	19.12	23.12	27.12	32.14
47	12.92	15.98	19.50	23.59	27.68	32.80
48	13.16	16.28	19.88	24.06	28.24	33.47
49	13.41	16.59	20.27	24.53	28.79	34.13
50	13.65	16.90	20.65	25.00	29.35	34.80
51	13.89	17.21	21.03	25.47	29.91	35.47
52	14.14	17.52	21.42	25.94	30.46	36.13
53	14.38	17.82	21.80	26.41	31.02	36.80
54	14.62	18.13	22.18	26.88	31.58	37.46
55	14.87	18.44	22.57	27.35	32.14	38.13
56	15.11	18.75	22.95	27.82	32.69	38.80
57	15.35	19.06	23.33	28.29	33.25	39.46
58	15.59	19.36	23.71	28.76	33.81	40.13
59	15.84	19.67	24.10	29.23	34.36	40.79
60	16.08	19.98	24.48	29.70	34.92	41.46
61	16.32	20.29	24.86	30.17	35.48	42.13
62	16.57	20.60	25.25	30.64	36.03	42.79
63	16.81	20.90	25.63	31.11	36.59	43.46
64	17.05	21.21	26.01	31.58	37.15	44.12
65	17.30	21.52	26.40	32.05	37.71	44.79
66	17.54	21.83	26.78	32.52	38.26	45.46
67	17.78	22.14	27.16	32.99	38.82	46.12
68	18.02	22.44	27.54	33.46	39.38	46.79
69	18.27	22.75	27.93	33.93	39.93	47.45
70	18.51	23.06	28.31	34.40	40.49	48.12

Exception: Parcels weighing less than 15 pounds, and measuring over 84 inches but not exceeding 100 inches in length and girth combined, are chargeable with a minimum rate equal to that for a 15-pound parcel for the zone to which addressed.

CURRENCY CONVERSION CHARTS*

Europe

Austria	Belgium	Czecho-slovakia*	Denmark	Finland	France	U.S.A.
Schilling Groschen	Franc Centime	Koruna Heller	Króner Ore	Markka Penni	Franc Centime	Dollar Cent
(S1=$.07)	(F1=$.0325)	(K1=$.10)	(K1=$.19)	(M1=$.25)	(F1=$.24)	$=
.70	1.55	.50	.25	.20	.25	.05
1.45	3.10	1.00	.50	40	50	.10
3.55	7.70	2.50	1.30	1.00	1.21	.25
7.15	15.40	5.00	2.60	2.00	2.45	.50
10.70	23.10	7.50	3.95	3.00	3.05	.75
14.30	30.75	10.00	5.25	4.00	4.85	1.00
28.60	61.55	20.00	10.55	8.00	9.70	2.00
42.85	92.30	30.00	15.80	12.00	14.55	3.00
71.40	153.85	50.00	26.30	20.00	24.25	5.00
107.15	230.75	75.00	39.45	30.00	36.40	7.50
142.85	307.70	100.00	52.60	40.00	48.50	10.00
214.30	461.55	150.00	78.95	60.00	72.75	15.00
285.70	615.40	200.00	105.25	80.00	97.00	20.00
357.15	769.20	225.00	131.60	100.00	121.25	25.00
428.60	923.10	300.00	157.90	120.00	145.50	30.00
571.45	1,230.80	400.00	210.50	160.00	194.00	40.00
714.30	1,538.45	500.00	263.15	200.00	242.50	50.00
1,071.45	2,307.70	750.00	394.75	300.00	363.75	75.00
1,428.60	3,076.95	1,000.00	526.30	400.00	485.00	100.00
3,571.45	7,692.30	2,500.00	1,315.80	1,000.00	1,212.50	250.00

Europe

Norway	Poland*	Portugal	Rou-mania*	Russia*	Spain	U.S.A.
Kroner Ore	Zloty Groszy	Escudo Centavo	Leu Bani	Ruble Kopeck	Peseta Centimo	Dollar Cent
(K1=$.20)	(Z1=$.03)	(E1=$.03)	(L1=$.08)	(R1=$1.45)	(P1=$.0135)	$=
25	1.65	2.03	60	.03	3.70	.05
50	3.30	4.05	1.20	.07	7.40	.10
1.25	8.30	10.15	3.00	.15	18.50	.25
2.50	16.65	20.25	6.00	35	37.05	.50
3.75	25.00	30.40	9.00	.50	55.55	.75
5.00	33.30	40.50	12.00	.70	74.10	1.00
10.00	66.65	81.00	24.00	1.40	148.15	2.00
15.00	100.00	121.50	36.00	2.05	222.20	3.00
25.00	166.65	202.50	60.00	3.45	370.35	5.00
37.50	250.00	303.75	90.00	5.15	555.55	7.50
50.00	333.30	405.00	120.00	6.90	740.75	10.00
75.00	500.00	607.50	180.00	10.35	1,111.10	15.00
100.00	666.65	810.00	240.00	13.80	1,481.50	20.00
125.00	833.30	1,012.50	300.00	17.25	1,851.85	25.00
150.00	1,000.00	1,215.00	360.00	20.70	2,222.20	30.00
200.00	1,333.30	1,620.00	480.00	27.60	2,963.00	40.00
250.00	1,666.65	2,025.00	600.00	34.50	3,703.70	50.00
375.00	2,500.00	3,037.50	900.00	51.70	5,555.55	75.00
500.00	3,333.30	4,050.00	1,200.00	69.00	7,407.40	100.00
1,250.00	8,333.30	10,125.00	3,001.00	172.40	18,518.50	250.00

Europe

Germany* East	Germany West	Gr. Britain	Greece	Holland	Hungary*	Italy
Ostmark Pfennig	Mark Pfennig	Pound Pence	Drachma Lepta	Guilder Cent	Forint Filler	Lire
(M1=$.52)	(DM1=$.52)	(£1=$2.00)	(D1=$.03)	(G1=$.48)	(F1=$.05)	(L1=.0012)
.10	.10	03	1.80	.10	1.03	41.65
.20	.20	05	3.60	.20	2.06	83.30
.50	.50	13	8.95	.50	5.15	208.30
95	95	25	17.85	1.05	10.31	416.65
1.45	1.45	40	26.80	1.55	15.46	625.00
1.90	1.90	.50	35.70	2.10	20.62	833.30
3.85	3.85	1.00	71.40	4.15	41.25	1,666.65
5.75	5.75	1 50	107.10	6.25	61.85	2,500.00
9.60	9.60	2.50	178.50	10.40	103.10	4,166.65
14.40	14.40	3.75	267.75	15.60	154.65	6,250.00
19.20	19.20	5.00	357.00	20.80	206.20	8,333.30
28.85	28.85	7.50	535.50	31.25	309.30	12,500.00
38.45	38.45	10.00	714.00	41.65	412.40	16,666.65
48.05	48.05	12.50	892.50	52.10	515.45	20,833.30
57.70	57.70	15.00	1,071.00	62.50	618.55	25,000.00
76.90	76.90	20.00	1,428.00	83.30	824.75	33,333.30
96.15	96.15	25.00	1,785.00	104.15	1,030.95	41,666.65
144.20	144.20	37.50	2,677.50	156.25	1,546.40	62,500.00
192.30	192.30	50.00	3,570.00	208.30	2,061.85	83,333.30
480.75	480.75	125.00	8,925.00	520.80	5,154.65	208,333.30

Europe/Middle East

Sweden	Switzer-land	Yugo-slavia	Iran*	Israel	Saudi Arabia	Turkey*
Kroner Ore	Franc Centime	Dinar Para	Rial Dinar	Pound Agorot	Riyal Halala	Lira Kurus
(K1=$.22)	(F1=$.63)	(D1=$.06)	(R1=$.014)	(£1=$.06)	(R1=$.30)	(L1=$.042)
.23	08	.80	3.50	83	.15	1.20
.45	15	1.65	7.00	1.66	30	2.40
1.15	40	4.15	17.50	4.15	80	5.95
2.25	80	8.30	35.00	8.30	1.65	11.90
3.40	1.20	12.50	52.50	12.50	2.50	17.85
4.55	1.60	16.65	70.00	16.65	3.30	23.80
9.10	3.20	33.30	140.00	33.30	6.65	47.60
13.65	4.75	50.00	210.00	50.00	10.00	71.40
22.70	7.95	83.30	350.00	83.30	16.65	119.05
34.10	11.90	125.00	525.00	125.00	25.00	178.55
45.45	15.85	166.65	700.00	166.65	33.30	238.10
68.20	23.80	250.00	1,050.00	250.00	50.00	357.15
90.90	31.75	333.30	1,400.00	333.30	66.65	476.20
113.65	39.70	416.65	1,750.00	416.65	83.30	595.25
136.35	47.60	500.00	2,100.00	500.00	100.00	714.30
181.80	63.50	666.65	2,820.00	666.65	133.30	952.40
227.25	79.35	833.30	3,500.00	833.30	166.65	1,190.50
340.90	119.05	1,250.00	5,250.00	1,250.00	250.00	1,785.70
454.55	158.70	1,666.65	7,000.00	1,666.65	333.30	2,380.95
1,136.35	396.80	4,166.65	17,500.00	4,166.65	833.30	5,952.40

Latin America

Argentina	Brazil*	Chile*	Colombia*	Costa Rica	Ecuador	U.S.A.
Peso Centavo	Cruzeiro Centavo	Peso Centesimo	Peso Centavo	Colon Centimo	Sucre Centavo	Dollar Cent
(P1=$.001)	(C1=$.055)	(P1=$.03)	(P1=$.03)	C1=$.12)	($1=$.04)	$=
50.00	.90	1.65	1.83	.43	1.25	.05
100.00	1.80	3.35	3.66	.86	2.50	.10
250.00	4.55	8.35	9.16	2.14	6.25	.25
500.00	9.10	16.65	18.32	4.29	12.50	.50
750.00	13.65	25.00	27.47	6.43	18.75	.75
1,000.00	18.20	33.35	36.63	8.58	25.00	1.00
2,000.00	36.35	66.65	73.25	17.15	50.00	2.00
3,000.00	54.55	100.00	109.90	25.75	75.00	3.00
5,000.00	90.90	166.65	183.15	42.90	125.00	5.00
7,500.00	136.35	250.00	274.75	64.30	187.50	7.50
10,000.00	181.80	333.35	366.30	85.75	250.00	10.00
15,000.00	272.70	500.00	549.45	128.65	375.00	15.00
20,000.00	363.65	666.65	732.60	171.55	500.00	20.00
25,000.00	454.55	833.35	915.75	214.40	625.00	25.00
30,000.00	545.45	1,000.00	1,098.90	257.30	750.00	30.00
40,000.00	727.25	1,333.35	1,465.20	343.05	1,000.00	40.00
50,000.00	909.10	1,666.65	1,831.50	428.80	1,250.00	50.00
75,000.00	1,363.65	2,500.00	2,747.25	643.20	1,875.00	75.00
100,000.00	1,818.20	3,333.35	3,663.00	857.65	2,500.00	100.00
250,000.00	4,545.45	8,333.35	9,157.50	2,144.10	6,250.00	250.00

*Indicates official government rate. Rates for all other countries are the market rates as of the date of printing.

Metric Equivalents

Weights

U.S.	U.S.
Ounce = 28.35 grams	1 gram = .04 ounce
Pound = .45 kilogram	1 kilogram = 2.20 pounds
Ton = .91 metric ton	1 metric ton = 1.10 tons

Length

U.S.	U.S.
Inch = 2.54 centimeters	1 centimeter = .39 inch
Foot = .30 meter	1 meter = 3.28 feet
Yard = .91 meter	1 meter = 1.09 yards
Mile = 1.61 kilometer	1 kilometer = .62 mile

To convert from kilometers to miles, divide the number of kilometers by 8 and multiply the result by 5.

Liquid Measure

U.S.	U.S.
Pint = .47 liter	1 liter = 2.11 Pints
Quart = .95 liter	1 liter = 1.06 Quarts
Gallon = 3.79 liter	1 liter = .26 Gallon

Temperature

Centigrade		Fahrenheit	
0°	(Freezing point)	32°	To compute to Fahrenheit: Multiply Centigrade by 1.8 and add 32.
5°		41°	To compute to Centigrade: Subtract 32 from Fahrenheit and divide by 1.8
10°		50°	
20°		68°	
30°		86°	
37°	(Normal body temp.)	98°	
40°		104°	
50°		122°	
60°		140°	
70°		158°	
80°		176°	
90°		194°	
100°	(Boiling point)	212°	

Clothing Sizes

MEN

Suits and Coats

American and British	34	36	38	40	42	44	46		
Continental	44	46	48	50	52	54	56		

Shirts

American and British	14	14½	15	15½	16	16½	17		
Continental	36	37	38	39	41	42	43		

Shoes

American	7	7½	8	8½	9	9½	10	10½	11
British	6½	7	7½	8	8½	9	9½	10	10½
Continental	39	40	41	42	43		44		45

Socks

American and British	9½	10	10½	11	11½	12	12½
Continental	39	40	41	42	43	44	45

Hats

American	6⅝	6¾	6⅞	7	7⅛	7¼	7⅜	7½
British	6½	6⅝	6¾	6⅞	7	7⅛	7¼	7⅜
Continental	53	54	55	56	57	58	59	60

(All size equivalents are approximate.)

Glove Sizes are the same as in the U.S.A. for men and women.

WOMEN

Blouses and Sweaters

American	32	34	36	38	40	42	44
British	34	36	38	40	42	44	46
Continental	40	42	44	46	48	50	52

Dresses and Coats

American	8	10	12	14	16	18	20
British	30	32	34	36	38	40	42
Continental	36	38	40	42	44	46	48

Shoes

American	5	5½	6	6½	7	7½	8	8½	9
British	3½	4	4½	5	5½	6	6½	7	7½
Continental	36		37		38		39		40

Stockings

American and British	8	8½	9	9½	10	10½
Continental	0	1	2	3	4	5

Deak-Perera
FOREIGN MONEY CONVERTER

*IMPORTANT NOTE: All currency values fluctuate. You must write to Deak & Co., Deak-Perera Building, 29 Broadway, New York, New York 10006, for a copy of the current conversion chart, or inquire at your local bank. Always use the current rate of exchange when ordering.

RATES OF DUTY ON IMPORTED GOODS*

ALCOHOLIC BEVERAGES

	Int. Rev. Tax	Customs duty
Beer	$ 9 bbl. (31 gal.)	6¢ per gal.
Brandy	$10.50*	50¢* to $5*
Gin	$10.50*	50¢*
Liqueurs	$10.50*	50¢*
Rum	$10.50*	$1.75*
Whisky*		
Scotch	$10.50*	51¢*
Irish	$10.50*	51¢*
Other	$10.50*	62¢*
Wine		
Sparkling	$2.40 to $3.40	$1.17
Still	17¢ to $2.25	31½¢ to $1

* Per U.S. gallon (128 fluid ounces) if under 100 proof. Duty and tax are based on proof gallon if 100 proof or over.

ANTIQUES produced prior to 100 years before the date of entry—Free
(Have proof of antiquity obtained from seller.)

AUTOMOBILES, passenger—3%

BAGS, hand, leather—8½ to 10%

BAMBOO, manufactures of—12½%

BEADS:
Imitation precious and semi-precious stones—7 to 13%
Ivory—10%

BINOCULARS, prism—20%
Opera and field glasses—8½%

BOOKS:
Foreign author or foreign language—Free

CAMERAS:
Motion picture, over $50 each—6%
Still, over $10 each—7½%
Cases, leather—8½ to 10%
Lenses—12½%

CANDY:
Sweetened chocolate bars—5%
Other—7%

CHESS SETS—10%

CHINA:
Bone—17½%
Nonbone, other than tableware—22½%

CHINA TABLEWARE, nonbone, available in 77-piece sets
Valued not over $10 per set—10¢ doz. + 48%
Valued over $10 but not over $24 per set—10¢ doz. + 55%
Valued over $24 but not over $56 per set—10¢ doz. + 36%
Valued over $56 per set—5¢ doz. + 18%

CIGARETTE LIGHTERS:
Pocket, valued at over 42¢ each—22½%
Table—12%

CLOCKS:
Valued over $5 but not over $10 each—75¢ + 16% + 6¼¢ for each jewel
Valued over $10 each—$1.12 ea. + 16% + 6¼¢ for each jewel

CORK, manufactures of—18%

DOLLS AND PARTS—17½%

DRAWINGS (works of art):
Original—Free
Copies, done entirely by hand—Free

EARTHENWARE TABLEWARE, available in 77-piece sets
Valued not over $3.30 per set—5¢ doz. + 14%
Valued over $3.30 but not over $22 per set—10¢ doz. + 21%
Valued over $22 per set—5¢ doz. + 10½%

FIGURINES, china—12½ to 22½%

FILM, imported, not qualifying for free entry is dutiable as follows:
Exposed motion-picture film in any form on which pictures or sound and pictures have been recorded, developed or not developed, is dutiable at 48/100ths of a cent per linear foot.
Other exposed or exposed and developed film would be classifiable as photographs, dutiable at 4% of their value.

FLOWERS, artificial, plastic—21%

FRUIT, prepared—35% or under

FUR:
Wearing apparel—8½ to 18½%
Other manufactures of—8½ to 18½%

FURNITURE:
Wood, chairs—8½%
Wood, other than chairs—5%

GLASS TABLEWARE valued not over $1 each—20 to 50%

GLOVES:
Not lace or net, plain vegetable fibers, woven—25%
Wool, over $4 per dozen—37½¢ lb. + 18½%
Fur—10%
Horsehide or cowhide—15%

GOLF BALLS—6%

HANDKERCHIEFS:
   Cotton, hand embroidered—4¢ ea. + 40%
   Cotton, plain—25%
   Other vegetable fiber, plain—9%

IRON, travel type, electric—5½%

IVORY, manufactures of—6%

JADE:
   Cut, but not set and suitable for use in the
      manufacture of jewelry—2½%
   Other articles of jade—21%

JEWELRY, precious metal or stone:
   Silver chief value, valued not over $18
      per dozen—27½%
   Other—12%

LEATHER:
   Pocketbooks, bags—8½ to 10%
   Other manufactures of—4 to 14%

MAH JONG SETS—10%

MOTORCYCLES—5%

MUSHROOMS, dried—3.2¢ lb. + 10%

MUSICAL INSTRUMENTS:
   Music boxes, wood—8%
   Woodwind, except bagpipes—7½%
   Bagpipes—Free

PAINTINGS (works of art):
   Original—Free
   Copies, done entirely by hand—Free

PAPER, manufactures of—8½%

PEARLS:
   Loose or temporarily strung and without clasp:
      Genuine—Free
      Cultured—2½%
      Imitation—20%
   Temporarily or permanently strung (with clasp
      attached or separate)—12 to 27½%

PERFUME—8¢ lb. + 7½%

POSTAGE STAMPS—Free

PRINTED MATTER—2 to 7%

RADIOS:
   Transistors—10⅝%
   Other—6%

RATTAN:
   Furniture—16%
   Other manufactures of—12½%

RECORDS, phonograph—5%

RUBBER, natural, manufactures of—6%

SHAVER, electric—6½%

SHELL, manufactures of—8½%

SHOES, leather—2½-20%

SKIS AND SKI EQUIPMENT—8 to 9%
   Ski boots—Free to 20%

STEREO EQUIPMENT
   depending on components— 5 to 10⅝%

STONES, CUT BUT NOT SET:
   Diamonds not over one-half carat—4%
   Diamonds over one-half carat—5%
   Other—Free to 5%

SWEATERS, of wool, over $5 per
   pound—37½¢ lb. + 20%

TABLEWARE AND FLATWARE:
   Knives, forks, flatware
      Silver—4¢ each + 8½%; stainless steel—1 to 2¢
      each + 12½ to 45%
   Spoons, tableware
      Silver—12½%; stainless steel—17 to 40%

TAPE RECORDERS—5½ to 7½%

TOILET PREPARATIONS:
   Not containing alcohol—7½%
   Containing alcohol—8¢ lb. + 7½%

TOYS—17½%

TRUFFLES—Free

VEGETABLES, prepared—17½%

WATCHES, on $100 watch, duty varies from $6 to $13

WEARING APPAREL:
   Embroidered or ornamented—21 to 42½%
   Not embroidered, not ornamented
      cotton, knit—21%
      cotton, not knit—8 to 21%
      linen, not knit—7½%
      manmade fiber, knit—25¢ lb. + 32½%
      manmade fiber, not knit—25¢ lb. + 27½%
      silk, knit—10%
      silk, not knit—16%
      wool, knit—37½¢ lb .+ 15½ to 32%
      wool, not knit—25 to 37½¢ lb. + 21%

WOOD:
   Carvings—8%
   Manufactures of—8%

*IMPORTANT NOTE: Rates of duty change, so you must write to the Office of Information and Publications, Bureau of Customs, Treasury Dept., Washington, D.C. 20226 and request booklets entitled "Know Before You Go," and "Trademark Information," which gives current duty rates and information on restricted trademarks.

ANIMAL

Most people end up doubling their expenses on pet supplies and equipment, simply because they don't know that everything sold in pet stores is available by mail at much lower prices.

Whether you have a cat or dog, fish or bird, pig, horse, goat or monkey, you can find everything you need in the catalogs, and you can also save money in unexpected ways: by giving your cat or dog its distemper shot yourself, you can save up to $20, or most of the cost of a visit to the vet.

The vast range of products for animals includes grooming equipment, shampoos, pest control products, wormers, dental and ear products, vitamins and supplements, collars, leads, runs, cages, traps, carriers, gates, feeding equipment, food, pet warning signs, toys, cat trays, animal clothing, breeding supplies, horse tack, training aids, colognes, deodorants, books, novelties, etc.

One caution when buying pet supplies: the FDA requires that you swear to the fact that your purchases of hypodermic syringes, needles, and antibiotics are for animal use only, and that you submit your vet's prescription with the order. Be sure to do this, whether the catalog states this regulation or not—it's now the law.

ANIMAL SPECIALTIES, INC.

P.O. Box 531
Camden, NJ 08101
(609) 662-8530
Catalog: $1, refundable
Discount: 20% off retail,
10% off specialty prices
with resale number
or letterhead
Goods: house, name
brand
Minimum Order: $5
Shipping, Insurance:
$2.00 sent by UPS
Sales Tax: NJ, IL, CA, TX
residents
Guarantee: satisfaction
Payment: check, MO,
MC, Visa, AE, C.O.D.
Resale #: necessary for
additional 10% discount
$$

Animal Specialties is the biggest mail order company in the world for dog and cat products. They have over 1,600 items, and have organized their catalog with informative introductions to each type of product. They have goods for everyone from pet owners to professional animal handlers. In the grooming section, they sell scissors, clippers, brushes, Lambert-Kay shampoos, showers, dryers, and grooming tables. There are insect control products, vitamins and supplements, whelping and breeding aids, training chokes, leads, collars, chains, cages and carriers, feeding dishes, signs, toys, and books. The information in the catalog alone is worth $1, and there are many things available here that are hard to find elsewhere.

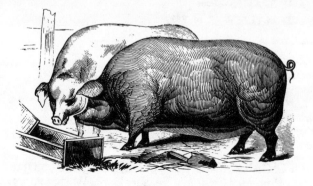

24

AQUA ENGINEERS

**250 Cedar St.
Ortonville, MI 48462
(313) 627-2877
Catalog: $1, pub. Jan.
and July, 25¢/WBMC
readers
Discount: 25% WBMC
Goods: brand, house name
Shipping, Insurance: free
Sales Tax: MI residents 4%
Payment: check, MC,
Visa, C.O.D.
$$$$**

Twice a year, Aqua Engineers issues a 24-page catalog full of supplies and equipment for fish and fish raising. The readers of WBMC, are in line for a 25% "free-stuff" discount—with every order of $10, you get $2.50 in free goods, or $25 per $100, which applies to everything except microscopes. In addition to fish paraphernalia, they sell fish cassettes, a fish magazine, fish medicine, fish books, and there is even a "tropical fish problem solver chart" to help you figure out why your fish is ill. Mr. Howard, the owner, says, "We do not pussyfoot around; we've been in business over 15 years. We are honest, and we sell good products. We accept customer returns—no squabbling. We call our catalog the 'everything' catalog because it should contain about everything a tropical fish hobbyist will ever need for his hobby."

KANSAS CITY VACCINE CO.

**Stock Yards
Kansas City, MO 64102
(816) 842-5966
*Small Animal Supply
Price List:* free
Discount: 25 to 33%
Goods: house name
Minimum Order: $10
Shipping, Insurance: extra
Sales Tax: KA, MO, NB, OK
Guarantee: replacement
of defective goods
Payment: check, MO
$$$**

This veterinary supply store was established in 1912, and has been going strong ever since. They carry all kinds of products for dogs and cats, including vaccines, wormer, calcium, flea powder, grooming tools, flea collars, stethoscopes, soap, tattoo markers (for identification purposes), vitamins, dietary supplements, and other related items. You can beat the high cost of having your dog or cat vaccinated for distemper by the vet by purchasing the vaccine from this company for $2.00 or $2.25 a dose and doing it yourself. Remember to enclose a prescription from your vet when ordering vaccines and syringes. Kansas City Vaccine Co. also sells rabies vaccine through the mail, but only where ordinances permit. Complete instructions are included with all orders.

LIBERTY LEATHER MANUFACTURERS

**P.O. Box 213
Liberty, TN 37095
(615) 597-7999
Brochure: 25¢ and SASE
Discount: up to 75%
Goods: handmade, house
brand
Minimum Order: none
Shipping: extra, UPS
Sales Tax: TN residents
Guarantee: unconditional
Returns: within 15 days
Payment: check, MO
$$$$**

Liberty makes leather collars for all sizes of dogs, from toy poodles to bull mastiffs. They are all handmade from genuine leather, and there are different weights and styles—plain, studded—to choose from. You can save up to 75% on a fine leather collar. There's no need to overspend on a cheap vinyl model at the pet store again.

PIEDMONT VETERINARY SALES

Box 1582
Salisbury, NC 28144
Catalogs: free
Discount: wholesale
Goods: house name
Minimum Order: $10
Shipping: included
Sales Tax: NC residents
Payment: check, MO

Piedmont has three catalogs that they will send free upon request—just specify Dog, Cat or Horse. They wholesale vet supplies such as vaccines, antibiotics, worm medications, vitamins, dietary supplements, equipment, etc. Unfortunately, their catalogs were in the process of being printed at this writing, so specific prices were not available, but the discount is wholesale and shipping is included, which brings the cost down even more.

STAR PROFESSIONAL PHARMACEUTICALS

11 Basin St.
Plainview, NY 11803
(516) 822-4621

Star carries a line of 29 health products for your dog, cat, or goldfish. There are pet vitamins, tearless shampoos, fur grooms, flea collars, fish food, rawhide bones for dogs, and even "happy breath," a dentrifice that sweetens the breath of your dog and helps prevent tartar deposits. For more information, see MEDICAL AND SCIENTIFIC.

THREE OAKS WORM RANCH

P.O. Box 26
Dresden, TN 38225
(901) 364-3755

Three Oaks sells several different kinds of worms, in lots of 1,000. They say the worms are excellent for breeding, and include a method of raising them in a soilless formula. See SPORTS AND RECREATION for the complete listing.

THE TIBETAN REFUGEE SELF HELP CENTER

Havelock Villa
65 Ghandi Rd.
Darjeeling, India

The Center breeds and sells rare pure Tibetan Apso Dogs, and can book orders in advance. Write to them for information. See HANDICRAFTS AND NATIVE PRODUCTS for the complete listing.

TOMAHAWK LIVE TRAPS

Box 323
Tomahawk, WI 54487
(715) 453-3550
Catalog: free
Discount: 25 to 50%
Goods: house brand
Minimum Order: none
Shipping: FOB
Tomahawk

Tomahawk makes box traps that catch animals without maiming or killing them. This kind of trap is used by state and federal conservation departments, dog wardens, universities, and anyone who wants to catch a critter humanely. You can trap anything from a mouse to a large dog in these traps. There are rigid and collapsible models from $6.95 to $89.15: fish and turtle traps, bird traps, transfer cages, and even a beaver trap for underwater use. You can also buy carrying cages for cats, raccoons, and dogs, from $12.65 to $40.50, and station wagon cages with swinging doors.

TOMAHAWK LIVE TRAPS

Sales Tax: WI residents
Guarantee: satisfaction
Payment: check, MO
$$$

Your price is about 33% less than the marked retail, and if you buy 6 traps or more of the same kind, it drops to about 50% less. Tomahawk also makes cages to order—just write with requirements.

UNITED PHARMICAL CO.

P.O. Box 1076
8693 La Mesa Blvd.
La Mesa, CA 92041
(714) 469-2112
Catalog: free
Discount: 10 to 30% plus
5 to 10% on quantity
Goods: house brand
Minimum Order: $5
Shipping, Handling:
$1.50 min.
Sales Tax: CA residents
Guarantee: satisfaction
Payment: check, MO,
MC, Visa, C.O.D.
$$$

When you add up the cost of keeping a pet, even the smallest kitten (not to mention a horse) can run you hundreds of dollars a year in visits to the vet, distemper shots, brushes, flea collars, etc. UPCO can save you money on just about any products associated with dogs, cats, or horses—antibiotics, wormers, instruments, vitamins, skin treatments, insecticides, grooming aids, horse tack, collars, feeders, books, etc. The goods range from the department store variety to specialized items sold to vets, groomers, and kennel operators. There are discounts of up to 50% off the retail price, and even larger discounts on quantity orders. You can buy distemper vaccine from UPCO and innoculate your dog or cat yourself for only $3 or $3.50, saving up to 90% over the vet's fee (you must send UPCO a prescription from your vet for the vaccine). Most people will find the ordinary accessories sufficient—flea collars, leashes, toys, feeders, books, coat brushes—for their needs, and you can combine orders with friends to get quantity prices.

VITAMIN QUOTA, INC.

14 E. 38th St.
New York, NY 10016
(212) 685-7026
or
1125 South Crenshaw
Blvd.
Los Angeles, CA 90019
(213) 936-7221

Vitamin Quota illustrates its description of pet vitamins with a picture of a "finicky cat" and a "hungry dog," both of whom, says Vitamin Quota, can use pet vitamins. Even if your cat, dog, or monkey is a hearty eater, he or she may not get the necessary nutrients for proper nutrition, and the multi-vitamins this company sells provide a good supplement. They cost $2.39 for 100, or $6.80 for 300. For more information, see MEDICAL AND SCIENTIFIC.

WATKINS AND DONCASTER

Four Throws
Hawkhurst, Kent,
England

They sell traps for catching insects and mounting specimens. See MEDICAL AND SCIENTIFIC for the complete listing.

APPLIANCES, TELEVISION, and VIDEO

Today there is absolutely no reason to pay list price for large and small appliances. Before the emergence of the consumers' movement, you had to depend for comparison shopping, on the veracity of a showroom salesman and a 10-second demonstration of an empty washer or mixer. Now, thanks to consumer magazines like *Consumer's Report* and *Consumer's Guide*, you can compare dozens of models in critical use-evaluations at home, order what you want by mail, and feel confident that guarantees and service policies will be honored.

Here you will find both large and small goods: washers, dryers, stoves, ovens, microwaves, broilers, dishwashers, disposals, compactors, refrigerators, freezers, air conditioners, humidifiers, vacuum cleaners, waxers, small kitchen appliances, personal care appliances, and related items. See chapters for AUDIO; OFFICE SUPPLIES; and TOOLS AND HARDWARE for additional appliances and machines.

As for TVs and video equipment, yes, Virginia, you *can* get Sony at a discount.

ARGUS RADIO & APPLIANCES

507 East 80th St.
New York, NY 10021
(212) 794-1705
Information: price quote
Discount: 20 to 30%
Goods: name brand
Minimum Order: none
Shipping: extra; UPS or FOB NYC
Guarantee: by manufacturer
Payment: check, MO, cashier's check
$$

Argus stocks large appliances (white goods), and TVs (brown goods). They carry appliances manufactured by such companies as G.E., Westinghouse, Hotpoint, Caloric, Garland, Kitchenaid, Indesit, Tappan, Whirlpool, Welbilt, Maytag, Amana, Wasteking, Frigidaire, Magic Chef, and Litton. Just call or write for a price quote. Argus also carries TV and video equipment by Quasar, RCA, Panasonic, Zenith, Philco, Sony, Sanyo, and Sylvania.

BLOOM & KRUP

206 First Ave.
New York, NY 10009
(212) OR3-2760
Information: price quote
Discount: 10 to 30%
Goods: name brand
Minimum Order: $25
Shipping: extra
Guarantee: by
manufacturer
Payment: check, bank
draft, MC, Visa
$$

Bloom & Krup sells appliances, TVs, furniture, and assorted goods for the home. They have been in business for over 50 years, and are used to selling by mail. In appliances, they carry lines by Amana, Caloric, Arkla, Charmglo, Country Squire, Frigidaire, G.E., Hotpoint, Indesit, Kitchenaid, Litton, Hoover, Eureka, Premier, Norelco, Moulinex, Oster, Waring, Hamilton Beach, Braun, Sub Zero, Tappan, Welbilt, Thermadore, and many others. If you are interested in a TV or video recorder by Magnavox, Panasonic, Quasar, RCA, Sony, Sanyo, Toshiba, Zenith, Admiral, or Sylvania write or call Bloom & Krup with the model number for a price quote. For more on what they carry, see the listings under HOME.

BONDY EXPORT CO.

40 Canal St.
New York, NY 10002
(212) 925-7785
Information: price quote
Discount: 30% minimum
Goods: name brand
Minimum Order: none
Shipping: extra
Sales Tax: NY residents
Warranty: by manufacturer
Payment: check, MO
$$$$

Brand name appliances, TVs, audio components, cameras, and luggage can all be found at Bondy. In large appliances, they carry G.E., Whirlpool, Tappan, Magic Chef, Westinghouse, Maytag, Caloric, and Sunbeam. There are Farberware mixers, plus blenders, irons, fans, and kitchen appliances. Just get the model and style number of the appliance you want and write them for a price quote. Bondy sells TVs and video equipment by Panasonic, Zenith, Sony, and Betamax, at a discount of at least 30% off list price. For more listings, see AUDIO; and LEATHER GOODS.

EBA ASSOCIATES

2329 Nostrand Ave.
Brooklyn, NY 11210
(212) 252-3400
Information: price quote
Discount: 10 to 40%
Goods: name brand
Minimum Order: none
Shipping, Insurance: extra;
UPS or FOB Brooklyn
Sales Tax: NY residents
Warranty: by
manufacturer
Payment: check, MO,
certified check, bank
check
$$$

EBA carries full lines of major appliances, small appliances, audio components, TVs and video equipment. They stock almost every manufacturer of large appliances, including Admiral, Amana, Caloric, Frigidaire, G.E., Hotpoint, Hardwick, Indesit, Jennair, Litton, Kitchenaid, Magic Chef, Maytag, Westinghouse, Whirlpool, Roper, Tappan, Wasteking, and Welbilt. They can special-order small appliances, and will accept phone orders. In addition, EBA carries TV and video equipment by Admiral, Panasonic, Sony, G.E., Toshiba, Zenith, RCA, Quasar, Sylvania, and Sharp. Write or call for a price quote. For further information on their stock, see AUDIO.

FLASH PHOTO ELECTRONICS

**1206 Ave. J
Brooklyn, NY 11230
(212) 253-7121
Information: price quote
Discount: 10 to 30%
Goods: name brand
Minimum Order: none
Shipping: $3.95
minimum charge
Guarantee: will exchange
defective goods with mfr.
within 10 days excluding
large appliances
Payment: check, certified
check, MC, Visa
$$$**

Flash Photo is a discount house that sells appliances, audio, TV and video equipment, and cameras made by hundreds of different manufacturers. In kitchenware and appliances they carry products by Amana, Tappan, Magic Chef, Westinghouse, Maytag, Avanti, Caloric, Chambers, Corning, Frigidaire, Hotpoint, Insinkerator, Kitchenaid, Salton, Speed Queen, Sub Zero, Thermadore, and many other top manufacturers. They also fill special orders, and will try to get the brand and model you want. In addition to large appliances, they sell smaller and personal appliances. Just write or call with the model number and color, and they'll give you a price quote. Flash Photo also sells TV and video equipment by Sony, Admiral, Zenith, G.E., RCA, Hitachi, and Panasonic, all at great discounts. For more on Flash Photo, *see* AUDIO; and CAMERA.

FOCUS ELECTRONICS

**4523 13th Ave.
Brooklyn, NY 11219
(212) 871-7600
Information: price quote
Discount: 10 to 30%
Goods: name brand
Minimum Order: none
Shipping: extra, $3.95
minimum
Guarantee: exchanges
within 10 days, along
with original cartons
Payment: check, MC,
Visa
$$**

Focus sells complete lines of large and small appliances, audio components, cameras, and TV and video equipment. The appliances are available in 220 volts for use overseas. In "white goods," they have G.E., Maytag, Amana, Frigidaire, Sub Zero, Magic Chef, Caloric, Whirlpool, Westinghouse, and Kitchenaid. In small appliances and kitchen goods they carry Farberware, Clairol, Gilette, Norelco, Remington, Sunbeam, Hamilton Beach, Oster, Waring, Connair, American, and Rival. If you are in the market for a TV or video equipment by Sony, RCA, Zenith, or Panasonic, be sure to call Focus for a price quote. For more on what Focus carries, *see* AUDIO; and CAMERA.

FOTO ELECTRIC SUPPLY

**31 Essex St.
New York, NY 10002
(212) 673-5222
Information: price quote
by mail
Discount: 30% minimum
Goods: brand name
Minimum Order: none**

Foto does very little advertising because their customers do it all for them. They have been written up in almost every New York shopping guide, and at this moment have the lowest prices in the city on Sony Trinitron TVs. They ship to Europe, Israel, South America, and other countries, as well as all over the U.S. Foto sells brand name TVs, video equipment, and videotape, and they carry the top names in large appliances: G.E., Westinghouse, Amana, Whirlpool, Maytag, Magic Chef, and were very enthusiastic over

FOTO ELECTRIC SUPPLY

Shipping Cost: FOB NYC
Sales Tax: inquire
Returns: on defective
goods
Warranty: by
manufacturer
Payment: check, MO,
Visa, MC
$$$$

their Thermadore ranges and Sub Zero refrigerators. You must *write* to them with the make and model number of what you need—they do not quote prices over the phone. Foto also stocks many other brand name goods—*see* AUDIO; and CAMERA.

INTERNATIONAL DISTRIBUTORS OF AMERICA

150 W. 28th St.
New York, NY 10001
(212) 989-7162

IDOA sells TV and video equipment by Zenith, Panasonic, Seiko, Sony, and many other top names, at discounts of up to 25%. For more information, *see* the listing under AUDIO.

INTERNATIONAL SOLGO, INC.

77 W. 23rd St.
New York, NY 10010
(212) 895-6996

INTERNATIONAL
SOLGO, INC. OF LONG
ISLAND
1745 Hempstead
Turnpike
Elmont, NY 11003
(516) 354-8815
Information: price quote
Discount: up to 40%
Goods: name brand
Minimum Order: $25
Shipping, Handling: extra
Sales Tax: NY residents
Guarantee: by
manufacturer
Returns: within 7 days
Payment: check, MO,
MC, Visa
$$$$

International Solgo is one of the pioneers of discounting, having been in business since 1933 selling goods at low, low prices. They sell appliances, audio components, cameras, jewelry, and luggage, as well as a complete line of TV and video equipment at discounts of up to 40%. The manufacturers they stock include Magnavox, Philco, Quasar, G.E., Zenith, Sony, Panasonic, RCA, and Hitachi. They carry large, small, and personal-care appliances by Amana, Brown, Eureka, Clairol, Hoover, Charmglo, Garland, Magic Chef, Tappan, Caloric, Admiral, Connair, Hotpoint, Sankyo, Norelco, Mr. Coffee, Maytag, Litton, Rival, Kitchenaid, Proctor Silex, Bunn, Norge, Sunbeam, Farberware, and many others. In addition, they carry things like pinball games, phone answering machines, and smoke alarms. Just write or call with model numbers for price quotes. For more information, *see* listings under AUDIO; CAMERA; and JEWELRY.

JILOR DISCOUNT

**1178 Broadway
New York, NY 10001
(212) 683-1590**

Jilor sells TV and video equipment by Sanyo, Magnavox, Hitachi, and Quasar, and also does special orders. For the main listing, see OFFICE SUPPLIES.

KUNST SALES

**45 Canal St.
New York, NY 10002
(212) 966-1909
Information: price quote
Discount: 10 to 50%
Goods: name brand
Minimum Order: none
Shipping: extra
Sales Tax: NY residents
Guarantee: by
manufacturer
Payment: MO, MC, Visa
$$$**

Kunst carries a wide variety of small kitchen and personal-care appliances, both in domestic current (110 volts) and overseas current (220 volts). Some of the brands available are G.E., Westinghouse, Sunbeam, Oster, Farberware, Norelco, and Clairol. Just call or write to Kunst for a price quote. In addition, Kunst has discounts of up to 50% on TVs by Sony, Panasonic, Zenith, RCA, Hitachi, and other manufacturers. For more on the goods Kunst carries, see CAMERA; AUDIO; and LEATHER GOODS.

LEWI SUPPLY

**15 Essex St.
New York, NY 10002
(212) 777-6910
Information: price quote
Discount: 20 to 40%
Goods: name brand
Minimum Order: none
Shipping: extra
Warranty: by
manufacturer
Sales Tax: NY residents
Payment: check, MO, AE
$$$$**

Lewi sells Brother sewing machines, Olivetti typewriters, and Sony products (a full line). They also have cameras by Yashica, Konica, and Canon. Their prices run from 20 to 40% off retail, but some of the discounts are even higher.

PHANTASMAGORIA

**311 South 11th St.
Tacoma, WA 98402
(206) 383-2041
Catalog: 50¢**

DISCOUNT

Jon and Karen Fayth who run Phantasmagoria are offering WBMC readers a 5% discount on top of their regular discounts of 20 to 25%. The discount covers their line of Alladin lamps and Champion juicers. They say that they carry the entire line of

PHANTASMAGORIA

Discount: 5% WBMC, reader discount on specified items plus original markdown
Goods: brand name
Minimum Order: $200 for WBMC discount
Shipping: FOB Tacoma, WA
Sales Tax: WA residents
Returns: all sales final
Warranty: by manufacturer
Payment: check, MO, bank check
$$$ on discounted items

Alladin lamps, including the turn-of-the-century model, antique decorator model, and Lincoln drape model. To qualify for the discount, *you must mention the WBMC when ordering*, and place a minimum order of $200 (computed on their selling price, not the higher retail price which they also list). Get your friends together to meet the minimum, and don't forget that Alladin lamps, which are kerosene or kerosene/electric convertible, are great for friends in the country and folks in the city, who never know when a blackout will leave them in the dark.

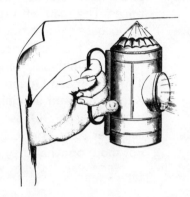

S & S SOUND CITY

58 W. 45th St.
New York, NY 10036
(212) 575-0210
Information: price quote
Discount: 10 to 40%
Goods: name brand
Minimum Order: none
Shipping, Handling, Insurance: extra
Sales Tax: NY residents
Warranty: by manufacturers
Payment: check, MO, MC, Visa, C.O.D.
$$$

S & S has been in business since 1975 selling appliances, audio components, and TV and video equipment. They claim to be "the nicest people in town," and will try to get anything you want (they will take special orders). S & S carries a complete selection of "brown goods"—TVs and video equipment—by Zenith, Toshiba, Sony, Quasar, G.E., and RCA. In large appliances, they carry lines by Maytag, G.E., Hotpoint, Whirlpool, etc. If you are in the market for surveillance equipment, write to S & S—they stock that too. For further listings see AUDIO.

SOUND MACHINE

2836 Kennedy Blvd.
Jersey City, NJ 07306

This store sells brand name TVs and video equipment. See AUDIO for main listing.

STEREO DISCOUNTERS

6730 Santa Barbara Ct.
Baltimore, MD 21227
(800) 638-3920, orders
(301) 796-5810 (MD
residents)

Stereo Discounters sells TVs by Sony, RCA, and Sinclair, at tremendous savings. They also have video receivers by RCA, Sony, Sanyo, Panasonic, and Zenith, and TV games by Atari. For more information, see AUDIO.

WISAN TV & APPLIANCES

4085 Hylan Blvd.
Staten Island, NY 10308
(212) 356-7700
Information: price quote
Discount: 10 to 40%
Goods: name brand
Minimum Order: $100
Shipping, Handling,
Insurance: extra
Sales Tax: NY residents
Warranty: by
manufacturers
Payment: check, MO,
MC, Visa, C.O.D.
$$$

Wisan has been in business for over 40 years, selling appliances, audio components, and TV and video equipment at discount prices. The man who runs Wisan said that "we shoot straight and try to get the best prices," and that they will take special orders. Some of the appliance manufacturers they stock are Frigidaire, Caloric, Whirlpool, Maytag, Magic Chef, Gibson, Westinghouse, Tappan, Speed Queen, Sub Zero, Amana, Chambers, Wasteking, Kitchenaid, and Jennair. Wisan also stocks TV and video equipment by Zenith, Quasar, G.E., RCA, Sony, and Panasonic. If you live near New York City, they can service your goods themselves. For more on what they stock, see AUDIO.

ART
and
ANTIQUES

Many people are not aware of the fact that antiques are bought at "wholesale," or more commonly, "dealer" prices, and are often passed from dealer to dealer (and marked up each time) before they reach the antique store. If you buy antiques directly from their sources in Europe, you will not only save shopping time and dealer markups, but you will also get the best selections.

The only problems with buying antiques and art by mail is that you rarely get more than a black-and-white photo of the item, so you have to use your imagination and the written descriptions as guidelines, and be prepared for surprises. Since items are usually subject to prior sale, give second and third choices when ordering. One thing you'll enjoy remembering is the fact that all antiques and art are imported duty free.

ANTIQUE EXPORT ESTABLISHMENT

P.O. Box 21 498
LF 9493
Mauren, Liechtenstein
Information: inquire
Discount: up to 90%
Shipping: air mail extra
Payment: bank draft

This company sells authentic antiques of every type and description, and also alarmingly authentic reproductions, which are identified as such. The Export Establishment says that unscrupulous antique dealers "age" these items and pass them off as the real thing. You're assured of getting the genuine item here, whether it is old hope chests, dolls, music boxes, biscuit barrels, miners' lamps, or clocks. They also sell reproductions of old silver, jewelry, furniture, and pewter (complete with marks). Write to them for information about their catalog.

BOYNE HOUSE LTD.

6 Bridge St.
Kingston, Herefordshire,
England
Catalog: $3.00,
refundable
Discount: up to 30%
Shipping: extra
Payment: bank draft
$$

The Boyne House specializes in 19th and early 20th century glass, china and tableware glass, china and tableware, with some real bargains. Write to them before ordering the catalog, as the price have changed.

DECOR PRINTS

111 Sulphur St.
Box 502
Noel, MO 64854
(417) 475-6367
Catalog: $1, refundable
Discount: 50%
Goods: house name
Minimum Order: $15 for discount
Shipping: postpaid on orders of 10 or more prints
Handling: $2 on orders of less than 10 prints
Payment: check, MO
Letterhead: necessary for wholesale quantity prices
$$

Decor Prints sells reproductions of well-known art prints for $2 and $3, with some a little higher. The company wrote that they had a "50% average discount on orders of $15 or more." Unfortunately, the handsome catalog that accompanied the letter had only code numbers and dimensions of the prints, no prices. Among the pictures were many classics: the Mona Lisa, Blue Boy, several ballet scenes by Degas, a Velasquez, a lovely landscape by Brueghel, and a frigate, among others. If you want to take a chance, Decor Prints has put together a potluck assortment of 25 prints for $22.50, which comes out to the bargain price of 90¢ a print—a great deal.

DODO

185 Westbourne Grove
London W.11
England
Information: inquire

Dodo sells things like orange crate labels, wine labels, jam labels, and chemist posters, at *what may be* very low prices. They also have other sorts of posters, which are described as old, and sound novel and unique; but as these may be out of stock, you must write to them for information.

GAND, LTD.

Dunmanway, County Cork, Ireland
Price Lists: $1 for 4; $2 for all 8
Discount: 30% minimum
Goods: antique and near antique
Minimum Order: varies
Shipping Cost, Insurance, and Packing: varies
Returns: within 3 days of receipt
Payment: cashier's check, bank MO
$$$

Antiques at wholesale prices? Gand, Ltd. supplies dealers who import and sell antiques in the U.S. at 30% to 100% markups, but will sell to anyone, and no resale number is necessary. Their range of goods is extensive: ancient objects of Egypt, Greece, Rome, Persia, and Paleolithic times, old keys (some to castles and prisons), lead figures, Victorian jewelry, pottery, glassware, Staffordshire china, silver, watches, clocks, etchings, maps, prints, and old legal documents. Prices are good: $27.50 for a 3x3-inch solid silver cigarette case, $9 for an ivory glove stretcher, $22.50 for a brass fireplace trivet (the kind selling for up to $100 in New York City), lead figures of horses about 2 inches tall for $2.75 each, a Neolithic flint hammerstone dating from 3,000 B.C. for $20, and so on. All the items are subject to prior sale, so it is best to include second and third choices. Some photos are included with the lists, and others are available on request. Minimum orders run from none at all to $40, and postage also differs from list to list.

E. GOLEMBERSKI

93 Whitemoor Rd.
Nottingham, NG6 OHJ
England
Catalog Subscription: 8
consecutive issues of the
catalog are approximtely
$4.00
Discount: to 50%, some
more
Goods: antiques,
collectibles
Minimum Order: none
Shipping: approx. $3.00
minimum
Payment: bank draft
$$$$

Mr. Golemberski issues subscriptions to his catalogs of antiques and collectibles in groups of 8 for about $4.00. He sells pottery and porcelain, glass, books and prints, dinnerware and drinking utensils, kitchenware, and a whole selection of "miscellany and curios." A Nottingham lace tablecloth is $12, old cookie tins are as inexpensive as 50¢, on up to $9.00, a pressed glass powder box is $2.50, a tobacco jar in gray stoneware is $22.00 (these cost over $50 here); and there are endless items like Staffordshire china cottages, Hogarth prints, bottles, tankards, magic lantern slides, postcards, biscuit barrels, Victorian door knockers, sewing boxes, and razors to delight you. The prices are amazingly low, and the quality and conditions of the pieces are all described in detail. Since they are actually selling the Staffordshire cottages for a fraction of what you pay today for them new, it's fair to assume that some real finds may be waiting in future issues of the catalogs. If you are interested in antiques in the least, be sure not to miss this source.

KEN LANGE

6031 N. 7th St.
Phoenix, AZ 85014
(602) 266-5637

For as little as $2.20, you can begin a collection of antique patented barbed wire. Lange sells wood plaques mounted with pieces of barbed wire, and the name of the patenter and date of patent is listed under each sample. The boards have from 5 to 22 pieces of wire on them, and some of the plaques are shaped like Western boots and the state of Texas. For $33, you can get a barbed wire clock, and there are even swizzle sticks and bracelets available in gold plated antique barbed wire. For more information, see the listing under JEWELRY.

LAURENCE CORNER

62/64 Hampstead Rd.
London NW1 2NU
England

In addition to surplus clothing and government goods, Laurence Corner sells art. Their Euston Gallery carries original oils, engraving, and prints, and they will send a catalog upon request. The current catalog contains pen and ink drawings by Lewis Baumer (for *Punch* magazine), Gould caricatures, paintings from Africa and Australia, some interesting watercolors by Phelan Gibb, a collection of Victorian paintings, a striking pen and wash of a woman, a good copy of Da Vinci's *Virgin of the Rocks*, a set of 15 lithographs by John Lennon, and much more. Prices are very reasonable, and Euston Gallery will advise you as to the general condition, artist, and market trends of any pictures you are interested in. For more information, see CLOTHING.

THE NEPAL CRAFT EMPORIUM

**G.P.O. Box 1443
Kathmandu, Nepal**

The Emporium sells beautiful statues of Buddhist gods and goddesses, copper sheet pictures, chakra and tantric paintings, and Nepalese inconographic and erotic scroll paintings. For more information, see listing under HANDICRAFTS AND NATIVE PRODUCTS.

ROCKWOOD INTERNATIONAL

**P.O. Box K-2337
Kowloon Central Post
Office
Hong Kong
Brochure: free
Discount: 30 to 70% off
U.S. prices
Goods: custom made
Shipping: included; air
$10 extra
Returns: within 30 days
Guarantee: full
satisfation
Payment: check, MO,
bank draft, cashier's
check
$$$$**

Rockwood International has 15 academy-trained artists from France, Italy, and the U.S. who will take the photo, negative, or slide you send then and immortalize its subject in an oil portrait, completed within 3 to 4 weeks. The portraits begin at $105 for a one-subject, 12x16-inch canvas, and go up according to canvas size and the number of subjects painted. Second subjects are 50% more, and third or fourth are 25% more each: a 24x30-inch canvas with three subjects would be $393.75. Slight alterations in hair, clothing or background can be done for a small charge. Rockford encourages you to give them "information as to physical makeup and personality that you think may be of aid to the painter." Satisfaction is guaranteed, and returns are accepted within 30 days. "For a truly unusual gift, so certain to please—give an oil portrait. Its pleasure cannot be worn out, outmoded nor consumed."

SAXKJAERS

**53 Købmagergade
1150 Copenhagen K,
Denmark**

This company sells those pretty collectors' plates by Royal Copenhagen, Bing & Grondahl, and other firms. The plates are lovely scenes and pictures done by artists in Sweden, and are wonderful gifts because their value increases each year—and at $11 to $22 per plate, it's a small investment, repaid in beauty alone. See HANDICRAFTS AND NATIVE PRODUCTS for the complete listing.

ART MATERIALS

Top quality art materials are not usually discounted, unless you buy in quantity. But there are many duplicate "house" brands manufactured by unknown firms that are cheaper and just as good.

Some of the goods available through art supply sources include pigments, paper, brushes, canvas, frames, pads, studio furniture, sculptors' goods, printmaking supplies, woodcarving tools, etc. For associated products, see CRAFTS AND HOBBIES.

ASHLEY ISLES, LTD.

Fenside
East Kirkby
Spelsby, Lincs, England
Catalog: free
Discount: 30 to 60%
Goods: handforged
Minimum Order: 3 tools
per size
Shipping: inquire
Warranty: full
Payment: inquire
$$$

Woodworkers will delight in this catalog of professional tools. They are hand forged and finished, made of manganese steel, and set in rosewood handles. There are many sizes and styles, from 1/16-inch to 1¼ inches wide, in straight, spoon bit, curved and fishtail pattern gouges. There are also handsome woodcarving tools and accessories like mallets, ground punches, woodcarvers' screws, slipstones, and bench stones. If you are a beginner, they suggest several tools ideal for getting you started. Their tools are unconditionally guaranteed, and will be replaced if defective. They cost from 57¢ (for a carver without a handle) to $91.49 for an 18-tool set, and average $5.50 for a carver or gouger. These would make wonderful gifts for the beginning or experienced woodcarver.

DICK BLICK

Box 1267
Galesburg, IL 61401
(800) 477-8192: orders
only
(800) 322-8183: IL
residents' orders only

Dick Blick lists over 20,000 items in its thick catalog of art supplies and equipment, which is geared toward schools but can be used by anyone. They have *everything*. Liquitex paints, Shiva pigments, Crayola crayons and finger paints, drawing tables, paintbrushes, Alfac transfer letters, Art Kraft paper, canvas, scissors, glue and cement, silk screen materials, display lighting, state flags,

DICK BLICK

(309) 343-6181: business
Catalog: $2
Discount: up to 25%,
plus quantity discounts
Shipping, Handling:
extra; UPS or FOB
Galesburg
Goods: house, name
brand
Minimum Order: none
Sales Tax: IL, PA
residents
Guarantee: "we stand
behind everything we
sell"
Payment: check, MO,
MC, Visa, C.O.D.
$$

printing equipment, woodcarving tools, molding materials, kilns, glazes, copper enamels, decoupage, materials, lapidary equipment, leather working kits, dyes, macrame material, looms, art slides, lecterns, blackboards, and learning aids. There are quantity discounts on certain items, and the selection here is hard to beat.

CROWN ART PRODUCTS

840 Broadway
New York, NY 10003
(212) 673-0150
Price List: free
Discount: 55%
Goods: house name
Minimum Order: none
Shipping, Insurance:
extra
Sales Tax: NY residents
$$$

Crown Art offers a discount on its metal section frames of 55% off list price. The frames are available in silver and gold, and in sizes from 5 inches to 40 inches. The prices begin at $1.86 and go up to $8.28. Custom-made sizes are available from 8 inches to 10 feet, and they will cut the frames to size and throw in the hardware and hangers free.

KARL HEIDTMANN

563 Remscheid 14
Postfach 140 309
West Germany

Mr. Heidtmann sells beautiful tools for woodcarving, in many sizes and blade styles. For more information, see the listing under CRAFTS AND HOBBIES.

FRANK MITTERMEIER, INC.

3577 E. Tremont Ave.
Bronx, NY 10465

Frank Mittermeier sells quality tools for sculptors, woodcarvers, engravers, ceramists, and potters. The carving tools, chisels,

FRANK MITTERMEIER, INC.

(212) 828-3843
Catalog: free
Discount: up to 30%
Goods: imported, name
brand
Minimum Order: none
Shipping, Insurance:
extra
Sales Tax: NY residents
Payment: check, MO,
bank draft
$$

gouges, and cut knives are all made by David Strasmann and Co. with top-quality workmanship and materials. They cost somewhat more than the professional tools you can buy from Germany, but since you save overseas postage and duty charges, they probably end up costing about the same. Mittermeier sells all kinds of different handles, sanders, buffers, scrapers, rasps, rifflers, Surform tools, hardwood calipers, hardwood potters' tools, wire loop ceramic and sculpture tools, rubber ceramic mixing bowls, German plaster tools, wax carvers, and other tools. They also have a Swedish anvil, routers, filter masks, vises, cutting wheels and points, oilstones, and Dremel power tools. There is a wide selection of books on engraving, cabinetry, upholstery, wood, sculpture, stonecarving, woodworking, repoussage, etc.

POLYART PRODUCTS CO.

1199 East 12th St.
Oakland, CA 94606
(415) 451-1048
Price List: free
Discount: 50 to 80%
Goods: house name
Minimum Order: $16.00
Shipping: included
Sales Tax: CA residents
Payment: check, MO,
cashier's check
$$$$

Polyart makes a high quality line of acrylic artist paints that contain the most permanent pigments known: phthalocyanine green and blue, cadmium yellow, quinacridone violet, etc. They say that most of their business is done with schools, but they sell to individuals at about 50% off retail price on a minimum order of $16.00. Orders of $40 get a further discount of 10%, $100 orders get 20% off, and $400 orders are discounted 30%. (These additional discounts are deducted from the initial 50%-off prices.) The paints are available in 12 colors, and cost $1.20 per 4 oz. and $3.20 per pint. Clear gloss and gel, gesso and modeling paste are also available at $3.20 to $4.00 per quart, $10.40 to $13.20 per gallon. Polyart will replace any defective paint or make a refund.

STU-ART PRODUCTS, INC.

2045 Grand Ave.
Baldwin, NY 11510
(516) 546-5151: NY
residents
(800) 645-2855: all other
orders
Catalog, Material
Samples: free
Discount: up to 50%
Goods: house brand

Stu-Art makes its own line of metal frames which come in three widths for flat mounting, stretched canvas mounting, and dimensional-art (deep) mounting. The frames are easily assembled and Stu-Art will cut frames to order. They are available in gold, silver, and pewter finishes. The prices run from $1.10 for a pair of 4-inch segments to $7.90 for a pair of 40-inch segments (two pairs make up one frame). Stu-Art also sells reversible duo-color, acid-free mats in 10 colors; regular mats in 18 colors; nonglare plastic to use in place of glass; wood and tenite section frames; shrink film and dispensers. By putting together your own frames, you can save

STU-ART PRODUCTS, INC.

Minimum Order: $15 to $25
Shipping: free on some goods
Sales Tax: NY residents
Payment: check, MO
$$$$

over 50% of the cost of buying the frame complete, and you can have it cut to order. If you have an odd size or very large picture, you'll be able to save even more, since some stores charge extra for unusual sizes.

UTRECHT LINENS CO.

33 35th St.
Brooklyn, NY 11232
(212) 768-2525
Catalog: free
Discount: 20 to 50%
Goods: house, name brand
Minimum Order: $25
Shipping, Insurance: extra, UPS or FOB NYC
Sales Tax: NY residents
Guarantee: "we stand behind everything we sell"
Payment: check, MO
$$$

Utrecht sells professional art, sculpture, and printmaking supplies and equipment. Their range of products includes canvas, stretchers, frames, pads, paper, brushes, tools, books, easels, tables, inks, paints, palettes, etc. The discount is very good—up to 50% off on some products—and they carry Grumbacher, Niji, Eberhard Faber, Pentell, and countless other brand names.

AUDIO

Before you buy any audio equipment, it pays to read as much as possible about the features of different systems and then evaluate your own needs in order to buy a system that's suited to you. When you are ready to purchase the components, start writing or calling the audio discount houses for price quotes on the goods you need. Remember to take into account shipping charges and sales tax when comparing prices. Guarantees are also very important; request warranty information at the same time you ask for the price quote so you can see how extensive the coverage is—the longer and more complete the guarantee is, the better buy you have.

Audio goods include turntables, receivers, speakers, amps, cartridges, styluses, headphones, mikes, cassette decks, reel to reel recorders, cleaners, treatments, changers, PA equipment, tuners, mixers, and disco equipment.

ANNEX OUTLET LTD.

43 Warren St.
New York, NY 10007
(212) 964-8661
Catalog: free (for tapes)
Discount: 35 to 40%
Goods: name brand
Minimum Order: none
Shipping: extra
Sales Tax: NY residents
Warranty: by
manufacturer
Payment: check, MO,
certified check
$$$

Annex Outlet has a large inventory of blank tapes made by companies like Maxwell, Scotch, TDK, and Ampex. Annex also sells audio equipment manufactured by Panasonic, Sanyo, Sharp, Fisher, Teac, Pioneer, and other companies. They have name brand car audio, Betamax, TV-video cameras, and other TV-video equipment. For the most part, their catalog lists only their tapes. If you are interested in brand name audio or TV equipment, you should write or call them for a price quote.

THE ARCHER AVE. STORE

4193 Archer Ave.
Chicago, IL 60632
(312) 523-2323

The Archer Ave. Store has a complete selection of Sony blank tapes, and are offering the line of tapes to readers of WBMC at 30% off the list price. Be sure to mention this catalog when you

43

THE ARCHER AVE. STORE

Price List: free
Discount: 30% WBMC
Goods: name brand
Shipping, Insurance:
extra, UPS
Sales Tax: IL residents
Guarantee: defective
goods replaced
Payment: check, MO,
bank draft, MC, Visa
$$$$

are requesting the price list and when you are ordering so that they will give you the discount.

BONDY EXPORT CO.

40 Canal St.
New York, NY 10002

Bondy sells audio equipment by Sansui, Fisher, and Sanyo. You must write to them for a price quote—they discount at least 30% off the retail price. For the complete listing, see APPLIANCES, TELEVISION, AND VIDEO.

T.M. CHAN & CO.

P.O. Box 33881
Sheung Wan Post Office
Hong Kong

If you're looking for radios or cassette decks, try T.M. Chan & Co. They sell Sony and Panasonic portable cassette recorders, radios, amplifiers, car cassettes, tape decks, transistor radios, and digital clock radios. For more information see the complete listing under CAMERA.

EBA ASSOCIATES

2329 Nostrand Ave.
Brooklyn, NY 11210
(212) 252-3400

EBA has access to *all* audio lines, which would make a listing of their brands a major undertaking. Write or call them for a price quote on any component you need. For more information, see APPLIANCES, TELEVISION, AND VIDEO.

FAR EAST CO.

K.P.O. Box TST 7335
Kowloon, Hong Kong

Far East is a Hong Kong company that sells cameras, watches, and audio equipment at a discount they say is up to 50% off U.S. list price. They carry Akai, Harman Kardon, JVC, Kenwood, Marantz, Pioneer, Sansui, Sony, Yamaha, Nakamichi, Sanyo, Teac, Shure, and Panasonic. The equipment includes receivers, amps, AM/FM tuners, speakers, cassette decks, turntables, reel to reel recorders, radios and dictating machines. They sell cassette tape in packs of 10 by BASF, Sony, and TDK, and also have a selection of name brand audio equipment for cars. For the complete listing, see CAMERAS.

FLASH PHOTO ELECTRONICS

1206 Ave. J
Brooklyn, NY 11230
(212) 253-7121

Flash has a full line of audio components, and carries equipment by Panasonic, Sony, Sansui, Pioneer, Teac, and all the top names. For more information, see listing under APPLIANCES, TELEVISION, AND VIDEO.

FOCUS ELECTRONICS

4523 13th Ave.
Brooklyn, NY 11219
(212) 871-7600

If you need audio components by Pioneer, Sansui, Marantz, BIC, Dual, Teac, or Akai, Focus sells them at up to 30% off list prices. For the complete listing, see APPLIANCES, TELEVISION, AND VIDEO.

FOTO ELECTRIC SUPPLY

31 Essex St.
New York, NY 10002
(212) 673-5222

Foto sells brand name audio equipment and stereo components at a good discount. They have many brand names, including Sony and Panasonic. See complete listing under APPLIANCES, TELEVISION, AND VIDEO.

INTERNATIONAL DISTRIBUTORS OF AMERICA

150 W. 28th St.
New York, NY 10001
(212) 989-7162
Information: price quote

IDOA is one of the "largest Pioneer dealers in the U.S." They sell full lines of name brand audio and TV equipment by makers like Sansui, Seiko, Panavision, Akai, Garrard, Marantz, BIC, Technics and many more. IDOA also runs week-long specials on

INTERNATIONAL DISTRIBUTORS OF AMERICA

Discount: 10 to 40%
Goods: name brand
Minimum Order: inquire
Shipping: extra, UPS or
FOB NYC
Sales Tax: NY residents
Guarantee: by
manufacturer
Payment: check, MO,
MC, Visa
$$$

certain items which brings the prices down even further. Write or call for a price quote. For more information, see APPLIANCES, TELEVISION, AND VIDEO.

INTERNATIONAL SOLGO, INC.

77 W. 23rd St.
New York, NY 10010
(212) 895-6996

Solgo is one of the biggest discounters in New York City, and carries a full line of audio components and equipment. They stock goods by Pioneer, Panasonic, Sankyo, Sanyo, JVC, Audiovox, Bearcat (CB), and many others. They also have phone answering machines made by Phonemate and Sanyo. For more information, see the main listing under APPLIANCES, TELEVISION, AND VIDEO.

KUNST SALES

45 Canal St.
New York, NY 10002
(212) 966-1909

Kunst has bargains of up to 50% off the retail price on their audio equipment. They carry brands such as Sansui, Marantz, Pioneer, and Akai. See APPLIANCES, TELEVISION, AND VIDEO for main listing.

S & S SOUND CITY

58 W. 45th St.
New York, NY 10036
(212) 575-0210

S & S carries audio components, radios, and CB equipment by Pioneer, Fisher, Sansui, Sony, Toshiba, and many other leading manufacturers. The also fill special orders. See APPLIANCES, TELEVISION, AND VIDEO for the main listing.

SOUND MACHINE

2836 Kennedy Blvd.
Jersey City, NJ 07306
NJ: (201) 963-6300

The Sound Machine carries brand name audio components, TVs, video equipment, CB, tapes, and phone machines. They also carry auto audio, scanners, radar detectors, computer games, and

SOUND MACHINE

NY: (212) 349-7070
All others: (800) 526-6070 (orders only)
Information: price quote
Discount: lowest price guaranteed
Goods: brand name
Minimum Order: none
Shipping: extra, FOB Jersey City
Sales Tax: NJ residents
Warranty: by manufacturer
Payment: check, MO, MC, Visa, DC, C.O.D.
$$$$

calculators. Brands incude Sony, Panasonic, Teac, Sansui, and all the major manufacturers. You are guaranteed the lowest prices; just write to them for a price quote.

STEREO CORP. OF AMERICA

1629 Flatbush Ave.
Brooklyn, NY 11210
(800) 221-0974: orders only
(212) 253-8888: quotes; orders from NY, HI, AL
Catalog: free
Discount: 30 to 70%
Goods: name brand
Minimum Order: none
Shipping, Insurance: extra; UPS or FOB Brooklyn
Handling: $1.50
Shipping, Handling, Insurance: $2 on headphones and cartridges
Sales Tax: NY residents
Warranty: by manufacturer
Payment: certified check, bank check, MO, MC, Visa
$$$

SCA has been selling audio components at rockbottom prices for 28 years. They carry over 60 name brands at real savings: 30% and more. Some of the manufacturers they carry are BIC, Dual, EPI, TEAC, Sansui, JBL, Marantz, Onkyo, Kenwood, Phase-Linear, Pioneer and Technics. In addition to audio components they sell headphones, cartridges, tapes, and the Sony Betamax. SCA puts out a 30-page catalog and sale flyers with discounts of up to 70%, and they also give price quotes by mail and phone.

UNIVERSAL SUPPLIERS

P.O. Box 14803
Hong Kong
Catalogs: free or $2.50
by air mail
Goods: brand name
Discount: 30 to 60%
Minimum Order: none
Shipping: extra
Insurance: included on
most items
Warranty: by
manufacturers
Payment: certified check,
IMO, bank draft
$$$$

Universal Suppliers is a Hong Kong house that sells a multitude of different things (see CAMERAS; MEDICAL AND SCIENTIFIC; HOME; and JEWELRY). They have brand name audio components and equipment. Some of the manufacturers they carry are Teac, Sony, Sansui, Garrard, Pioneer, and Sharp. Specify the audio catalog when you write, as they have several different catalogs.

STEREO DISCOUNTERS

6730 Santa Barbara Ct.
Baltimore, MD 21227
(800) 638-3920
(301) 796-5810 (MD
residents)
Catalog: free
Discounts: 30% plus
Goods: brand name
Minimum Order: $10 on
charges
Shipping, Insurance: 5%
Sales Tax: MD residents,
5%
Returns: authorized only
Warranty: by
manufacturer
Payment: check, MO,
MC, Visa, C.O.D.
$$$

Stereo Discounters has tremendous discounts on name brand audio equipment, records and tapes, cameras, TVs, and video recorders. They carry Pioneer, Panasonic, Marantz, Jensen, Kenwood, Akai, Sansui, Sherwood, Dynaco, Shure, O'Sullivan, BIC, Dual, Sony, Garrard, KLH, Teac, and Pickering audio components. There are blank tapes by Scotch, Fuji, Memorex, BASF, TDK, and Ampex. There is also a full line of audio equipment for cars. For further listings, see APPLIANCES, TELEVISION, AND VIDEO; CAMERAS; and BOOKS AND RECORDS.

WAREHOUSE SOUND CO.

Railroad Square
Box S
San Luis Obispo, CA
93405

Warehouse Sound has everything that you could possibly want in the way of audio equipment and supplies. The list includes turntables, receivers, amps and tuners, power amps, changers, cartridges, cleaning and preservative devices, speakers, record-

WAREHOUSE SOUND CO.

(805) 544-9700,
Catalog: free, pub. 3
times yearly
Discount: 15 to 30%
Goods: name brand
Minimum Order: $12
Shipping: FOB San Luis
Obispo
Sales Tax: CA residents
Returns: authorized
Payment: check,
cashier's check, postal
MO, MC, Visa
Guarantee: by
manufacturer
$$$$

ers—cassette, 8-track, and reel to reel, microphones, public address equipment, auto audio, etc. There are 48 brands to chose from, all top name—Akai, BSR, Garrard, JBL, Marantz, Maxwell, Metrosound, Micro Acoustics, Phase Linear, Pickering, RTR, Sansui, Sanyo, Scott, Shure, Sony, Sound Guard, TDK, Teac, Technics, Toshiba, and Watts, to name a few. They also carry a line of disco equipment and recording studio equipment and supplies, and video tape recorders and tape. For those who demand the very best and whose stereo systems are sensitive enough, Warehouse Sound offers a line of direct discs, also at discount prices. (Direct discs are made without the use of tapes, so the sound is very good.) They also have music enhancement equipment that emulates the sound quality of direct discs through machines. If you're into audio, you can't afford to miss this company.

WISAN TV & APPLIANCES

4085 Hyland Blvd.
Staten Island, NY 10308
(212) 356-7700

Wisan's extensive line of goods includes audio components, of which Zenith is their major line. They will fill special orders on appliances, and can also get audio equipment by other makers—inquire. For the complete listing, see APPLIANCES, TELEVISION, AND VIDEO.

AUTOMOTIVE and MARINE SUPPLIES

You can save more than 50% on the cost of new parts for cars and motorcycles by buying them used from "salvage" centers. The procedure for getting parts is simple: just call or write to the center with the manufacturer, model, and stock numbers of the part, and they will give you a price quote if they have the part on hand, and put you on a waiting list if it's out of stock. Even when you have repairs done by someone else, you can supply the parts yourself through the salvage centers and save that much off the bill. For all you know, the mechanic may have been buying salvage parts all along and charging you for new goods.

You can save up to 40% off list price by buying tires by mail for your car, RV, or motorcycle. The top names and specialized-function brands are available from most tire suppliers, and brands include Michelin, Pirelli, Goodyear, Goodrich, Semeperit, and Monarch.

Car maintenance supplies and other automotive equipment such as batteries, mufflers, shock absorbers, and engines are also available from these companies at 20% to 40% off list price.

After you spend hundreds or even thousands of dollars on a canoe, sailboat or yacht, the last thing you want to have to anticipate is high maintenance costs and constant repairs. The marine industry is well supplied with discounters who stock *everything* necessary for a watertight ship, a stylish crew, and finely furnished cabins.

The typical range of goods in a marine catalog includes hull finishes and sealants, deck treatments, fiberglass and resins, winches, boat stoves, sails, galley equipment, navigation instruments, communications equipment, boat clothing, hardware, teak cabin accessories, dinghies, books, and much more. Many of the items, such as clothing, hardware, and galley equipment, are very well designed and can be used in the home and on dry land, and cost less than when purchased from landlubbers.

BELLE TIRE DISTRIBUTORS, INC.

Competition Division
12190 Grand River
Detroit, MI 48204
(800) 521-7544
Information: price quote
Discount: 25 to 30%
Goods: name brand
Minimum Order: none
Shipping: free on orders
of 4 tires or more
Sales Tax: MI residents
Payment, Check, MO
$$

You can buy radial tires by Michelin, BF Goodrich, Pirelli, and Trans Am here for 25 to 30% below list price. Write or call Belle Tire with the model number of the tires you want, and they will give you a price quote.

CAPITAL CYCLE CORP.

2328 Champlain St. NW
Washington, DC 20009
(202) 387-7360
Price List: free
Discount: 20% plus
Goods: BMW motorcycle
parts
Minimum Order: $5
Shipping: extra, free on
orders over $250
Sales Tax: DC residents
Guarantee: 6 months on
all parts
Payment: check, MO
$$

Capital Cycle is an importer of BMW motorcycle parts. They have original spare parts and they also service transmissions, and rebuild engines. Write for the free price list.

CHERRY AUTO PARTS

**5650 N. Detroit Ave.
Toledo, OH 43612
(419) 476-7222: OH
residents
(800) 537-8677: all
others
Information: price quote
Discount: up to 70% over
new parts
Goods: used foreign parts
Minimum Order: none
Shipping: extra, UPS or
FOB Toledo
Sales Tax: OH residents
Payment: certified check,
MO
$$$**

Why pay top dollar for new car parts if you can get perfectly good ones used, for up to 70% less? To find out if they have what you need, write and ask for it, or call toll-free on their WATS line.

CLINTON CYCLE & SALVAGE, INC.

**6709 Old Branch Ave.
Camp Springs, MD
20031
(301) 449-3550
Price List: free
Discount: up to 50%
Goods: used salvage
Minimum order: none
Shipping: included on
orders over $100
Sales Tax: MD residents
Guarantee: satisfaction
Payment: MO, MC, Visa,
C.O.D., AE
$$$**

Clinton handles used parts for road bikes only, 250cc or larger. They stock parts for cycles by Honda, Yamaha, Suzuki, and Kawasaki. They also have a waiting list for large parts, such as engines, and will notify you when they get the part you need.

CRYSTAL SONICS

**535 North Brand Blvd.
Glendale, CA 91203
(213) 240-7310
Catalog: $1
Discount: up to 40%
Goods: name brand
Minimum Order: none
Shipping: free
Insurance: Packing
$2.28 per order
Sales Tax: CA residents
Returns: within 14 days
Guarantee: satisfaction
Payment: check, MO,
cashier's check, MC,
Visa
$$$**

For $1, Crystal Sonics will send you what they call a "boogie handbook," which states on the cover that it is published in extremely poor taste. That may be so, but the bargains inside and the detailed instructions on how to install a car stereo are worth risking your aesthetics for. They have cassette and 8-track in-dash and under-dash models made by companies like Pioneer, Panasonic, MetroSound, Craig, Sanyo, and AudioVox. There are speakers by Jensen, KLH, and Blaupunkt, and CB equipment by other top names. There are also a few pieces of stereo equipment for the home by Teac and Garrard. The catalog lists its price as "high price $1 but worth every penny," and it is—get it before you buy any car audio equipment.

DEFENDER INDUSTRIES

**255 Main St.
P.O. Box 820
New Rochelle, NY 10801
(914) 632-3001
Catalog: $1.00
Discount: up to 45% in
catalog; they "will not be
undersold"
Goods: house, brand
name
Minimum Order: $10.00
Shipping: FOB factory or
New Rochelle
Sales Tax: NY residents
Warranty: by
manufacturer
Payment: check, MO,
C.O.D.
$$$$**

This catalog is crammed cover-to-cover with boat supplies, sailing accessories, tools and hardware, navigation instruments, boat maintenance equipment, and fishing goods. Although they have fewer luxury items than Goldberg's Marine, they carry more maintenance supplies. Several pages of the catalog are devoted to boat and hull finishes, and a guide to applying fiberglass and resin is also included. They will not be undersold, and say they will beat any price that is lower than theirs. Between this company and the other discount houses, you should be able to get everything you need in order to set sail and stay afloat, with money left over. For further listings, see BOOKS AND RECORDS; CAMERAS; CLOTHING, FURS, AND ACCESSORIES; and SAFETY AND SECURITY.

EASTERN CYCLE SALVAGE, INC.

**87 Park St. Dept. W
Beverly, MA 01915
(617) 922-3707**

Eastern Cycle sells used and reconditioned motorcycle parts "at savings of up to 50% off retail." They ask that you call at the hours listed to see if they have the part you need and how much it

EASTERN CYCLE SALVAGE, INC.

Price Quote: call Tues thru Sat 9AM to 5PM; Thurs 9AM to 8PM
Discount: up to 50% off retail
Goods: used and reconditioned
Minimum Order: none
Shipping: UPS, extra
Returns: within 3 days
Guarantee: none on used parts
Payment: deposit: check, MO balance: C.O.D.
$$$

is. "All the parts are in good used condition when sent and may be returned within 3 days for refunds, less shipping, if not found satisfactory to the customer."

EDGEWOOD NATIONAL, INC.

6603 N. Meridian
Puyallup, WA 98371
(206) 927-3388
Catalog: $2, refundable
Discount: 10 to 40%
Goods: name brand
Minimum Order: $5
Shipping, Handling: FOB Puyallup
Sales Tax: WA residents
Warranty: manufacturer
Returns: authorized only
Payment: certified check, MO, MC, Visa
$$

Edgewood puts out a catalog that is chock full of everything and anything you need for your 4-wheel drive vehicle. The new catalog was at the printers as of this writing, but the prices are true discount, and, as the manager himself said, "the selection is tremendous."

GOLDBERGS' MARINE

**202 Market St.
Philadelphia, PA 19106
(800) 523-4506: orders
only
(800) 523-2926:
customer hotline
(215) 627-3700: main
office
Catalog: $2.00, pub. in
Jan.
Discount: to 40%
Goods: name, house
brand
Minimum Order: $25 on
phone orders, $10 on
mail orders
Shipping: extra, UPS
Handling: $1.00, all
orders
Sales Tax: PA and NY
residents
Returns: authorized, 10
days
Warranty: by
manufacturer
Payment: check, MO,
MC, AE, Visa
$$$**

If it's used for sailing, Goldbergs' probably has it. They carry everything from anchors to zinc collars, and a lot in between: rope, bilge pumps, rigging, knives, lifeboats, preservers, navigation instruments, boat covers, winches, and even a kitchen sink. The emphasis is on yacht and sailboat equipment, although much of the boating gear—sweaters, sunglasses, boots, caps, slickers— would appeal to landlubbers, and there are quite a few items in the maintenance and hardware section that would function fine on dry land. They also have a ''gift boatique,'' and a selection of stylish galley gear, teak bulkhead racks, and other yacht accessories. The discounts run around 20 to 30%, although there are many things with greater reductions, like a hand-held compass at 40% off. Their sales catalog lists some discounts of 50% and more. For further listings, see CLOTHING, FURS, AND ACCESSORIES; HOME; and TOOLS AND HARDWARE.

KARZ UND PARTZ

**P.O. Box 9295
Greensboro, NC 27408
(919) 373-1498: NC
residents
1-800-334-0808: all
others
Catalog: $3
Discount: 10 to 50%
Goods: name, house brand
Minimum Order: $10
Shipping: included on
orders over $100
Sales Tax: NC residents, 4%
Payment: certified check,
MC, Visa, AE, C.O.D.
$$$**

If you own a foreign-made car, you can probably get parts for it here, in addition to Ansa exhaust systems, Cibie accessory lighting, Amco tops, Recaro seats, Karz and Partz own BMW products, and more, at up to 50% off list prices. The $3 you invest in a catalog can save you hundreds of dollars in the long run.

MANUFACTURER'S SUPPLY

**Box 157-W
Dorchester, WI 54425
(715) 654-5821**

Manufacturer's has 11 different kinds of motorcycle tires at savings of 20 to 40%. They also have batteries for Honda, Yamaha, Kawasaki, Suzuki, Harley, BMW, and other bikes. They also carry a whole range of products by Petrochem to keep both your motorcycle and snowmobile functioning smoothly. Don't miss the foot pegs, engines, breaker points, condensers, magnetic coils, carburetor repair kits, mufflers, valves, wheels, tracks, spark plugs, and dozens of other items for repairing and maintaining motorcycles, snowmobiles, lawnmowers, tillers, and chain saws. For the complete listing, see TOOLS AND HARDWARE.

SAILING EQUIPMENT WAREHOUSE

**P.O. Box 2575
Olympia, WA 98507
(206) 754-9353
Catalog: $2
Discount: 30% plus
Goods: house, name
brand
Minimum Order: none
Shipping: extra, UPS or
FOB Olympia
Sales Tax: WA residents
Payment: check, MO,
MC, Visa
$$$**

The Warehouse sells a 200-plus page catalog that opens with a letter to the customer in the voice of the catalog itself which says, "I started out as the 1977 Warehouse Catalog. It was my first year and I was very scared, but the boating magazines ran my picture, said I was wonderful, and the people who bought me were great!" Fortunately, the rest of the catalog is written from a more conventional point of view, describing its no-nonsense line of goods for boat maintenance and repairs, finishes, cordage, anchors, windlasses, buoys, horns, seacocks, winches, electronics, communications, navigation instruments, lumber, hardware, etc. They also have boating clothes, teak and mahogany furnishings, and a complete selection of galley gear. The catalog itself reminds you to keep it handy all year, "because I really can save you *lots* of money. Besides, I'd hate to get stuck away, forgotten in a bookcase or squished under a pile of heavy old magazines." Don't argue with this one—put it on the coffee table.

MICKEY THOMPSON TIRES

Dept. W.
1133 W. Portage Trail
Extension
Akron, OH 44313
(216) 928-3326
Catalog and Decals: $1,
refundable
Discount: up to 40%
Goods: house brand
Minimum Order: none
Shipping, Insurance:
extra
Sales Tax: OH residents,
4%
Warranty: limited, pro-
rated
Payment: check, MO,
MC, Visa
$$$

Mickey Thompson carries a unique line of tires that they have designed, engineered, and manufactured. They have the widest tires available on the market, and an exclusive lineup of high performance radials, plus 70-60-50-series sizes with matching heights. They also have a complete line of on- and off-road RV tires, featuring wraparound tread for extra traction, and racing slicks. The materials and workmanship are warrantied, and credits on returned tires are pro-rated. If you're looking for super-wide, high-performance tires, this is the place to find them.

THE TIRE CONNECTION

110 W. Mt. Royal Ave.
Baltimore, MD 21201
(800) 638-4770
MD residents: 252-
8585
4WD and RV catalog:
free
Catalog: free
Discount: 25 to 40% off
Goods: brand name
Minimum Order: none
Shipping, Insurance:
included
Sales Tax: MD residents
Warranty: by
manufacturer, limited
Payment: check, MO,
certified check, MC, AE,
Visa, C.O.D.
$$$$

Jay Roberts' Tire Connection has been in business for over 57 years, so you know they know what they're doing. Their catalog features 32 pages of brand name tires for all American cars and imports, pickups, vans, campers, RVs, and four-wheel-drives. In addition, they stock shock absorbers, quartz iodine driving lamps, mag and custom wheels, exhaust systems, and other accessories. The discounts range from 25 to 40%. The catalog also incudes a section on tire-care tips, and a chart that unravels the mysteries of tire rotation. The tires are all covered by nationally honored manufacturer's warranties, and there are no shipping, insurance, or handling charges to inflate the prices.

TUGON CHEMICAL CORP.

**P.O. Box 31
Cross River, NY 10518
(203) 762-3953
Price List and Literature:
free
Discount: exclusive
goods; comparable items
30% more
Goods: house name
Minimum Order: none
Shipping: included
Handling: 25¢ on all
orders
Sales Tax: NY State
residents
Returns: within 90 days
Payment: check, MO,
C.O.D.
$$$**

Tugon Chemical makes a line of products oriented toward owners of older wooden boats. They include epoxy primer, caulking, decking, sealant, glue, filler, and rotted wood aid. Many of the products can be used in low temperatures and on damp or wet wood and still cure effectively. They are designed to resist water, sun, salt, barnacles, temperature changes and fuel spills. Tugon's products are more durable, versatile, and seem to be of a much higher quality than those made by other firms. If you have tried ordinary compounds and your boat problem hasn't been solved, write to Tugon with specifics and they will be able to recommend an effective compound that will save you time and money.

U.S. GENERAL SUPPLY CORP.

**100 General Place
Jericho, NY 11753
(516) 333-6655**

U.S. General carries all kinds of car maintenance supplies at discount prices. They also sell some optical devices suitable for marine use—binoculars, etc. For the complete listing, see TOOLS AND HARDWARE.

YACHTMAIL CO., LTD.

**5/7 Cornwall Crescent
London W11 1PH,
England
01-727-2373
Price Lists: free
Discount: 30%
Goods: house, brand
name
Minimum Order: none
Shipping: minimum of
$8, FOB U.S. port
Guarantee: by
manufacturer
Payment: check, MO,
bank draft
$$$**

Yachtmail specializes in cruiser yacht gear and inflatables. They sell navigation instruments, winches, pumps, lights, clocks, barometers, and more. The English brands are equal to or superior to American makes, but are often hard to get here, and very expensive. On small items like navigators' instruments, the postage and insurance charges are low and the savings well over 30%. Their prices on Avon inflatable dinghies and rafts are 30% less than American discount prices, but you must place your order in England and then have it delivered here (or have someone do it for you). If you are about to outfit your yacht or boat, be sure to write for this catalog and check out their prices.

BOOKS, RECORDS, EDUCATIONAL SUPPLIES, CARDS and STATIONERY

You can get current bestsellers, out-of-print editions, magazine subscriptions, encyclopedias, and records and tapes at savings of up to 83% off retail, or "list" prices. You can even get services—printing, photo offset copying, Xeroxing, stamp-making, labels, etc.—at a substantial discount.

Some of the best book buys around are from the houses that stock remainders and closeouts, and from the magazine subscription services. You can buy subscriptions to weekly magazines for one year at rates that are often as low as the price of a few copies bought at the newsstand. If you need a rare or out-of-print book, sources like Strand in New York City can help you locate what you want—and if it's not too valuable, it's probably right there on their shelves along with 1,000,000 other old and new books.

There are also discount sources for records and tapes, where you can save up to 50% over list price. Some audio discounters have huge selections of top label records and tapes, and blank cassettes and reel to reel, so check AUDIO for these listings as well.

The cards and stationery you can buy from craft and foreign sources are beautiful as well as original. Hallmark step aside. Your friends and family wil love these, and won't have seen anything similar before.

Party supplies are also included in this section. Paradise Products is the first and last word in party goods of all kinds—they carry items for just about every conceivable kind of party, and their prices are excellent.

AMERICAN EDUCATIONAL SERVICES

University House
419 Lentz Court
Lansing, MI 48917
(517) 371-5550
Information: inquire
Discount: up to 50%
Goods: nationally
distributed magazines
Minimum Order: none
Payment: check, MO,
MC, Visa, budget plan
$$$

This magazine service sells subscriptions to students and educators at what they call the "lowest educational rates anywhere." There are over 50 magazines offered, including *Time, Modern Photo, Apartment Life, The New Yorker, Road & Track, Teacher,* and *Forbes.* You must be a student or an educator to qualify for these rates, which are up to about half of the regular or discount rates.

AMITY HALLMARK LTD.

P.O. Box 929, Linden
Hill Station
40-09 149th Place
Flushing, NY 11354
(212) 939-2323
Catalog: free
Discount: up to 30%
Goods: services
Minimum Order: $8.95
Shipping: free in NY Tri-
State area; extra, by UPS
elsewhere
Sales Tax: NY residents
Payment: check, MO
$$$

Amity Hallmark offers offset printing services at very good prices, and will ship all over the U.S. at a nominal rate—even shipments to California are only $2 per 1,000 8½x11-inch sheets. All the standard services are available, including offset printing for camera-ready material in letter and legal sizes, with special papers and colors offered at extra charge. They also do business cards, 11x17-inch paper runs, 3½x5½-inch cards, envelopes, short run specials, and snap-out forms. Some of the extra services (at nominal extra charge) are cutting (75¢ per 1,000 sheets), colored inks, heavy ink coverage, halftones, folding, hole punching, numbering, perforating, collating, and packing. Shipment to all the New England states is absolutely free, and small charges are made for goods delivered elsewhere, Amity is constantly upgrading their machinery, and they pass on the savings of increased efficiency to you by reducing prices.

CAPRILAND'S HERB FARM

Silver St.
Coventry, CT 06238
(203) 742-7244

You can buy notepaper printed with verses and quotes about rosemary, lavender, thyme, Easter, and the winter, which is available only at Capriland's. For $1.25, you can get 8 sheets and envelopes, which compares well with any exclusive stationery. For more information, *see* COSMETICS AND PERFUMES.

CHESTERFIELD MUSIC SHOPS, INC.

12 Warren St.
New York, NY 10007
(212) 964-3380
Catalog: free, pub. 3 or 4
times a year
Discount: to 70%
Goods: brand, house
name
Minimum Order: none
Shipping, Packing,
Insurance: $1.00
Sales Tax: NYC residents
Returns: after 1 playing
only
Payment: check, MO,
MC, C.O.D., Visa
$$

Chesterfield sells classic, jazz, popular and folk music at discount prices. Most of the records are also available in cassette form. They have English medieval carols for $3.79, the soundtracks of *A Chorus Line*, *Annie*, and *Threepenny Opera* for $6.29, jazz greats at $2.49 each, imports from England, and 3 pages of classical music at good prices. There are also children's records by Folkways and Tom Glazer with old favorites like "Jimmy Crack Corn," "This Old Man," and "Skip to My Lou." You are allowed to return records after one playing only, with a credit or replacement given. Gift certificates are also available.

COPEN PRESS

100 Berriman St.
Brooklyn, NY 11208
(212) 235-4270
Brochure: free
Discount: varies
Goods: to order
Minimum Order: varies
Shipping Cost: FOB
Brooklyn, NY
Sales Tax: NY residents
Payment: check, MO,
C.O.D.
$$

Copen Press is "a complete web offset operation" that prints books, booklets, leaflets, and flyers. They have red and black ink, and offer a folding service. Material must be camera-ready, but they will give you a guide on typing the layout for your book or leaflet. An 8½x11-inch letter in black ink done in a run of 1,000 is $24, 5,000 is $53, and 50,000 copies are $338. The book and booklet services are reasonable. For shipping, they provide charts for weight, UPS zones, and carrier rates, so you can estimate the cost to the penny. C.O.D. is 85¢ extra.

DEFENDER INDUSTRIES

255 Main St.
P.O. Box 820
New Rochelle, NY 10801

Defender has a wide selection of books on sailing and boating. See AUTOMOTIVE AND MARINE SUPPLIES for more information.

FREEDOM PRESS

(in Angel Alley)
84b Whitechapel
High St.
London E1
Catalog: free
Discount: up to 30%
Goods: exclusive,
privately published books
Minimum Order: $2
Shipping: 15% of order
value
Payment: bank draft
$$

The Freedom Press call themselves a seller/publisher of material on anarchy, and even put out their own paper, *Freedom*, which costs $10 a year by subscription. Their book list includes writings by Emma Goldman, William Godwin, Peter Kropotkin, Herbert Read, Mary Wollstonecraft, Tolstoy, Thoreau, Oscar Wilde, Wilhelm Reich, Erich Fromm, George Orwell, and many other authors whose works could be seen as "anarchist," or at least "free-thinking." Several books, by Kropotkin, Enrico Malatesta, and Rudolf Rocker, are published or distributed by Freedom Press themselves, and hard to get in the U.S. Because of this, it's difficult to determine how much you save by buying here. But the prices on certain items—60¢ for Thoreau's *On the Duty of Civil Disobedience*, $1.10 for *On the Road* by Jack Kerouac, and $1 for Orwell's *Animal Farm* are up to half what they cost when bought here. If you'd like to open your mind a little, this catalog can serve as book supplier and reading list.

GOLDEN EARTH WHOLESALE

512 E. Lambert
Brea, CA 92621
(714) 990-0681

Golden Earth has about 40 books on practical topics, with many related to plants and gardening. They are 20% off list price, with no minimum order. For more information, see FARM AND GARDEN.

HACKER ART BOOKS, INC.

54 W. 57th St.
New York, NY 10019
(212) 757-1450
Catalog: free, pub. March
and Oct.
Discount: 30% minimum
Goods: name brand
Minimum Order: none
Shipping, Handling: $1
for the first book; 50¢
each additional, plus $1
per each 6 books
Sales Tax: NY residents
Returns: on all books in
good condition
Payment: check, MO
$$$

The current catalog from Hacker Art Books lists almost 200 titles of books on art, ranging from *Art of the Ancient World* to *Late Modern*. There is art criticism, art history, books on architecture, primitive and folk arts, photography and theater, cartoons and collage. Many of the books are currently on sale in bookstores for 30 to 40% more than they cost here, and most bookstores don't accept returns—Hacker does.

KONN'S FINE ARTS

Mail Order Department
The Hong Kong Hilton
Hotel
Hong Kong
Samples and Price List:
free
Discount: 50%
Goods: handmade house
brand
Minimum Order: 100
cards
Shipping: included
Insurance: extra
Guarantee: satisfaction
Payment: certified check,
IMO, bank draft
$$$

This Hong Kong firm makes greeting cards decorated with pictures of birds, flowers, children, boats, and scenes handpainted on silk. You can have them printed with your name and a message inside, and have the envelopes printed with your name and address for a nominal charge.

KEN LANGE

6031 N. 7th St.
Phoenix, AZ 85014
(602) 266-5637
Returns: undamaged
goods only

The Navajo and His Blanket, Sheridan's Troops on the Borders, and *Indian Stories from the Pueblos* are a few of the 65 titles Ken Lange carries among his books on Indian history and Western Americana. Some are reprints of old classics and cover a wide range of topics: Navajo weaving, Indian missions, the Sun Dance ceremony, Pikes Peak, pioneers, gold and silver mines, Taos Indians, an account of frontier Colorado by a pioneer woman journalist, and more. The books are discounted 40% off retail prices, and *any* book can be returned within 14 days for a refund, exchange, or credit. The minimum order is $25. The books are priced at $4.40 to $24.20. For more information, see the listing under JEWELRY.

LITERARY MART

1261 Broadway
New York, NY 10001
(212) 684-0588
Price Lists: free
Discount: 10 to 75%
Goods: used
Minimum Order: none
Shipping: extra, $2 to
$15
Sales Tax: NY residents

Anyone with school age children has probably investigated buying an encyclopaedia or other reference system and been shocked at the prices: the cheapest *Britannica* is $800, the *Americana Encyclopaedias* is $650, and even the one-volume *Columbia* goes for $80 (retail). Literary Mart will sell you this year's edition of a major encyclopedia for $600, 25% off list price. The books get cheaper as they get older—you can buy the 14th edition of the *Britannica*, published between 1929 and 1939, for $30. They carry encyclopaedias by Americana, International, Collier, Columbia, Random House, World Book, Comptons, Funk & Wagnall,

LITERARY MART

Payment: check, MO
$$$

Merit, Grolier, and New Standard. They also have yearbooks, dictionaries, children's reference texts, atlases, and specialized texts on natural history, biography, music, the military, religion, architecture, Americana, etc. Some of these works never go out of date, and all are well priced and in conditions that vary from good-used to brand new. Before you give that salesman a down payment on a new set (on which you could pay 18% in finance charges), write to Literary Mart for their current price list.

MAGAZINES AT DISCOUNT

P.O. Box 601
Broomall, PA 19008
Information: inquire
Discount: up to 50%
Goods: nationally
distributed magazines
Minimum Order: none
Payment: check, MO
$$$

This magazine service carries a huge selection of well-known magazines at discounts of up to 50%. You can get *Business Week, Car and Driver, MS,, Redbook, Time, TV Guide*, and many others at prices equal to the cost of just several issues at newsstand prices. Write to them for information.

MARBORO BOOKS, INC.

Dept. WBM
205 Moonachie Road
Moonachie, NJ 07074
(201) 440-3800
Catalog: free
Discount: up to 90%
Goods: major publishers,
reprints, imports
Minimum Order: $5
Shipping, Handling:
$1.95
Sales Tax: NY, NJ
residents
Payment: check, MO,
MC, Visa, AE, CB, DC
Guarantee: satisfaction
or money back
Returns: within 10 days
$$$$

Marboro is one of the best-known chains of discount bookstores in this country, and does a whopping mail order business. They carry all kinds of books, from current bestsellers to obscure reprints. The current catalog has *Prehistoric Art of Australia* for $5.95 (originally priced at $17.50), *A Pictorial History of the SS* at $6.98 (originally $14.95), an 845-page book on nostalgia for $5.95, reduced from $24.95, and many more at comparable savings. There are books here for every taste, including art books, Judaica, history and politics, hobby books, world literature and fiction, biography, Americana, science, art and architecture, psychology, and more. Don't miss this source if you're stuck with a long Christmas gift list, or want to catch up on your reading.

MOHR WF-78

24725 Butler Rd.
Junction City, OR 97448
(503) 998-8233
Catalog: free
Discount: to 70%
Minimum Order: $6.00
Shipping, Handling:
orders under $10, 50¢;
free on orders over $10.00
Guarantee: "100% money
back"
Payment: check, MO
$$

If you enjoy books on moneymaking schemes or eroticism, this company is right up your alley. Willis Mohr puts out a catalog full of titles like *Successful Little Known Businesses, How to Invest in Gold Coins, Nudes in Color*, etc. There are many how-to books, as well as directories of drop-shippers, wholesale book sources, freebies, closeouts, and more. Mr. Mohr guarantees satisfaction or your money back, and includes bonus books with orders of $10 and $20.

THE PENDLETON SHOP

P.O. Box 233
407 Jordan Rd.
Sedona, AZ 86336
(602) 282-3671

There are 54 books on weaving alone in the Pendleton Shop bookshelf. Three are by Mary Pendleton herself, including the comprehensive *Navajo and Hopi Weaving Techniques*. There are books on backstrap weaving, card weaving, Oregon looms, Flemish weaving, patterns, Inkle weaving, and many others. There are also 14 books on spinning, including one on how to spin with dog hair. These books are sold at retail prices, but many are hard to find elsewhere and well worth the price. For the complete listing, see CRAFTS AND HOBBIES.

PUBLISHERS CENTRAL BUREAU

Dept. WBM
1 Champion Ave.
Avenel, NJ 07131
(201) 382-7960
Catalog: free
Discount: to 83%
Goods: nationally sold
books; privately
published
Minimum Order: $5.00
Shipping, Handling:
$1.95
Sales Tax: NY, NJ
residents
Guarantee: satisfaction
or money back
Returns: within 14 days
Payment: check, MO
$$$

Publishers Central is a clearinghouse for publishers and record manufacturers, and also stocks new editions which are identical to the originals. They have books on every topic—the Irish, codes and ciphers, prehistoric animals, film, comics, boxing, boating, trivia, occult and magic, bookbinding, gardening, diet and beauty, ships, plain and fancy cooking, Americana, art and architecture, the Civil War, and much more. Most of the books are overstock, and they also sell new editions and bestsellers. If you buy from their big catalog, they make you part of their "family" and will send you private sale catalogs throughout the year. They also sell cassettes from Olympic Records, the Longines Symphonette series, and an assortment of records from Paganini to polkas. There are first-rate bargains here, and you can return books within 2 weeks—something bookstores don't usually allow.

S & C HUBER, ACCOUTREMENTS

**82 Plants Dam Rd.
East Lyme, CT 06333**

S & C Huber specialize in authentic country crafts and crafts supplies. They have a large bookshelf on many of the early American crafts that are becoming popular once again, but about which very little is known. They have books on bookbinding, early American costume, dyeing, folk art and painting, needle-crafts, quilting, rugs, spinning, stenciling, weaving, and textiles. There are a whole slew of cookbooks with titles like *Best Shaker, American Frugal, Pot Stirred*, etc. Their list of books about women included *Sampler, Seasonal Hearth*, and *Woman on Frontier*, and are bound to make any woman thankful for things like washer/dryers and vacuum cleaners. For more information, see CRAFTS AND HOBBIES.

S & P OF NEW YORK BUDO INC.

**P.O. Box 2
Depew, NY 14043
(716) 681-7911
West of the Mississippi:
California S & P, Inc.
479 Ninth St.
San Francisco, CA 94103
(415) 626-1811**

S & P has 130 books on different kinds of martial arts—aikido, judo, kendo, karate, tae kwondo, hapkido, and kung fu. There are weaponry books and some reference texts on taoism, the Samurai, biorhythms, Bruce Lee, and all kinds of related topics. The books can be combined with goods in 2 other categories to get the volume discount of 30 to 40%, so it's easy to save without buying a lot. For the main listing, see SPORTS AND RECREATION.

STEREO DISCOUNTERS

**6730 Santa Barbara Ct.
Baltimore, MD 21227**

Stereo Discounters sells hit records at more than 30% off list price. They carry Columbia, Reprise, Atlantic, Asylum, Capitol, Arista, A & M, and RCA and other top labels represented by current artists, and the selection is great. They also sell blank tapes. For the complete listing, see AUDIO.

THE STRAND BOOKSTORE

828 Broadway
New York, NY 10003
(212) GR3-1452
Catalogs: free
  Art Book Specials
  Books
  Reviewers' Copies
  Literature
Discount: up to 75%
Goods: nationally known
and private publishers
Minimum Order: none
Shipping, Handling: 75¢
per book on orders under
$20
Sales Tax: NY residents
Payment: check, MO
$$$$

If you live in New York City and have ever needed an out-of-print book, chances are you went to Strand for it. They have a 30-page catalog of literature, with books by Yeats, Faulkner, Mailer, Mary McCarthy, and many others. If you're fond of books about the books—commentary, critique, biography—you'll find them here among the 600 titles. For those with diversified interests, there is the all-purpose catalog of over 700 specials, including out-of-print books and books on history, architecture, politics, food, drama, Americana, etc. If you are interested in art, the art catalog has over 1,300 listings of books on the fine arts, crafts, and every possible related topic. Strand completes the partial roundup of its 8 miles of books in its catalog of reviewers' copies, which contain over 10,000 titles. Every book is 50% off list price, so don't put off reading current bestsellers until they come out in paperback. And if you can't find what you want in the catalogs, write to them—they advertise that "particular attention is paid to your special want lists." Remember Strand for gifts—the reviewers' catalog alone could solve all your Christmas problems.

THE TIBETAN REFUGEE SELF HELP CENTER

Havelock Villa
65 Ghandi Rd.
Darjeeling, India

The Center sells various cards which are handpainted on hand-made paper for 46¢ each with envelope. There are also letter pads and bookmarks. See HANDICRAFTS AND NATIVE PRODUCTS for a complete listing.

WATKINS AND DONCASTER

Four Throws
Hawkhurst, Kent,
England

This company sells books on naturalistic topics, from fungi to fossils, at good prices. See MEDICAL AND SCIENTIFIC for the complete listing.

PARADISE PRODUCTS, INC.

P.O. Box 568
El Cerrito, CA 94530
Catalog: $2, pub. in Feb.
Discount: up to 25% off
comparable store list
prices, plus quantity
"Paradise
Discount"
Goods: domestic,
imported
Minimum Order: $25 net
(after discount)
Shipping: 10% of
merchandise costs
Guarantee: shipments
will arrive on time; goods
as represented in catalog
Payment: PMO, MC, Visa
$$$

There is no way to give a calm, rational explanation of the goods Paradise Products carries. Any catalog that pictures thousands of favors, decorations, and costumes for over 120 kinds of parties should be given only to certifiably adult, practical people, as it will drive the child in you crazy. The parties are classified by country and by theme. Four pages are devoted to Oktoberfest goods—steins, Alpine cow horns, Tyrolean hats, Kaiser helmets, wigs, lederhosen, beer-drinking music records, streamers, signs, papergoods, posters, lamps, bunting, Alpine boot cigarette lighters, and much more. Every conceivable country and traditional theme is represented. Some of the more unusual are Calypso, Old South, Parisienne, "Las Vegas Night," Pirate, "A Night on the Delta Queen," Safari, Western Chuck Wagon, and the Roaring 20's. There is a quantity discount, and prices are already lower than retail on many items, so your savings are as good as the time you're going to have deciding what to order.

CAMERAS, PHOTOGRAPHIC EQUIPMENT, and OPTICALS

Contrary to popular belief, prices on cameras and photographic equipment are, for the most part, better here in the United States than they are in Hong Kong. Even a firm that has only a small camera department in addition to an extensive appliance or audio inventory can probably offer discounts of up to 40% off list prices. The large camera and photographic supply houses carry much more than cameras, bulbs, and film. Some of the specialized goods available from these firms are lighting equipment, screens, film editors, splicers, projection lamps, batteries, projection tables, lenses, filters, adapters, meters, albums, camera bags and cases, enlargers, color analysers, darkroom equipment and supplies, and film processing services.

Even if you don't need custom work done, you can have your film processed by a mail order discount lab at about half the price a drugstore or retail outlet would charge, and you usually get credit for unprintable negatives.

ASHREH SUPPLY CORP.

473 Broadway
New York, NY 10013
(212) 925-9507
Catalog: free
Discount: 50%
Goods: brand name
Minimum Order: none
Shipping: extra
Sales Tax: NY residents
Warranty: by manufacturer
Payment: check, MO
$$$

Ashreh carries the top brands in cameras—Kodak, Pentax, Nikon, Canon, Amaya, etc. They also carry Kodak and Polaroid film, and Eveready and Mallory batteries. Because their catalog was in preparation, there was no way to obtain specific prices, but the discounts are very good—up to 50%.

BONA FIDE NOVELTIES

Photographic Division
1123 Broadway
New York, NY 10010
(212) 242-5442
Price List: free
Discount: up to 70%
Goods: house, brand name
Minimum Order: $5.00
Shipping: extra
Sales Tax: NY residents
Payment: check, MO
$$$$

Bona Fide has a large selection of camera film and developing paper. They carry Printonfilm, Plus-X, Veraspan, Kodachrome, Ektachrome, Ansochrome, Tri-X, and other kinds of film, in sizes from 16 to 70mm. They sell enlarging paper in sheets and rolls, contact paper, and miscellaneous photographic developing supplies. The prices are incredibly low: 8 rolls of black-and-white 35mm film in 50-foot segments that sells for $3.00 is a typical example. Bona Fide also sells film for television recording.

CAMBRIDGE CAMERA EXCHANGE, INC.

7th Ave. and 13th St.
New York, NY 10011
(212) 675-8600
Information: price quote
Discount: to 60%
Goods: brand name
Minimum Order: $20
Shipping: extra
Sales Tax: NY residents
Returns: within 20 days
Warranty: by manufacturer
Payment: check, MO, MC, Visa
$$$$

The man who runs the show at Cambridge Camera says that they carry everything you can think of in the way of photography equipment: lenses, enlargers, projectors, chemicals, bulbs, and much more. He read off a dizzying list of camera lines that are available, including Nikon, Kodak, Vivitar, Bell and Howell, Leica, Pentax, Shinan, Elmo, Yaschica, Hassleblad, Fujica, Komure, Bolex, Sigma, Eumig, and many more. Write for a price quote.

T.M. CHAN & CO.

P.O. Box 33881
Sheung Wan Post Office
Hong Kong
Catalog: free
Discount: 30% plus
Goods: name brand
Minimum Order: none

T.M. Chan and Co. is a Hong Kong firm that sells brand name cameras and accessories, binoculars, and other goods. They carry cameras by Asahi-Pentax, Canon, Contax, Fujica, Konica, Kowa, Mamiya, Minolta, Vivitar, and Yaschica. There are lenses by Sigma, Soligor, Tamron, and Vivitar, filters by Kenko and Hoya, and tripods by Vivo and Topman. They also sell movie cameras by Canon, Elmo, Fujica, Minolta, Nikon, and Sankyo, and brand

T.M. CHAN & CO.

Shipping: surface freight included, air $3.80/lb.
Insurance: 2%
Payment: bank check, certified check, IMO

name movie slide projectors, exposure meters, flash units, and enlargers. The binoculars they carry are made by Asahi Pentax, Canon, Nikon, Hoya, and Carl Zeist. Chan and Co. invite inquiries about equipment not illustrated as they carry things not listed in the catalog. For more on what they sell, see the listings under AUDIO and JEWELRY.

DEFENDER INDUSTRIES

255 Main St.
P.O. Box 820
New Rochelle, NY 10801

Defender sells binoculars and other special devices used at sea but which are perfectly good used on land as well. For complete listing, see AUTOMOTIVE AND MARINE SUPPLIES.

DIGNAN PHOTOGRAPHIC, INC.

Box 4338
12304 Erwin St.
North Hollywood, CA 91607
(213) 762-7139
Price List: free
Discount: 40 to 60% below retail labs
Goods: house brand
Minimum Order: $25
Shipping: included
Sales Tax: CA residents
Guarantee: "satisfation"
Payment: check, MC, Visa
$$$

At Dignan, you not only bypass the high cost of retail photo processing, but save over the discount cost, too. Dignan sells kits for developing your color film yourself which start at $9.95, and sells all the replacement chemicals and supplies you will need for further use. You may want to invest in a subscription to their report on how to use the chemicals and general information on developing color film, which costs $24 a year.

EXECUTIVE PHOTO

884 Sixth Ave.
New York, NY 10001
(212) 532-1277
Catalog: $3
Discounts: up to 50%
Goods: name brand
Minimum Orders: $25
Shipping: extra
Sales Tax: NY residents
Guarantee: by
manufacturer
Returns: within 2 weeks
Payment: check, MO,
MC, Visa, AE
$$$$

Executive sells all the name brands in cameras and accessories—Nikon, Pentax, Sigma, Hassleblad, Minolta, etc. Unlike most U.S. camera discounters, they have a catalog, which saves you the trouble of writing or calling for a price quote. Their discounts are true wholesale—50% and more off list price.

FAR EAST CO.

K.P.O. Box TST 7335
Kowloon, Hong Kong
Catalog: free, $1 air mail
Discount: "30 to 50%"
Goods: brand name
Minimum Order: none
Shipping, Handling,
Insurance: included; air
mail extra
Guarantee: 1 year
Payment: check,
cashier's check, bank
draft
$$

Mr. Stephen Woo of Far East says that you can save 30 to 50% over U.S. list prices by buying from Hong Kong. The only expenses not included in the prices are customs charges, which are nominal. In cameras, Far East carries Canon, Fujica, Konica, Mamiya, Nikon, Olympus, Pentax, Yaschica, Vivitar, Soligor, Tamron, Bronica, and Nikkormat. There are accessories like filters, lens hoods, exposure meters, flashes, and a wide variety of lenses. They also carry movie projectors, binoculars, and underwater cameras. For additional listings, see AUDIO; and JEWELRY.

FLASH PHOTO ELECTRONICS

1206 Ave. J
Brooklyn, NY 11230
(212) 253-7121

Flash Photo carries full lines of cameras by Nikon, Minolta, Canon, Yaschica, Mamiya, Leica, Kodak, Polaroid, Hassleblad, Olympus, Eumig, Sigma, Soligar, Bell and Howell, and other top names. They also have film by Agfa, Kodak, Ilford, Fuji, and Polaroid. See the main listing under APPLIANCES, TELEVISION, AND VIDEO for more information.

FOCUS ELECTRONICS

4523 13th Ave.
Brooklyn, NY 11219
(212) 871-7600

Focus carries cameras by all the major manufacturers, plus film by Kodak, Fuji, Agfa, and Polaroid. For more information, see the listing under APPLIANCES, TELEVISION, AND VIDEO.

FOTO ELECTRIC SUPPLY

31 Essex St.
New York, NY 10002

Foto sells cameras and photographic supplies. Some of the brands available are Pentax, Canon, Nikon, Minolta, Bell and Howell, Kodak, and Eumig. See APPLIANCES, TELEVISION, AND VIDEO for complete listing.

GARDEN CAMERA

345 Seventh Ave.
New York, NY 10001
(212) 868-1420
Information: price quote
by phone or mail
Catalog: $1.00
Discount: 30 to 50% plus
Goods: name brand
Minimum Order: $40.00
Shipping, Insurance:
extra
Warranty: full, by
manufacturer
Payment: check, MO,
MC, Visa
$$$

Garden sells cameras by Nikon, Pentax, Minolta, Olympus, Vivitar, Canon, Mamiya, Hassleblad, Eumig, Leica, Bell and Howell, Sankyo, Yaschica, Minox, and Confax. They have Kodak, Agfa, and Fuji film, and calculators by Texas Instruments and Hewlett Packard. They also stock all darkroom equipment and accessories. All the merchandise is factory packed and brand new.

PHOTOGRAPHER.

INTERNATIONAL SOLGO, INC.

77 W. 23rd St.
New York, NY 10010
(212) 895-6996

Solgo sells thousands of different items at discounts of 25 to 40%, among them a full line of brand name cameras. They have Polaroid, Nikon, Minolta, Canon, Yaschica, and many others. See APPLIANCES, TELEVISION, AND VIDEO for more information.

MINIFILM PHOTO

167 W. 32nd St.
New York, NY 10001
(212) 695-8100
Catalog: 50¢
Discount: 25 to 40%
Goods: name brand
Minimum Order: $10
Shipping: extra
Warranty: by
manufacturer
Payment: certified check,
MO, MC, Visa
$$$

Minifilm sells all the top names in cameras—Minox, Bell and Howell, Nikon, Canon, Eumig, Pentax, Minolta, Vivitar, Kodak, Polaroid, etc. They also sell film by Kodak, Agfa, Polaroid, and Ilford, and darkroom equipment and binoculars.

ORIENTAL FILMS

P.O. Box 5784 TST
Kowloon, Hong Kong
Price List: free
Discount: 30% minimum
Goods: name brand
Minimum Order: $25
Shipping, Insurance:
included
Guarantee: 1 year
Payment: certified check,
bank draft, MO, cashier's
check
$$$

Oriental Films sells brand name cameras, lenses, accessories, and projectors. They carry Asahi, Pentax, Canon, Konica, Minolta, Olympus, Yaschica, Miranda, Bronica, Rollei, and Nikon. There are lenses by Vivitar, Nikkor, Soligor, Sigma, and other companies. The prices are lower than U.S. discount houses, and much lower than the list price. There are 3 prices given—the store price if you bought it there, the cost of the camera plus sea freight, and the cost plus air mail postage. If you are shopping for a camera, don't buy one until you look at this catalog.

SOLAR CINE PRODUCTS, INC.

4247-49 South Kedzie
Ave.
Chicago, IL 60632
(312) 254-8310
Catalog: free, pub. twice
yearly
Discount: up to 40%
Goods: name brand
Minimum Order: $5
check or MO; $5 charge
card

Solar Cine's 74-page catalog is packed cover-to-cover with all kinds of photographic equipment and accessories. It starts with still and movie film by Kodak, Fuji, and Polaroid, and film processing by Solar and Kodak. In equipment, there are Super 8 cameras, projectors, lights, 35mm and cartridge cameras, studio lights, screens, instant cameras, editors, splicers, reels and cans, flashguns and bulbs, lenses, filters, tripods, meters, and enough darkroom equipment and accessories to fill most photographers' needs, including color printing supplies. The brands Solar Cine carries include Bell and Howell, Minolta, Yaschica, Kodak, Canon, Eumig, Bauer, Elmo, Sankyo, Chinon, Sylvania, Kenco, Smith

SOLAR CINE PRODUCTS, INC.

Shipping: extra, UPS, PP, or FOB Chicago
Sales Tax: IL residents
Warranty: by manufacturer
Returns: on defective goods, authorized
Payment: check, MO, MC, Visa
$$$

Victor (studio lights), Praktica, Rollei, Vivitar, Olympus, Pentax, Konica, Nikon, Argus (slide projectors), Ciro, Soligor, Braun, Metz, Hoya, Gossen, Durst, etc. In addition to the excellent discounts in the catalog, there are "specials" at extra low prices. Be sure to look here for specialized equipment and supplies, and all kinds of film processing.

STEREO DISCOUNTERS

6730 Santa Barbara Ct.
Baltimore, MD 21227
(800) 638-3920
(301) 796-5810 (MD residents)

Stereo Discounters sell cameras by Yaschica at savings of over 30%. For the complete listing, see AUDIO.

UNIVERSAL SUPPLIERS

P.O. Box 14803
Hong Kong
Price List: free, $1.80 by air

Universal sells brand name cameras, binoculars, telescopes, riflescopes, and other optics. When you write to request a catalog, specify "camera" because they have several brochures. For a complete listing, see AUDIO.

WESTSIDE CAMERA, INC.

2400 Broadway
New York, NY 10024
(212) 877-8760
Information: price quote
Discount: 10 to 40%
Goods: name brand
Minimum Order: $18
Shipping: extra, UPS
Sales Tax: NY residents
Payment: check, MO, MC, Visa
Guarantee: 1 yr. from the store; also from manufacturer
$$

Westside carries a full line of name brand cameras, darkroom supplies and equipment, and film. Some of the brands they offer are Nikon, Kodak, Minolta, Olympus, Konica, Omega, B & H, Canon, Ilford, Vivitar, Leica, Rollei, and Minox. They also sell film made by Kodak, Agfa, Ilford, and Polaroid. Westside stresses the fact that their line of darkroom supplies and equipment is full and complete, so hobbyists should take note. They also offer the top quality quartz movie and stills lighting equipment made by Lowel Lighting. Write to them for a price quote.

CIGARS, PIPES, and TOBACCO

If you're going to smoke, you might as well enjoy it as much as possible and try to save money while doing it. You can buy everything except cigarettes at a discount—pipes, tobacco, rolling machines, and cigars. Even the "leisure" smoker will find a good selection of paraphernalia which should enhance smoking pleasure with the least amount of pain in the right hip pocket.

FAIR & SQUARE

22 Huron St.
Port Jefferson, NY 11776
(516) 928-8707: NY
orders
(800) 645-1160: all
others
Catalog: free
Discount: 20 to 50%
Goods: name brand
Minimum Order: $50
Shipping: included on
prepaid orders
Sales Tax: NY residents
Payment: check, MO,
C.O.D.
$$$

Fair & Square carries all the paraphernalia that will make your "leisure smoking" really pleasurable. They have all kinds of pipes, roach clips, rolling papers, power hitters, coke kits, spoons, straws, and papers. They even have glow-in-the-dark "bongs." Fair & Square carries the popular Bambú, E-Z Wider, and wired papers. Bambú regulars are 15¢ per pack, about half of what they cost in New York.

76

FEDERATION

Box 2047
Pittsburgh, PA 15230
Information: inquire
Discount: up to 90%
Goods: house, name brand
Minimum Order: $1
Shipping: inquire
Guarantee: satisfaction
Payment: check, MO
$$$$

Federation sells incense, 100 sticks for an incredible $1—and it's already sorted and all guaranteed. Since incense at headshops costs up to 10¢ a stick, this is a real bargain—and how can you lose for a dollar?

GREEN RIVER TOBACCO CO., INC.

Box 1313
Owensboro, KY 42301
(502) 684-4737
Brochure: 30¢
Discount: up to 30%
Goods: house brand
Minimum Order: none
Shipping: extra, UPS
Sales Tax: KY residents
Guarantee: by manufacturer
Payment: check, MO, MC, Visa
$$$

If you can't quit, maybe you can slow down and enjoy the cigarettes you do smoke by rolling them yourself. Green River sells 10 kinds of cigarette tobaccos and roll-your-own machines, which not only allow you to control the blend of tobacco, but save you up to 30% over the cost of prepackaged cigarettes. You can also get accessories from Green River: cigarette cases, flints, lighters, etc. Pipe smokers are not forgotten—there are 25 pipe blends available here, also at discount prices.

HAYIM PINHAS

P.O.B. 500
Istanbul, Turkey
Catalog: free
Discount: 25 to 30%
Goods: handmade
Miminum Order: 2 pipes
Shipping: $1.50 per pipe;
FOB Istanbul
Payment: certified check
$$$$

The little catalog from this company shows photos of 52 different styles of meerschaum pipes and cigarette holders. Meerschaum is stone that comes from fossilized sea animals. It is ivory in color, and gains a rich brown color with years of smoking. Many of the pipes are carved so that the bowl looks like the head of a famous person. Some of the characters shown are D'Artangnan, Cleopatra, Shakespeare, Bacchus, Socrates, Lincoln, and Ramses. There are also sea-woman, Viking, fisherman, lion, Indian, dog, priest, and hand designs. The prices run from $4 to $300 but are mostly $12.50 to $25.00. Cigarette holders are $1.50, and pipes with masonic symbols are available for $25.00. Pinhas includes a complete guide to breaking in and caring for a meerschaum, and all his work is guaranteed.

J-R TOBACCO CO.

108 West 45th St.
New York, NY 10036
(212) 869-8777
Catalog: free
Discount: to 75%
Goods: house, name
brand
Minimum Order: $10.00
Shipping: 50¢ per box
Guarantee: absolute
Payment: check, MO, MC
$$$

J-R calls itself "the world's largest tobacco store," and judging from their selection, this is probably true. They have direct factory arrangements with a long list of brand name cigar manufacturers (Te-Amo, Alfred Dunhill, Don Alvaro, Palicio, etc.) that allow them to give you savings of 30 to 40% as a matter of course. In the catalog, there are articles about cigars and the pleasures of smoking that make interesting reading. In addition to cigars, there are tins of smoking tobacco, lighters, humidors, ashtrays, pens, and cigar cutters, all at discounts of over 50%. Don't miss their "deals for gamblers," which are potluck selections of cigars at prices even lower than usual, up to 60%.

NURHAM CEVAHIR

Istiklal Ceddesi
Bekar sokak No. 12/4
Beyoglu, Istanbul, Turkey
Catalog: free
Discount: 30% WBMC
reader discount
Goods: handcarved
Minimum Order: none
Shipping: 75¢ to $6.00
per item
Payment: bank draft to
Cevahir's bank
$$$$

DISCOUNT

Nurham Cevahir sells meerschaum pipes, with bowls carved into various shapes, and named things like Laughing Bacchus, Dragon, Lion, Tulip, Mermaid, Apache, and Women. Most of the pipes appear identical to those sold by Hayim Pinhas. They also have a good selection of plain meerschaum pipes, and some just etched with designs. The pipes are available in 4 sizes, and cost from $4.90 to $21.00, including the WBMC discount. Giftboxes are extra. There is a set of three handsome pipes, giftboxed, offered "for publicity," at $19.60. There are also black and white meerschaum chessmen. Don't forget to mention WBMC to get the discount.

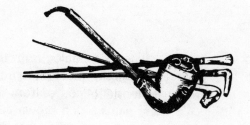

CLOTHING, FURS, and ACCESSORIES

You can buy some of the most beautiful clothing made anywhere from foreign firms, and often get it made to order for very little extra. There are alpaca sweaters from Ecuador here, and slickers from New York, surplus military clothing from the U.S. and England, sweaters from New Zealand, Denmark, and the British Isles, underwear from the Lower East Side in New York City, tams from Ireland, cashmere sweaters from Hong Kong, furs from New York, Amish clothing from Indiana, ponchos from Iceland, wooden shoes from Holland, and much more.

Most of the discounts are substantial, from 30% to 90%, and the goods include not only under and outer wear, but ties, shoes, boots, scarves, mittens, belts, and other accessories.

ANDEAN PRODUCTS

Apartado 472
Cuenca, Ecuador
South America

Andean Products sell heavy sweaters of thick wool that are found in import and department stores here for twice as much. Most of them are cream-colored, with designs such as Indian motifs woven into them. There are also macramé purses, leather "saddle bags," and belts. The artisans weave their own fabric to vibrant stripes to make shawls, ponchos, sashes, and horse-blankets. There is a large selection of hand-embroidered clothing in the familiar peasant styles, with puffy sleeves and drawstrings, square neck yoke tops, and hostess sets with deeply embroidered sleeves and hems. For more information, see main listing under HANDICRAFTS AND NATIVE PRODUCTS.

JOS. A. BANK CLOTHIERS, INC.

109 Market Pl.
Baltimore, MD 21202
(301) 837-1700

"You save 30% . . . in season" is the motto of Bank Clothiers. They carry good-looking men's clothing with a full line of well-priced suits in 2 and 3 button styles, sportscoats, a variety of classic

JOS. A. BANK CLOTHIERS, INC.

**Catalog: free, pub. 2 or 3
times a year
Discount: 30%
Goods: house name
Minimum Order: none
Shipping, Insurance,
Handling: up to $2.25
per item
Sales Tax: MD residents
Returns: within 30 days
Payment: check, MO,
MC, Visa
$$$**

shirt styles, straight leg pants, sports shirts, ties, belts, shoes, tuxedos, underwear, and tennis gear. There are also 3 pages of clothing for women. The men's suits are available in wool and wool blends, lightweight blends, poplin, seersucker, and denim. Prices run from $89.50 for summerweight suits to $165 for an all-wool suit (vests are extra and suits come unaltered). The sportscoats and blazers run from $69.50 for a seersucker check to $175 for an ultrasuede jacket. There are plaids and madras for the more daring, but even these are tastefully done. The ties offered are in solid colors, stripes, and English prints. They have a "Churchill collection" of ties in stripes inspired by Winston Churchill's medals. Most of the ties are silk and run from $6 to $8.50. There are dress shirts in 3 styles, including 100% cotton buttondowns, from $12 to $27.50, all kinds of slacks from $17.00 to $35.00, and casual clothes at good prices. Gift certificates are available, and you can return any item within 30 days if you aren't satisfied.

BUDGET UNIFORM CENTER, INC.

**941 Mill Rd.
Cornwells Heights, PA
19020
(215) 245-0300: main
line, PA orders
(800) 523-6582: medical
and individual orders
(800) 523-5750: group
orders
Medical Catalog: free,
pub. 3 times a year
Restaurant Catalog: free,
pub. twice a year
Discount: 25 to 35% on
jewelry; up to 35% on
clothing
Goods: house, name
brand
Minimum Order: none
Shipping: included,
prepaid orders
Handling: $2.25 max.
Sales Tax: PA residents
Payment: check, MO,
MC, Visa, C.O.D.
$$$**

Budget Uniform sells uniforms and accessories for the restaurant industry and medical professions. The medical catalog is filled with page after page of smart nurses' uniforms in all kinds of styles, plus smock tops, caps, shoes, pantyhose, sportswear, nightwear, lingerie, and jewelry. The jewelry is very pretty—gold-filled chains, bracelets, watches, monograms, and gold-plated service pins for RNs, candy stripers, PNs, aides, dental technicians, and emergency technicians, at just $5.95 each. There are also several pages of "Mr. Budget" consultation coats, jackets, pants, and labwear, and a section of useful items such as stain remover, a lighted pen, stethoscopes, a pocket timer, and a blood pressure kit. There are quantity discounts of 10% on orders over $100. Budget's restaurant catalog has uniforms and outfits for waiters, waitresses, bartenders, and kitchen help, in styles from short-skirted low-cut costumes to modestly tailored blazer suits. There are quantity discounts on medical and restaurant goods of 5 to 20% which make their low prices even lower. For more information, see MEDICAL AND SCIENTIFIC.

I. BUSS AND CO.

50 West 17th St.
New York, NY 10011
(212) 242-3338
Information: inquire
Discount: 30%
Goods: surplus
Minimum Order: none
Shipping: extra
Sales Tax: NY residents
Guarantee: satisfaction
Returns: unworn goods
Payment: MO, MC, Visa,
AE

I. Buss sells surplus clothing and goods for camping. They have sailor pants, military greatcoats, fatigue pants, capes, pea jackets, field jackets, and all kinds of accessories. They have no catalog, so you must write or call with a description of the goods you want, and they will tell you whether they have them in stock.

CAMBRIDGE WOOLS, LTD.

P.O. Box 2572
16-22 Anzac Ave.
Auckland, New Zealand

Cambridge makes sweaters of natural New Zealand wool in Aran styles. The colors are black, gray, and white, and the sweaters cost $35. They will make them to order for $45—a very low price indeed. See CRAFTS for complete listing.

V. JUUL CHRISTENSEN AND SON

17 Livjaegergade
DK-2100 Copenhagen
Denmark
Catalog: free
Discount: 30 to 50% plus
Goods: handknitted
Minimum Order: none
Shipping, Insurance:
included
Guarantee: satisfaction or
money back
Payment: check, MO, AE,
DC
$$$

Christensen and Son sells several styles of striped Icelandic sweaters in the natural wool colors of white, gray, brown, and black. There are zippered jackets, ponchos, pullovers, and matching scarves and hats. These cost from $10 for mittens to $98 for a hooded zipper jacket. The real show stealers in the brochure are four sets of sweaters for men and women which are shown in color. These are cardigans and pullovers done in stunning yoke designs and utterly beautiful colors. All the sweaters are available in several color combinations, and in cardigan and pullover styles. It would be hard to exaggerate how handsome these sweaters are, and how well priced at $58 to $66 (they would sell in stores for easily over $100). All the sweaters are made from the fleece of the famous Icelandic sheep, which produces wool that is light, yet wind- and waterproof, and a pleasure to wear.

LOUIS CHOCK, INC.

74 Orchard St.
New York, NY 10002
(212) 473-1929
Information: price quote
Discount: 25 to 35%
Goods: name brand
Minimum Order: none
Shipping: included in
price quote
Sales Tax: NY residents
Guarantee: satisfaction or
money back
Returns: resaleable
merchandise only
Payment: check, MO
$$$

Louis Chock carries underwear for men and children, and loungewear and nightwear for women. Some of the brand names he stocks are Hanes, BVD, Jockey, Burlington, Munsingwear, Berkshire, Vassarette, Lollipop, Mayer, and Carters. He asks that you write to him with the brand name, style number, and the color, and he will quote you a price that includes shipping, tax, and handling. It's a good idea to write or call with several choices, since he doesn't stock full lines of each brand.

D & A MERCHANDISE

22 Orchard St.
New York, NY 10002
(212) 226-9401
Information: price quote
Discount: to 30% and
more
Goods: brand name
Minimum Order: none
Shipping: extra
Sales Tax: NY residents
Returns: cash
Payment: check, MO
$$$

D & A sells brand name lingerie, socks, hosiery, and men's underwear. Most of their prices are discounted from 20 to 30% and more, which is very good on the items they are selling. The man who runs the store asked that the brand names not be listed because he is underselling the large stores. The brands are ones you know and love, and all you have to do is find the article you like in a store and make a note of the style and color numbers, as well as being sure of the size you want, and write D & A a letter or give them a call.

DAVID AND JOE TRADING CO.

P.O.Box 8189
Shamshuipo, Kowloon,
Hong Kong
Catalogs: free; $1 air
Discount: 30 to 90%
Goods: handbeaded,
custom made
Minimum Order: none
Shipping: FOB

David and Joe sell beaded and embroidered sweaters for women, and beaded bags and gloves. The sweaters are delicate and beautiful, and there are many different designs to choose from. Some are embellished with embroidery and sequins, and all the sweaters are available in a fur blend wool or cashmere. The prices are very low: $9.50 to $20 for fur/wool blends and $12.50 to $24 for cashmere. The sweaters would look lovely with long skirts or over evening wear. There are also beaded handbags to match priced at $1.20 to $12, and beaded gloves from $1 to

DAVID AND JOE TRADING CO.

**Payment: check, MO,
bank check
$$$$**

$2.50. For day, they offer more casual sweaters and custom-made shirts. The shirts are made to collar and chest size and sleeve length, and are unbelievably cheap: 2 longsleeved shirts in pima cotton cost $5.60, and monograms are 80¢ each. If you can find pima shirts here, they often cost at least $30 and monograms are often $5 each in department stores. You must request catalogs for men's clothing, and ask for information about their complete custom tailoring services. See also the listing under CRAFTS AND HOBBIES.

DEFENDER INDUSTRIES

**255 Main St.
P.O. Box 820
New Rochelle, NY 10801**

Defender carries stylish boating clothes that are waterproof and good looking. Some of the clothes, like the striped French fishermen's sweaters, are much cheaper here than elsewhere, and everything has the added feature of being practical and hardwearing. For more information, see AUTOMOTIVE AND MARINE SUPPLIES.

EILEEN'S HANDKNITS

**Ardara, Donegal, Ireland
Brochure: free
Discount: about 30%
Goods: handmade
Minimum Order: none
Shipping Cost: $2.50/
sweater surface; $5.50/
sweater airmail
Returns: alterations to
suit or money back
Payment: cashier's
check, MC, AE
$$**

Eileen sells sweaters that come "from the cottages of Ireland," handknitted in patterns that differ from knitter to knitter. There are 4 styles for women and 3 for men—cardigans, pullovers, and jackets. A matching tam and mittens are available. Almost all the sweaters are $45 each, compared to $75 and more charged in New York for comparable items. Eileen's knitters also do custom work at a small extra charge.

EISNER BROTHERS

**76 Orchard St.
New York, NY 10002
(212) 475-6868
Brochure: free
Discount: to 75%**

This business occupies a long, narrow little store that is stocked floor to ceiling with T-shirts in a rainbow of colors, all spilling off the shelves. The people who run it are serious and very businesslike. They sell to schools, clubs, athletic teams, and individuals all over the U.S., so they are very experienced in mail order. Most of

EISNER BROTHERS

Goods: house, brand name
Minimum Order: one dozen
Shipping: FOB warehouse NY
Sales Tax: NYC residents
Payment: cashier's check, C.O.D.
Resale #: necessary for sales tax exemption
$$$

the shirts they sell come from the mill that makes brands like Fruit of the Loom and Hanes, but there are no labels. All the shirts are American made. This is a good way to stock up on men's and boy's underwear at $11.50 to $22 a dozen. The minimum is one dozen shirts of the same size and color; remember that *anyone* can wear a T-shirt, and they make great gifts when you iron on transfers or embroider them.

HY FISHMAN FURS

305 Seventh Ave.
New York, NY 10001
(212) 244-4948
Information: inquire
Discount: 50% off store prices
Goods: house name, made to order
Shipping, Insurance: extra
Sales Tax: NY
Payment: certified check, MO, MC, AE, Visa
$$$$

Hy Fishman has a huge inventory of all kinds of furs and will make you a coat to order at no extra charge. He carries opossum, lynx, all kinds of mink, all kinds of fox, raccoon, nutria, fitch, and curly lamb. Write to him with your preferences and your measurements, and he will tell you what he has and how much it will cost. His prices are about half of what is charged in department stores for the same kind of fur—an unbelievable savings.

FURRIER.

G & G PROJECTIONS

53 Orchard St.
New York, NY 10002
(212) 431-4531,
226-9513
Information: by price
quote
Discount: up to 35%
Goods: name brand
Minimum Order: none
Shipping: extra
Guarantee: replacement
or refund on defective
goods
Payment: check, MO,
MC, Visa
$$$

G & G sells name brand men's shirts by makers like Oleg Cassini, Egon von Furstenburg, Phillip Venet, and Ferrari. They also carry Stanley Blacker blazers, Viceroy jeans, suits by Geoffrey Beene and Egon von Furstenburg, Robert Louis sheepskin coats, and much more. Their store is closed Saturdays and open Sundays, so don't phone in your order on a Saturday.

GENTLEMEN'S FURNISHER.

GOHN BROTHERS

Middlebury, IN 46540
(219) 825-2400
Catalog: free
Discount: 20 to 70%
Goods: house, brand
name
Minimum Order: none
Shipping: up to $2.90 on
orders under $40; free on
orders over $40
Sales Tax: IN residents
Returns: within 30 days
Payment: check, MO,
C.O.D.
$$$$

Reading the Gohn Bros. catalog takes you back into a world where bonnet board, buckram, quilting sheeting, crinoline, suspender webbing, and frock coats were stock items in the general store. The prices recall better days too, with bow ties at 98¢, 100% cotton sanforized blue denim in 10 to 13¾ weights from $2.39 to $2.59 a yard, muslin at 98¢ per yard, chambray at $1.69 per yard, and thread for 39¢ a spool. This company is a source for Amish clothing (some of the shirts fasten with hooks and eyes), and the clothes are work-tailored, sturdy, and cheap. Men's cotton chambray workshirts are $4.98, broadfall pants (denim) are $9.98 per pair, and men's underwear ranges from $1.69 for an undershirt to $8.19 for a thermal union suit. Men's cotton dress socks, $2.50 in New York stores, are 59¢ here. In addition, there are work gloves, sensible shoes, handkerchiefs, diapers, infant clothing, and, to shade your horse-drawn carriage, a large black buggy umbrella for $12.79. For more information, see CRAFTS AND HOBBIES listing.

GOLDBERGS' MARINE

202 Market St.
Philadelphia, PA 19106

Goldbergs' carries lovely Breton sweaters, French fisherman's striped sweaters for men and women, oiled wool sweaters, and bright yellow raincoats and waterproof boots. All the clothing is pictured in color in their catalog, and priced at a good discount. For the complete listing, see AUTOMOTIVE AND MARINE SUPPLIES.

HANDART EMBROIDERIES

**Hing Wai Building,
Rd. 106
36, Queen's Rd. Central
Hong Kong
Information: inquire
Discount: minimum of
30%
Goods: handmade
$$**

Handart Embroideries is an associate of Duk Kwong Opticals, who recommended them. They make hand-embroidered table-cloths, handkerchiefs, clothing, and pyjamas, and silk and satin bed sheets, tapestries, neckties, ivory, wood carvings, and other handicraft items. You must write to them for information on catalogs and shipping. They accept Visa cards and Diners Club. They do a brisk trade with U.S. customers, like most Hong Kong companies.

HUDSON'S

**105 Third Ave.
New York, NY 10003
(212) 475-9568
Catalog: $1.00
Discount: up to 40%
Goods: name brand
Minimum Order: none
Shipping: extra
Sales Tax: NY residents
Guarantee: on defective
mdse.
Warranty: by
manufacturer
Payment: check, MO,
MC, Visa, AE
$$$**

Hudson's sells name brand clothing for camping and casual wear like jeans, shirts, and Western shoes and boots. They also sell top brand camping equipment and hiking shoes. The discounts are very good and the selection is vast.

HYDE PARK TRADING CO.

DISCOUNT

**Colonial Shopping
Center, Rte. 9
Hyde Park, NY 12538
(914) 229-7900
Catalog: free, pub. in
April
Discount: 30% WBMC
Goods: name brand
Minimum Order: none
Shipping, Handling: $1
Sales Tax: NY residents
Payment: check, MO,
MC, Visa
$$$$**

Hyde Park Trading sells Quoddy handsewn moccasins at a 30% discount to readers of this catalog. They have the famous boat moccasins that are laced with rawhide and feature a nonskid white deck sole, at $20 less than other stores even before you take off 30%. There are styles for men and women, and they cost just $21 to $27 with the discount. Hyde Park also sells hiking shoes with Vibram soles, ring boots, casual shoes, fringed boots, and real leather boots for women at only $24 to $31 with the discount. They also have a large selection of beautiful Indian-style moccasins, some with beading, some in suede, and some suitable for outdoor wear. There are also wonderful fleece-lined slippers that would make great gifts for anyone who lives in a cold climate. Remember to mention the WBMC when requesting the catalog *and* when ordering, so you are sure to get your 30% discount.

ICEMART

**P.O. Box 23
Keflavik International
Airport
Iceland
Catalog: $1 airmail, pub.
in Sept.
Discount: minimum of
30%
Goods: handmade
Minimum Order: none
Shipping Cost: included
Guarantee: satisfaction,
or refund or exchange
Returns: within 30 days
Payment: check, IMO,
MC, AE, DC, Eurocard,
Access
$$$**

Airport stores are notoriously seductive, enticing the traveler to spend the last of his money on beautiful products, duty free, just as he's about to leave the country. Icemart is no exception. They sell beautiful sweaters in natural colors—white, gray, brown, and black. They carry "Lopi" sweaters, made of unspun wool and knitted with geometric yoke and cuff designs. Each sweater is different in shade and design. Prices are $29.70 to $50.60. There are also sweaters in teased wool, with stripes and Icelandic symbols knitted in, at $35 to $45 each, plus capes, ponchos, jackets, an opera cape, and more. Accessories are available: hats, socks, and mittens, from $5 to $12. For listings of other goods that Icemart sells, see CRAFTS AND HOBBIES; FOOD; HANDICRAFTS AND NATIVE PRODUCTS; HOME; and JEWELRY.

KENNEDY'S OF ARDARA

**Ardara Co. Donegal,
Ireland
Catalog: free
Discount: up to 80%
Goods: handmade
Shipping: $3.50 per
garment; $7 air mail
Payment: IMO, bank
draft
$$$**

Tucked away in the mountains of Donegal are 900 cottage knitters who create sweaters and accessories of pure Aran wool in unique designs taken from Irish symbols and history. The sweaters pictured in the brochure are classic cardigans and pullovers for both men and women. With average care, they are supposed to grow softer with every wash, keep shape, and not wear out. They cost from $35 to $49 each, much lower, say the Kennedys, than the prices in Lord and Taylor, Saks Fifth Avenue, and Bloomingdales, *where their sweaters are sold at retail prices.* There are also shawls at $15, Aran mitts at $3.50 per pair, and other knitted things.

LAURENCE CORNER

**62/64 Hampstead Rd.
London NW1 2NU
England
Catalog: $2.50
Discount: varies
Goods: surplus, original
art
Minimum Order: none
Shipping: extra, min. of
$4.40**

Laurence Corner sells what looks like tons of surplus goods which are all pictured haphazardly in their big catalog. Their main line is clothing: parkas, jackets, greatcoats, military raincoats, hunting clothes, beach shorts, camouflage clothing, and overalls. There are menacingly heavy Wellington boots, woodsmen boots with silent treads, long johns, vests, police capes and a whole section of "surplus chic" clothing that looks like top fashion but costs a lot less. In addition, there are belts, pullovers, mittens, hats and scarves. Laurence carries a line of new clothing—leather coats and jackets, Levi's and Wranglers, and cowboy hats. Some prices

LAURENCE CORNER

**Guarantee: satisfaction
or money back
Payment: check, MO,
Barclaycard
$$**

are very low, while others are more in line with the value of the goods. The catalog is a fascinating mishmash of item descriptions, photographs, and quips like "it's crazy but it's fun" and "trends to suit all pockets" jumbled across the pages. For more listings, see ART AND ANTIQUES; SPORTS AND RECREATION; MEDICAL AND SCIENTIFIC; and SURPLUS.

D. MacGILLIVRAY AND COY.

**Muir of Aird
Benbecula
Western Isles, Scotland
PA88 5NA**

MacGillivray sells clothing for men, women, and children, both ready-to-wear and custom made. For children there are baby shawls, Fair Isle bordered sweaters, cardigans and lumber jackets from $10.50 to $14.00, and accessories. Women's clothing includes Fair Isle lumber jackets, $20 each, jumpers at $19, berets and gloves at $5 each, and a Kilspindie sweater in Fair Isle design in 3-color combinations for $36. There are also Harris wool pullovers, heavily oiled and waterproof for $20 and $24. These are available in sizes for men also, as are the Kilspindie sweaters and a group of Aran sweaters. For men there are tartan ties, tams, and caps. In addition, MacGillivray can make cashmere and lambswool clothing to order—send $1.00 for brochure and samples. They have a personal tailoring service that will copy a garment from style plates, photos, or illustrations. Cost, including everything but fabric, runs from $22.50 for a plain lady's skirt, to $100.00 for a man's 3-piece suit. And for those interested in the absolutely authentic article, MacGillivray sells handtailored tartan kilts for men, women, and children, in 2 grades of wool, from $80 to $130. For complete listing, see CRAFTS AND HOBBIES.

THE NEPAL CRAFT EMPORIUM

**G.P.O. Box 1443
Kathmandu, Nepal**

The Craft Emporium sells beautiful Nepalese handicrafts, including some clothing and accessories. There is a woolen bakkhu jacket, which is sleeveless with woven trim and pockets, for $3.00. The same jacket with sleeves and trimmed cuffs is $5.25, and is recommended for skiing. There are also shoulder bags of jute, cotton, wool, and silk, which cost from 30¢ to $1.75. The goods are very simple in design, yet very handsome. For the complete listing, see HANDICRAFTS AND NATIVE PRODUCTS.

A.W.G. OTTEN

Albert Cuypstraat 102-104-106
Amsterdam, Holland

Otten makes and sells functional and decorative wooden shoes, which are worn in Holland even today by gardeners, dairy workers and other people. They also sell modified clogs which are quite attractive. For the complete listing, see HANDICRAFTS AND NATIVE PRODUCTS.

RAMA JEWELRY LTD.

P.O. Box 858
987 Silom Rd.
Bangkok, Thailand

This company sells jewelry of semiprecious stone, and also carries a line of Thai silk clothing. For the complete listing, see JEWELRY.

SCHACHNER BROTHERS

98 Orchard St.
New York, NY 10002
(212) 674-6910
Information: price quote
Discount: 30 to 60%
Goods: name brand
Minimum Order: $100.00
Shipping: extra
Sales Tax: NY residents
Payment: MO
$$$

Schachner Brothers sell the top names in ladies' gowns and lingerie, hosiery, and robes, plus men's underwear and socks and children's underthings. Because of agreements with their suppliers, they can't have the names listed; but if you write to them with a model or style number, they will tell you if they have it and give you a price quote.

THE TIBETAN REFUGEE SELF HELP CENTER

Havelock Villa
65 Ghandi Rd.
Darjeeling, India

The Center sells wool and cotton blend clothing—coats and shawls in simple styles, plus Tibetan soldiers' caps and lovely boots. See HANDICRAFTS AND NATIVE PRODUCTS for a complete listing.

TRADE EXCHANGE CEYLON, LTD.

72 Chatham St.
Colombo 1, Sri Lanka
Catalog: $5 airmail
Discount: 30%
Goods: handmade
Shipping: FOB India
Payment: bank transfer
$$$

Trade Exchange sells batiked fabric that is created by the traditional wax-dyeing methods. They make the fabric into clothing, bedspreads, lampshades, and hangings. Their "Lakloom" brand clothing comes in Indian styles, primarily full-length dresses that make use of the spectacular patterns that the batiking produces. The sarees are distinctly ethnic and quite flamboyant, but there are also Western styles in brilliant colors and border prints. There is even a beach coat and trunks ensemble for men, and caftans for everyone. The catalog itself was at the printers at this writing, but prices are guaranteed to be low. See the listing under HOME for more information.

COSMETICS and PERFUMES

If you love French perfume but hate the high prices, take heart: you can buy directly from France at savings of up to 60% off U.S. list. Most of the famous name perfumes are available at Grillot, including Nina Ricci, Lanvin, Paco Rabanne, and Guy Laroche. You can also buy Scottish perfume, "natural" grooming products, and a variety of scented candles, potpourris, and sachets. Incense materials and scented wreaths are also included here.

Several of the firms sell cosmetic preparations in addition to scents, also at good discounts. The strangest cosmetic product around is also recommended highly by several people as the most effective—"Bag Balm," a treatment for sore or chapped cows' udders that is said to work miracles on hands in the same condition.

CAPRILAND'S HERB FARM

Silver St.
Coventry, CT 06238
(203) 742-7244
Catalog: 25¢ or SASE
Discount: 50% on some items
Goods: homegrown
Minimum Order: none
Shipping: $1 minimum
Sales Tax: CT residents
Payment: check, MO
$$$

Capriland's grows over 300 kinds of herbs and scented geranium, plus roses and other flowers. They sell the dried flowers in many forms—sachet pillows, wreaths, dolls, and in loose quantity. The half-pounds of rose buds and lavender are $4.00, half of what they cost in New York City, and lemon verbena, frankincense, and myrrh are $5.00 per half-pound. Essential oils, enough to make one pound of potpourri, are $2 each and come in 13 scents. There are other fragrances—patchouli leaves, vetiver root, sandalwood, etc., in packages for $1. You can also buy clove, orange, or apple pomander balls for $1.75, or get a kit that makes 6 to 8. Capriland's also sells seeds, plants, herb stationery, and books. For information on these, see BOOKS AND RECORDS; FARM AND GARDEN; HANDICRAFTS AND NATIVE PRODUCTS; TOYS AND GAMES.

DAIRY ASSOCIATION CO., INC.

Lyndonville, VT 05851
(802) 626-3610
Brochure: free
Discount: 50%
Minimum Order: none
Shipping: included
Payment: check, MO
$$$$

The Dairy Association makes a unique product that is used to treat the sore udders of cows. It is called, appropriately, "Bag Balm," and it also works miracles on weatherbeaten, chapped, or just plain dry hands. It costs $2 for a 10-ounce container of the cream, which is sold by other companies for $3.95. The man who runs Dairy Association says that "Bag Balm" stains, so you should use it at night with protective gloves.

GRILLOT

10, Rue Cambon
Paris 1er, France
Price List: free
Discount: up to 60%
Goods: brand name
Minimum Order: none
Shipping, Insurance:
$3.00 per package
seamail, $6 by air
Payment: check, MO,
bank draft
$$$$

Grillot carries a list of perfumes that includes scents by such famous names as Balenciaga, Dior, Patou, Nina Ricci, Jean Desprez, Lanvin, Paco Rabanne, and Guy Laroche. Most of the perfumes are available in pure perfume, cologne, and eau de toilette forms. Grillot also sells the green cypress scented candles by Rigaud. They cost $18.35 for the complete candle and $13.35 for the refill. Lest this seem somewhat expensive, note that in New York City the complete candle is $35 and the refill is $25 (the smell is wonderful and the candle is something of a status item). Grillot also sells a few skin creams by Dior, also at substantial savings. Some of the perfumes listed are Ma Griffe, Miss Dior, Joy, Calandre, Je Reviens, Givenchy III, Gucci No. 1, Eau Savage, Bal à Versailles, Fidgi, Arpege, L'Air du Temps, and Amour Amour. Grillot states that you can have certain small items sent as "unsolicited gifts," which makes them exempt from duty charges. In the end, the additional charges often amount to less than the sales tax paid on the same items bought in the U.S.!

D. MacGILLIVRAY AND COY.

Muir of Aird
Benbecula
Western Isles, Scotland
PA88 5NA

MacGillivray sells eight Hebridean perfumes which are "crofter made, hand blended, and highly concentrated," with names like "Plaid," "Dark Glen," "Tangle," "Love Lilt," and "Caluna." Prices are $1.50 for 1cc; 5cc's for $4; and 10cc's for $5.50. See CRAFTS AND HOBBIES for complete listing.

PURE PLANET PRODUCTS

1025 N. 48th St.
Phoenix, AZ 85008

Pure Planet carries all kinds of natural soaps and shampoos, including a full line of Dr. Bronner's well-known peppermint and almond castile soap that's so pure you can brush your teeth with it. They also have aloe vera soap, cucumber soap, and a foot-long bar of castile soap. There are also combs and brushes of "natural" materials, and everything is very cheap with the 30% WBMC reader discount. See FOOD for complete listing.

DISCOUNT

S & C HUBER, ACCOUTREMENTS

82 Plants Dam Rd.
East Lyme, CT 06333

These people sell simple potpourris in 3 scents: "spices of life," "wisps of roses," and "citrus grove." There are also 4 soaps: plain, oatmeal, cornmeal, and soap-on-a-rope. The sachets cost $4 to $6.30 per 4-ounce bag, and the soaps run from 50¢ a bar to $1.50 for soap-on-a-rope, all of which are low prices (comparable sachets in New York cost $10 and $12, and the soaps begin at $2 a bar). For complete listing, see CRAFTS AND HOBBIES.

STECHERS LTD.

62 Independence Square
Port-of-Spain,
Trinidad, W.I.

Stechers sells, among other lovely items, perfume from famous French houses such as Lanvin, Dior and Raban at 30 to 50% off. For more information, see HOME.

CRAFTS and HOBBIES

When we showed the crafts catalogs to some of our craftspeople friends, their eyes began to water, and so did, we assume, their mouths. You don't have to be stuck with paint-by-number and plasticene, even if you live in a small town, for these sources are inexpensive, reliable, and offer a great range of products. The foreign suppliers are especially low cost and high quality. You're certainly not going to find the yarns, for example, in your local Woolworth's.

The hobby catalogs are really delightful. They take you back to the wonder of childhood and free time and doing things for fun. Even if you're not a hobbyist, you may want to send for the catalogs as small gifts to someone who is, or perhaps to interest your child in a new pursuit. You will also find other relevant listings in ART MATERIALS; JEWELRY, GEMS AND WATCHES; and TOOLS—and scattered throughout several other sections.

AAA SCALE CO.

P.O. Box 496
Paramount, CA 90723

Triple A Scale makes a hand scale that comes in very handy when measuring things like dyes and scents for candles, cosmetic preparations, etc. See OFFICE for the complete listing.

AMERICA'S HOBBY CENTER, INC.

146 West 22nd St.
New York, NY 10011
(212) 675-8922
Catalogs: boat models,
$1.50
airplane models, $1.50
train models, $1.50
plastics, 50¢

The people at America's Hobby are putting together a new catalog, and the discounts are said to range from 10 to 40%. Virtually all the goods are brand name. The discounts are figured on a legitimate list price and not a grossly exaggerated figure, so the discounts represent true bargains. The catalogs listed contain information on the models and the retail price, but if you send them a stamp, they will send you a brochure that comes out every 3 or 4 months that has the reductions. The man at America's said

94

AMERICA'S HOBBY CENTER, INC.

discount brochure, 1 stamp
Discount: 10 to 40%
Goods: brand name
Minimum Order: none
Shipping: included in U.S.
Handling: $1.00
Insurance: 50¢
Sales Tax: NY residents
Returns: 14 days, less postage (no returns on electronics)
Warranty: by manufacturer
Payment: check, MO
$$

that they carry all kinds of brand names, and rattled off a whole list of them (Tyco, Cox, etc.). When you order the catalog, don't forget to send a stamp to get the brochure with all the special low prices.

AQUA ENGINEERS

250 Cedar St.
Ortonville, MI 48462
(313) 627-2877

Aqua Engineers sells all kinds of supplies, equipment, and esoterica related to raising tropical fish. They also carry new lines for dogs, cats, hamsters and "crawlers." Aqua Engineers offers a "free stuff" discount of 25% to WBMC readers. See ANIMALS for main listing.

BERJE CHEMICAL PRODUCTS, INC.

43-10 23rd St.
Long Island City, NY 11101
(212) 937-1280
Price List: free
Discount: up to 41% off
Goods: house brand
Minimum Order: 1 lb. scent or 1 case sticks
Shipping: FOB L.I.C., NY
Sales Tax: inquire
Payment: check, MO
$$$

Berjé sells essences and fragrances for use in scenting candles and incense. The essences are very concentrated; Berjé suggests a mixture of 3 to 5% of fragrance to cutting oil. The scents range in price from $7.25 to $13.90 per pound, and the cutting oil is $1.00 per pound (in 30 lb. cans only). Unscented incense sticks are available in 9½-, 11-, and 19-inch lengths and 10,000 11-inch sticks are $31. If you buy a drum of cutting oil for $30, a pound of fern essence for $10, and a case of sticks for $31, you can make around 10,000 incense sticks at 70¢ per hundred—and since 10 cost as much as 70¢ in "head shops," this is a savings of up to 90%. You can also use the scents for candle-making. There are over 90 fragrances listed, and if you don't find what you need among "blossom of spring," jasmine, maple, "French fantasy," cedarwood, and tuberose, then inquire—they probably stock it.

BUCKLE SHACK, USA

1173 Alpharetta St.
Roswell, GA 30075
(404) 993-2100
Catalog: free
Discount: 30% plus
Goods: name brand
Minimum Order: $25
Payment: check, C.O.D.
$

Buckle Shack claims that they have the largest variety of belt buckles at one source in the entire United States. They sell leather tools, snaps, rivets, key rings, etc. The catalog was unavailable, but a talk with the manager verified that the selection is unparalleled and the prices fantastic—wholesale and below.

CAMBRIDGE WOOLS, LTD.

P.O. Box 2572
16-22 Anzac Ave.
Auckland 1, New Zealand
Leaflet and Samples: free
Discount: 30 to 70% off
U.S. list
Goods: house name,
custom made
Minimum Order: none
Shipping: included
Returns: money back if
not satisfied
Payment: IMO or bank
draft
$$$$

In addition to wool and yarn, Cambridge Wools sells an Ashford spinning wheel in standard and upright models which is sent partly assembled. They throw in 4 bobbins and a "lazy Kate" bobbin holder, and a booklet on how to spin—all for $66, less than half the U.S. price. Wool carders are $11, compared to $30 and more in the U.S. Cambridge also sells greasy (natural) and scouted carded wool in white, black, and gray, at $2.50 and $3.50 per pound. Their quantity discount is 10¢/lb. on 100 to 500 lb. orders, and 20¢/lb. on orders over 500 lbs. If you want to dispense with carding, spinning, and dyeing, Cambridge sells weaving and knitting yarn at 35¢ and 40¢ an ounce, much lower than U.S. equivalents. The knitting yarn is available in over 30 jewellike colors, and a brilliant bundle of samples is enclosed with the price list. Cambridge even offers sheepskin rugs dyed to match the yarn. See HOME for further information, and CLOTHING for a listing on their sweaters.

ALBERT CONSTANTINE AND SON, INC.

2050 Eastchester Rd.
Bronx, NY 10461
(212) 792-1600
Catalog: 50¢
Discount: 10 to 30%
Goods: house, name
brand
Minimum Order: $5
Shipping: extra; UPS, PP,
or FOB Bronx
Sales Tax: NY residents
Payment: check, MO
$$$

Constantine carries every precut wood-picture kit made in America—over 60, including handsome country scenes, animal pictures, praying hands, antique cars, Americana, the Florida Everglades, and even the seal of the United States. Prices start at $1.95 for a 5x7-inch picture and run up to $75 for a detailed 21x38-inch reproduction of Da Vinci's *Last Supper*, which uses 577 pieces of wood. Constantine sells sheets and pieces of veneer, and tools for woodworking. You can buy a box of samples of common and exotic veneers, from ash to zebrawood, for only $7.75. These are good for small crafts projects and wood identification. Large pieces of veneer are available from 20¢ to $1.25 a square foot, plus craft boxes, tools, hardware, cabinet woods, finishes, glues, and specialty items like lamp finials, clockhands, and Shaker pegs. For more on what they carry, see FARM AND GARDEN; TOOLS AND HARDWARE; and TOYS AND GAMES.

CRAFTSMAN WOOD SERVICE CO.

**2729 South Mary St.
Chicago, IL 60608
(312) 842-0507
Catalog: 50¢
Discount: up to 30%
Goods: house, name
brand
Minimum Order: $6
Shipping: extra, UPS or
FOB Chicago
Sales Tax: IL residents
Guarantee: by
manufacturer
Payment: check, MO,
MC, Visa
$$$**

Craftsman has over 4,000 items in its 150-page catalog. There are comprehensive selections of Dremel woodworking tools and accessories, Stanley routers, all kinds of lathes, drill presses, shapers, files, abrasives, and cabinet hardware. Lamp craftsmen or anyone trying to refurbish a worn lamp will find just about everything they need in Craftsman's 5 pages of lamp supplies. There are also upholstery materials and tools, wood-carving trimmings for furniture, picture frame moldings, wood stains, cabinet woods and veneers, and all kinds of finishes and glues. Craftsman sells beautiful clock kits that cost from $11.95 to $79.95, plus all the necessary faces, hands, and movements to build one; miniature furniture kits, and handsome wood inlay marquetry kits. The prices are excellent, and the tools and supplies can be used by craftspeople of every ilk, in addition to saving homeowners money who make their own repairs on furniture, lamps, clocks, etc.

DAVID AND JOE TRADING CO.

**P.O. Box 8189
Shamshuipo, Kowloon,
Hong Kong**

This Hong Kong firm has incredible prices on their fabrics. They are selling pure silk fabric, 42 inches wide, for $2.50 a yard. Their silk mix brocade, 28 inches wide, is $2.10, and acetate and rayon brocades are $1.50 and $1.00 per yard. These are available in colors and checks, and are 75 to 90% lower in price than comparable goods in the U.S. Don't miss the main listing in CLOTHING AND ACCESSORIES for their low prices on beaded sweaters and custom clothes.

EMPIRE MODELS

**Dept. C, P.O. Box 42287
Tucson, AZ 85733
(602) 881-1257
Catalog: $1.50
Discount: 10 to 40%
Goods: name brand
Minimum Order: none
Shipping, Insurance: 95¢
to $4.50
Sales Tax: AZ residents
Payment: check, MO,
MC, Visa, C.O.D.
$$$**

Empire's catalog is chock full of radio-controlled model airplanes at discounts of 10 to 40% off list price. In addition to the planes, radios, and engines, they have complete lines of accessories, Du-Bro parts, and Dremel tools. The planes are made by Fox, Carl Goldberg, K & B, Kraft, Lanier, Mark's Models, Midwest Products, MRC, Steve Muck, Bud Nosen, Dave Platt, Soarcraft, Sterling, and others. There are also radio-controlled boats by Dumas. Some of the models are pictured, but most are listed by name, size, and model number, so you have to know what you want when you order. Look in high-priced model shops for the kits you want, then write to Empire with the information.

FABRICS CUTAWAYS

Darlene's Originals
P.O. Box 424-7
Arcadia, SC 29320
(803) 579-2033
Catalog: 35¢
Discount: to 80%
Goods: fabric remnants
Minimum Order: none
Shipping: 50¢ per
assortment
Sales Tax: SC residents
Guarantee: satisfaction
Returns: refund
Payment: check, MO
$$$

If you do quilting and patchwork, you've probably bought yards of goods to cut into scraps and then sew back into a quilt—which was not the way Grandma did it. She used scraps. If you want to carry on in that thrifty tradition, consider Fabric Cutaways which sells cloth and scraps by the pound. These are leftovers and seconds from dressmaking and fabric factories: one pound of dress-weight cotton blend = 4 yards of fabric. One quilters' special is 6 lbs. for $6.00, which averages out to 25¢ a yard. Velvet, satin, and knits are also available at low prices. These are good for doll clothes, pillow covers, and the like. Polyester batting for filling quilts is also sold here at $2.00 per yard in 102-inch widths. Remember this source for materials for Christmas bazaar toys, etc., when you don't need yard lengths.

FORT CRAILO YARNS

2 Green St., Dept. 3
Rensselaer, NY 12144
(518) 465-2371
Sample Cards: 4 wool
sample cards, $1.20;
cotton sample card, 50¢
Discount: 30%; quantity
discounts of 5% and 10%
Goods: 100% virgin wool
Minimum Order: none
Shipping, Packing: 85¢
plus UPS charges
Guarantee: satisfaction
Payment: check, MO
$$$$

Fort Crailo sells a large line of yarns suitable for handweaving and rugmaking which are available in different weights and 33 exquisite colors. The sleek folding sample cards show Zephyr Worsted (fine, $2.48 per ¼ lb.), Crailo Lite-Spun (thicker, $1.96 per ¼ lb.), Crailo Rya (thick, for Rya rugs, $1.92 per ¼ lb.), and Crailo-Spun (thin, tightly spun, at $1.80 per ¼ lb.). The cotton yarn is *very* fine, comes in 17 colors, and costs from 98¢ to $1.28 per ¼ lb. Fort Crailo also makes novelty yarns and wool/synthetic blends, which are incredibly cheap at $2.75 a pound. The yarn comes in skeins or is wound on 4-ounce cones, and approximate yardage per pound is also given for each yarn type. This company is a must for weavers and knitters looking for good supply sources.

GLORYBEE HONEY AND SUPPLY

1001½ Terry St.
Eugene, OR 97402
(503) 485-1649
Catalog: 25¢, pub. in Jan.
Discount: quantity
discounts of 5 and 10%
on low prices
Goods: house, name
brands

Glorybee sells a complete line of equipment and supplies for keeping bees, and also sells live bees and assembled hives. In addition, Glorybee gives a course covering the essentials of beginning beekeeping, and they advertise that they pay the highest price for beeswax. They sell all the equipment you need to set up a hive: foundations, hive frames, hardware, extracting equipment, an observation hive, queen and drone traps, honey dabbers, veils, gloves, tools, smokers, escapes, excluders, repellants, bee feed and stimulants, and honey pumps. The prices are great to begin

GLORYBEE HONEY AND SUPPLY

Minimum Order: none
Shipping: FOB Eugene,
OR
Sales Tax: OR residents
Guarantee: satisfaction
or replacement
Payment: check, MO,
bank draft
$$

with, and there are quantity discounts of 5 and 10% on orders over $200 and $300. Glorybee also has books on beekeeping, bee coloring books, a Pooh Cook Book, labels for your honey jars, and T-shirts that read "Support Your Local Honey."

GOHN BROTHERS

Middlebury, IN 46540

Gohn Brothers sells all kinds of fabric, thread, and things like 100% cotton bed sheeting, quilt sheeting, tailor's canvas, haircloth, and more. They have batiste at $1.89 a yard, rayon gabardine at $1.29 a yard, plisse crepe, voile, cracker barrel, and some double knits. Prices are all very low. Cotton thread too, if they can get it runs from 39¢ to 95¢ a spool. There is embroidery floss for 15¢ a skein, pillow tubing at $1.29 a yard, stiffening, all kinds of denim and chambray, suit lining, and wool coat material. The prices are about as low as any you'll get anywhere on dress goods, and many of these things are almost impossible to get elsewhere. For the complete listing, see CLOTHING, FURS, AND ACCESSORIES.

JOHN HATHAWAY

Box 1287
San Pedro, CA 90731
(213) 833-9853
Catalog: free, pub. in
June
Discount: up to 50% over
specialty stores
Goods: imported,
domestic
Minimum Order: none
Shipping, Insurance:
extra, UPS
Sales Tax: CA residents
Guarantee: satisfaction
Returns: refunds on
resaleable goods
Payment: check, MO
$$$$

For a mere $5.35 you can buy a whole German village with 21 houses and a fountain; or, if you're strapped for cash, you might want the Lichtenstein Castle for only $2.25. When wood, metal, and even plastic models get expensive and overly complicated, take a break with John Hathaway's paper models of castles, towns, churches, historical sites, animals, ships, cars, aircraft, warships, or his working clock. The models are printed on a light cardboard and are imported from England, France, and Germany. Mr. Hathaway even designs his own models and is working on a bi-plane. Prices run from $1 to $25, but most are under $5, making paper modeling one of the cheapest hobbies around. Mr. Hathaway sent a model of the Lichtenstein Castle as a sample of his goods, which proved irresistible and was promptly assembled, turning out beautifully. Most of the models are colored, and foreign models come with guidelines in English. You can choose from dozens of models, including some dramatic flying birds described as "taxidermy in paper." A word of warning—be prepared to become totally addicted to the art of paper modelling.

KARL HEIDTMANN

563 Remscheid 14
Postfach 140 309
West Germany
Catalog and Price Lists:
2 IRC's
Discount: 30 to 50% off
U.S. prices
Goods: high quality tools
Minimum Order: 100DM
($50)
Shipping, Packing,
Insurance: included in
invoice
Returns: correspond
within 1 week
Payment: bank draft, or
transfer
$$$$

Karl Heidtmann makes old-world quality woodcarving tools in all sorts of shapes and sizes. There are straight and skew chisels, straight and curved gouges, parting tools, and spoon bit chisels and gouges. The tools are pictured in good line drawings, and their shapes—up to 40mm—are represented by curved or straight lines. Hornbeam handles for the tools are available from 55¢ to $1.10 each. The tools themselves run from $3.25 to $25.75. They are priced in deutschemarks, so you must obtain the current conversion rate when you order in order to set the price in dollars. Mr. Heidtmann has assembled 2 sets of tools for beginners, 1 with 18 tools and handles and 1 sharpening stone for about $100, and the other with 32 tools and handles and 2 stones for about $175. This averages out to about $5.50 per tool, which is much less than what you'd pay here for tools of comparable quality. And to wrap everything up, there are canvas rolls that hold 12, 24, or 36 tools, which cost from $10 to $22.50. If you are a beginner or an experienced woodcarver, don't miss this excellent source for superior tools.

THE HOBBY MARKET

P.O. Box 2172
Fort Worth, TX 76113
(817) 738-2301
Catalog: free
Discount: 30%
Goods: name brand
Minimum Order: none
Shipping: included
Handling: $2 on prepaid
orders, $5 on C.O.D.
Sales Tax: TX residents
Payment: check, MO,
MC, Visa, C.O.D.
$$$

The Hobby Market carries airplane models by over 160 manufacturers. Their prices are consistently low—30% and more—and they run specials throughout the year at up to 40% off. The catalog is not illustrated, so you have to know the model you want by name or model number to order. In addition to radios, engines, and airplanes, Hobby Market sells items like sanders and paper, tools, airbrush equipment, resins, fiberglass equipment, fiberglass cloth, and paint. Shipping is included, so you end up saving even more, especially on large orders.

HOBBY SHACK

18480 Bandilier Circle
Fountain Valley, CA
92708
(714) 963-9881
Catalog: $2.00, pub. in
March
Discount: 20 to 30%
Goods: house, name
brand
Minimum Order: none
Shipping: extra
Sales Tax: CA residents
Payment: check, MO,
MC, Visa, C.O.D.
$$$

HOLE IN THE WALL

229 E. 14th St.
New York, NY 10003
(212) 533-1350
Catalog: none; inquire
for information
Discount: 30% plus
Goods: house brand
Minimum Order: dozen
or gross, depending on
item
Shipping: extra
Sales Tax: NY residents
Guarantee: satisfaction
Payment: check, MO
$$

ICEMART

P.O. Box 23
Keflavik International
Airport
Iceland

Hobby Shack sells radio-controlled airplanes, boats, cars, and the accessories to make them work. They have Hobby Shack kits and kits by Pilot, plus Cirrus radios. They also carry Fuji engines and Saito steamboat engines. Once your name is on their mailing list, you get 30-page seasonal catalogs with specials and the newest model equipment.

STEAM-ENGINE.

If you are an artisan or craftsman interested in buying dozens or grosses of findings and jewelry hardware, Hole in the Wall is interested in you—write to them stating what you need and they will give you a price quote. They have all kinds of jewelry tools, findings, and chains, and specialize in what they call "Art Deco-Nouveau filigree." Because they sell in quantity, prices are rock bottom.

JEWELLER.

A kit for an Icelandic sweater in hand-twisted Lopi wool, cardigan or pullover style, in natural colors of white, gray, brown, or black is available here for $24.90. Instructions are included. For a complete listing, *see* CLOTHING, FURS, AND ACCESSORIES.

KASURI DYE WORKS

P.O. Box 7101
1959 Shattuck Ave.
Berkeley, CA 94704
(415) 841-4509
Catalog: 75¢
SASE: samples of Ikat
yarn and tape, samples of
cloth, $2.00
Discount: up to 40% in
quantity
Goods: housebrand
Minimum Order: none
Shipping: extra, UPS
Handling: 25¢ to 50¢
Sales Tax: CA residents
Payment: check, MO
$$$

Kasuri is one of the few sources in the United States that sells supplies for Ikat, which is a form of Japanese weaving. They also sell Japanese fabrics, cotton yarn, indigo dyes, seaweed starch, patterns for weaving, tools, and much more. They offer one of the few books available on Ikat, with photographs, instructions, and diagrams, for $3.20. The fabrics are described as being printed in Japanese "folk art" patterns, are 14 inches long and 28 inches wide, and cost (as of this writing) from $1.90 to $4.75 per yard. Although many of the goods—yarn, dye, fabric—are good for other crafts, this company is a real find for the Ikat weaver who has trouble locating materials even through the most specialized craft supply houses.

KOHLMAN'S MINIATURES SHOP

33 Newton Rd.
Rochester, NY 14626
(716) 225-0754
Catalog: inquire
Discount: 50% to
dealers; "nice" discounts
to retail
Sales Tax: NY residents
Payment: check, MO

Kohlman's Miniatures sells dolls, books, dollhouses, miniatures, and the X-acto Collector's series. They wrote (on miniature-sized paper) to say that their catalog was at the printer, but they sell to dealers and retail customers at different rates. They've been in business for almost 10 years and make a point of answering all letters, so you're sure to get a reply if you inquire about the goods and the discount.

STAVROS KOUYOUMOUTZAKIS

Workshop Spun Wools
166 Kalokerinou Ave.
Iraklion, Crete, Greece
Price List and Samples:
free
Discount: to 60%
Goods: hand spun
Minimum Order: $20
Shipping: included
Insurance: $1 per pkg.,
extra
Payment: cashier's check
in dollars
$$$

Mr. Kouyoumoutzakis sends out a price list bulging with four bunches of lush-colored yarn samples included free of charge. The yarn is $3.50 to $4.00 per pound for orders over $20, and 10% more for orders under $20. There are two types of natural colored yarn (brown, black, and cream) from Crete, one of which is made from spun goat's hair. There is a sample of Australian 2-ply yarn in a cream color, and a whole bundle of vibrant colored strands of Greek wool. Be sure to order enough of the colored yarn for whatever you're making, as dye lots are sure to be different.

E.C. KRAUS

P.O. Box 7850
Independence, MO
64053
(816) 254-7448
Catalog: free
Discount: up to 50% over
wines purchased at
liquor stores
Goods: name brand
Minimum Order: none
Shipping: included
Sales Tax: MO residents
Guarantee: satisfaction
Returns: authorized only
Payment: check, MO,
MC, Visa
$$$

You can save up to half the cost of wine by making it yourself, and even more on special items such as liqueurs. Krause sells books, supplies, and equipment for making all kinds of beer and wine, and their catalog even includes some recipes. They sell the yeasts that you need to begin fermentation, additives, clarifyers to improve wine flavor, purifiers and preservatives, fruit acids, acidity indicators, hydrometers, bottle caps, corks and corkscrews, fermenters, barrel spigots and liners, and dozens of extracts and flavor enhancers. Their book on "First Steps in Winemaking," should help you toward your first gallons of custom-made concoctions, and there are 20 other books of recipes and tips for the experienced brewer. If you like drinking it, you'll probably have a ball making it and saving money at the same time.

LIQUOR-DEALER.

LEATHERCRAFTERS SUPPLY CO., INC.

Dept. WM
25 Great Jones St.
New York, NY 10012
(212) 673-5460
Catalogs and Price List:
$1.50
Discount: up to 40%
(quantity discounts)
Goods: house, brand
name
Minimum Order: $25.00
Shipping: FOB
warehouse NYC
Sales Tax: NY residents
Guarantee: satisfaction
Returns: authorized only
Payment: certified check,
MO, MC, Visa
$$

Leathercrafters Supply has a tremendous selection of leatherworking tools, equipment, and supplies. They carry tools by Craftool, Osborne, Ramparts, Baron, Basic, Century, and tool kits for beginners made by top companies. They sell books on leatherworking, buckles, brass rings, and many types of hardware. They also sell all kinds of leather: buckskin, Swedish elk, shearling, reverse suede, chamois, latigo, natural cowhide and lining. There are, when available, bags of tooling and carving leather scraps for small projects. Leathercrafter also sells dyes, finishes, leather cement, and lacing. Their discounts are largest on enormous quantities of goods, but some of their single-item prices are well below comparable retail.

D. MacGILLIVRAY AND COY.

Muir of Aird
Benbecula
Western Isles, Scotland
PA88 5NA
Brochure and Price List:
free
Shetland swatches:
$1.00; cashmere and
lambswool brochure and
pricelist: $1.00
Discount: 30 to 70% and
more
Goods: handmade,
custom made
Minimum Order: none
Shipping, Insurance:
$10.00; A.P.O., F.P.O.:
$4.00
Returns: money back
guarantee
Payment: check, MO,
bank draft, postal MO,
IMO
$$$$

D. MacGillivray is one of the companies that makes shopping by mail so worthwhile. Their fabrics are bargains even by Scottish standards. The handwoven Harris tweed is 28 inches wide and costs $7.00 per yard. They send swatches free on request. They also sell cashmere, pure wool Shetland tweeds, Donegal tweeds, and many others, which are 54 inches to 60 inches wide. Send $1.00 for the price list and swatches. For good Scottish plaids and tartans in a huge selection of colors and patterns, MacGillivray can't be beat, and the price is only $6.00 a yard. They also sell Aran oiled knitting wool, 50¢ per ounce, and pure Shetland wool, "very soft and fine," at 60¢ per ounce. All the fabrics are preshrunk and can be cold water washed. MacGillivray's services seem to go far and beyond the call of dry goods, as the note under "Holidays in the Highlands and Islands" in the brochure indicates: "If you are thinking of spending your holidays in the Scottish Highlands or Islands, we shall be delighted to help you in any way possible. Please tell us where you wish to go and we will send you all the information you require." For additional listings, see CLOTHING, FURS, AND ACCESSORIES; COSMETICS; HANDICRAFTS AND NATIVE PRODUCTS; HOME; JEWELRY; and MUSIC.

DRY GOODS.

DISCOUNT

L. MARTIN COINS

31 Garden St.
Hyde Park, NY 12538
(914) 229-7286
Price List: free
Discount: 30% WBMC
Goods: coins, tokens,
and medals
Minimum Order: none
Shipping, Insurance:
$1.50 on orders over $10
Sales Tax: NY residents
Payment: check, MO,
bank draft
$$$$

Mr. Martin carries copper and silver coins, mainly from the 19th and 20th centuries, in addition to tokens and medals. He specializes in coins of the British Commonwealth and South Africa, and will also seek out coins of special interest to you. There are also specials of 50% off on selected coins for his regular customers. With your first order, you get a free Swiss coin. Don't forget to mention the WBMC when writing to Mr. Martin and ordering; this entitles you to a 30% reader discount.

MILAN LABORATORY, INC.

57 Spring St.
New York, NY 10012
(212) 226-4780
Catalog: $1.25
Discount: 50% on
manufactured goods;
10% quantity discount
Goods: house brand
Minimum Order: $7.50
Shipping: $1.95 to $2.95
on light orders; heavy
equipment FOB NYC
Guarantee: by
manufacturer
Payment: check, MO,
bank check
$$$

Making your own wine and beer is now becoming as popular as making your own bread, yogurt, ice cream, and pasta became in recent years. Milan Lab not only supplies all the chemicals, preservatives, supplies and equipment you will need to make wine, beer, liqueurs, brandies, and whiskeys, but also carries books that give you all the information you need. The Lab is operated by the third generation of Miccios, who are about as experienced as any winemaking supply firm. They've been selling in the heart of Little Italy for almost 100 years. They can even take samples of your homemade wine and tell you what's gone wrong with it, and prescribe corrective chemicals that will make a bitter wine sweet, cloudy wine clear, or a sweet wine dry. Their line of supplies include keg taps, sulphur strips, corks, bungs, bottles, brushes, champagne labels, and much more. Milan also sells extracts and flavors—see the listing under FOOD for more information.

NATIONAL HANDICRAFT CO., INC.

337 Lincoln Rd.
Miami Beach, FL 33139
(305) 534-7314
Catalog: free
Discount: to 30%
Goods: house, brand
name
Minimum Order: none
Shipping: extra; FOB
Miami
Sales Tax: FL residents
Guarantee: on Osborne
tools
Payment: check, MO
$$$

This company supplies schools, community centers, and YMCAs with crafts materials. Most of what they sell is for leatherworking. There are leather stamps for $2.50 each, belt buckles from 45¢ to $1.50 for solid brass, leather shears, cutters, lacing, rivets, dyes, punches, and other tools. The Osborne line of leather embossing tools are guaranteed to be perfect in materials and "to do the work for which they are intended." Leather pieces and skins are sold here from $2.20 to $3.00 per square foot, and there are leather belts at $2.00 to $3.00 each, and rawhide laces in 9 colors at 50¢ per 72-inch pair. National sells felt squares at $2.20 per dozen, lanyard hooks, key chains, pipe cleaners, and "craft sticks"—unused popsicle sticks. At $2.20 per 1,000, this last item should be a lifesaver to anyone who's spent a summer saving and washing sticky sticks for some child's project that called for "just" 152.

NATURALCRAFT, INC.

2199 Bancroft Way
Berkeley, CA 94704
(415) 841-4909
Catalog: $1, refundable

Naturalcraft, Inc. found mail order business so profitable that they closed their shop and are now selling only by mail. They have dyes by Putnam and Inkodye, Versatex paints, fibers for basketry, cane, cordage, and assorted jewelry findings. There are eight

NATURALCRAFT, INC.

**Discount: 25 to 33%,
quantity discounts
Goods: house brand
Minimum Order: none
Shipping: extra, UPS
Sales Tax: CA residents
Payment: check, MO,
C.O.D., MC
$$$**

pages of beads—camel bones, mother-of-pearl fetishes, clam shell, porcelain, Ecuadorian clay, ceramic, olivewood, maple, glass, abalone, copal amber, and genuine Art Deco beads shaped like bows and flowers and other novel designs and studded with rhinestones. There are camel bells, elephant bells, and feathers: ostrich, goose, eagle (imitation), guinea hen, marabou, and chinchilla coque. They also carry unique crafts supplies like Austrian lead crystal hearts, antique silk Peking tassels, and whole pheasant skins. Almost everything is illustrated with photographs, and the catalog is great idea material if you are interested in crafts.

NEW ENGLAND EARTH CRAFTS

**882 Massachusetts Ave.
Arlington, MA 02174
(617) 646-2450
Catalog: $1, refundable
Discount: 40% plus, with
quantity discounts
Goods: house brand
Minimum Order: none
Shipping, Insurance:
extra, UPS
Handling: 50¢ on orders
under $15
Sales Tax: MA residents
Payment: check, MO,
MC, Visa
$$$**

New England Earth carries materials, equipment, and supplies for spinning, weaving, pottery, candle making, rugmaking, basketry and batiking. They have a wide range of professional-quality goods. There are 5 kinds of looms at $40 to $999, all kinds of loom accessories, knitting and crochet tools, quilting frames, unsized fabric, Naphthex, Procion, and Putnam dyes, chair cane and rush, rug canvases, Kemper clay tools, and much more. Yarn is very well priced at $3.00 to $4.50 per pound for 100% wool rug yarn; heavy cotton yarn is $3.50 and $6.00 per pound; Shetland weaving yarn is $6.50 per pound, etc. New England Craft also gives basic instructions on handling several kinds of dyes, batik tools, and dyeing processes in the back of the catalog, information which is worth at least the price of the booklet, especially to a craftsperson.

THE PENDLETON SHOP

**P.O. Box 233
407 Jordan Rd.
Sedona, AZ 86336
(602) 282-3671
Price List: 65¢ refundable
Discount: 30% plus
Goods: handspun
Minimum Order: $10
Shipping, Insurance:
extra
Sales Tax: AZ residents
Payment: check, MO
$$$$**

Weavers of every kind will find something of interest in the Pendleton Shop. The sample sheet that Mary Pendleton sends out comes laden with tufts of wool, strands of yarn and warp thread, and a handful of long handspun strands. The wool is the kind used in Navajo rugs, and comes straight from the hogans of the Indian women on the reservation. The wool comes from the longhaired Navajo sheep, and is available in natural colors— white, grays, browns, and golds. There are other kinds of wool, including a single-ply yarn that can be substituted for Navajo and is available in many colors. Mary Pendleton carries not only the wool, but also looms and a large assortment of books. The looms are very well priced—a 30x42-inch standing Navajo-type loom with rods, shed sticks, battens, comb, and cord is $37.00, post-

THE PENDLETON SHOP

paid. This is an ideal way to get started in Navajo or Hopi weaving, and there are enough books in the bookshelf to answer any questions you have. See BOOKS AND RECORDS for more information.

S & C HUBER, ACCOUTREMENTS

**82 Plants Dam Rd.
East Lyme, CT 06333
(203) 739-0772
Catalog: 75¢
Discount: 20% to much
more (some goods
exclusive)
Goods: handmade
Minimum Order: none
Shipping: FOB East
Lyme, UPS, extra
Sales Tax: CT residents
Returns: within 10 days
Payment: MO, C.O.D.
$$$**

S & C Huber calls itself a center for early country arts and produces hand-crafted goods of 18th and 19th-century design on its small 1710 farm. They carry all kinds of crafts supplies, books, and some finished items. In spinning, dyeing, and weaving, they have a large selection of tools such as the Saxony spinning wheel, drop spindle carder, a niddy-noddy, distaff, 3 kinds of looms, shuttles, wooden combs, and more. The fibers for spinning and weaving that they offer include fleece, flax, cashmere, llama, alpaca, and *even silk cocoons at 5¢ each*! There are yarns already spun of the same materials, and fabrics like monks cloth, linen, and 4 Williamsburg fabrics in the colonial spirit. There are over 50 dyes to choose from, all of which are natural: alder bark, bearberry, marigolds, nettle, eucalyptus, indigo herb, meadowsweet, St. John's wort, tansy, turmeric and more. For the candlemaker, they sell waxes of bayberry, tallow and beeswax, plys, wicks and scents. There are paper-making supplies too, including the frame and deckle. For additional listings, please see BOOKS AND RECORDS; FOOD; COSMETICS AND PERFUMES; and HOME.

SAMARTH GEM STONES

**P.O. Box 6057
Colaba, Bombay 400 005
India**

Samarth sells a wide variety of cut and polished stones that would be suitable for mounting or further work, at very low prices. For more information, see listing under JEWELRY.

SOME PLACE

**2990 Adeline St.
Berkeley, CA 94703
(415) 843-7178
Catalog: 50¢
Discount: up to 50%;
quantity discounts on
yarn**

The Kliots own and run Some Place, which sells supplies and equipment for lacemaking, weaving, rugmaking, basketweaving, and various needlecrafts. They carry handspun, Navajo, worsted, and mill end rug yarn, cotton warp cord, twine, jute, marline, linen, nylon, and sisal fibers. Mill end yarn is as cheap as $3.50 per lb. and even handspun is only $8. You get a 10% discount if you buy 50 lbs. of mill end yarn or 10 lbs. of any other kind. The

SOME PLACE

Goods: house brand
Minimum Order: none
Shipping: $1 and up,
UPS
Insurance: 40¢ to 80¢
Sales Tax: CA residents
Payment: check, MO,
C.O.D.
$$$$

selection of tools and other supplies is vast: there are carders, flickers, niddy-noddies, spindles, scrim, tatting shuttles, crochet hooks, knitting needles, kume himo goods, slay hooks, winders, bobbins, and much more. There is a whole leaflet devoted to bobbin lace, and there are books on all the textile crafts. The Kliots sell all kinds of spinning wheels and looms, including 2 they designed themselves—both cost less than $30 each. This is one source no textile craftsman should overlook.

STRAW INTO GOLD

5533 College Ave.
Oakland, CA 94618
(415) 652-7746
Catalog: $1
Discounts: up to 30% in
volume
Goods: house brand,
name brand
Minimum Order: none
Shipping, Insurance:
extra, UPS
Handling: $1
Sales Tax: CA residents
Guarantee: returns
accepted, must be
authorized
Payment: check, MO,
C.O.D.
$$$

Straw Into Gold is a well-known store and mail order source for what they call "textile crafts" supplies. They sell fibers for handspinning, dyes, mordants, yarn, fabrics for dyeing and batiking, and basketry materials. They also offer equipment for spinning, weaving, and dyeing. Their catalog lists prices for small amounts and single items, and discount rates for volume orders. There are 900 books on crafts in their bookshelf, some of which are discounted. They are true professionals, and are sure to have the answer to any questions you might have about the textile crafts.

TEST FABRICS, INC.

P.O. Drawer O
200 Blackford Ave.
Middlesex, NJ 08846
(201) 469-6446
Price List: free
Swatch Booklet: $4.50
Discount: good
Goods: house, name
brand
Minimum Order: $25

Test Fabrics sells fabric primarily to the labs of major textile companies, but will also sell to anyone who needs a yard or more of plain cotton, wool, silk, "regenerated cellulose," taffeta, satin, twill, and challis. Prices run from $1.00 a yard for cotton filter cloth to $7.50 for spun silk when you buy 1 to 14 yards, and 70¢ to $7.00 per yard on orders of 100 yards or more of the same fabric. The cottons and silks are excellent for batik work and tie-dyeing, because there is no finish on them. They are also good for silkscreening, handpainting, and textile painting. Some of the cloth is bleached, and it ranges in weight from duck to batiste. There is

TEST FABRICS, INC.

Shipping: 10% of order
Sales Tax: NJ residents
Payment: MO, bank
draft, C.O.D.
$$$

also velveteen, sheeting, and tubular T-shirt material. Unless you are very familiar with general textile descriptions, it's a good idea to invest $4.50 in the swatch booklet so you can see just what "#10 cotton duck, griege" looks like before you order.

U.S. GENERAL SUPPLY CORP.

100 General Place
Jericho, NY 11753
(516) 333-6655

Tucked away in its catalog of tools and hardware, U.S. General has some low-priced hobby supplies and books: a rock polisher, ship models, leatherworking tools, and more. For the complete listing, see TOOLS AND HARDWARE.

THE VILLAGE TINKER

377 Boston Post Road
Sudbury, MA 01776
(617) 443-3330
Catalog and price list:
$2.50
Discount: 20 to 30%
Goods: name brand,
imported
Minimum: none
Shipping: $2.50 on
orders under $50; free on
orders over $50
Sales Tax: MA residents
Guarantee: missing
pieces or defective goods
replaced
Payment: check, MO,
MC, Visa
$$$

For $2.50 you get four beautiful catalogs of model railroad trains, tracks, buildings and accessories. The Hornby "00" catalog shows locomotives, train sets, coaches, wagons, track systems, power systems, and many kinds of buildings, vehicles, and even miniature people. There are also catalogs for Peco N, HO, 00, 009, and 0 models and accessories, plus books on putting together a model railroad layout, and histories of some famous railways. From Germany, there are the Fleischmann line of model trains, and beautiful railroad accessories and buildings by Kibri. Don't miss this source if you have a European model railroad and want to add trains or accessories, or would just like a windmill in the middle of your layout.

WATKINS AND DONCASTER

Four Throws
Hawkhurst, Kent,
England

Try Watkins and Doncaster for hard-to-find taxidermy supplies at good prices. See complete listing under MEDICAL AND SCIENTIFIC.

FARM and GARDEN

If you go to 5 local stores for plants, you'll probably find the same variety in every store, and at about the same prices (and you'll often get only local plants). But go the mail route and you'll save money while you swoon amidst the exotica of leaves and flowers you've never seen before. These are definitely the sources for gifts for your green-thumb friends. No one on earth feels slighted by a present that grows and gives off oxygen.

Be sure what you get will grow where you live.

Though we're interested in saving you money, improvements in your landscaping can also *make* you money. A well-planned investment of 50 to 100 dollars in "environmental" improvement of your property can increase its value by 500 dollars, especially if you've got something "rare" for your locality.

THE AMERICAN GARDEN GUILD

Garden City, NY 11530
(516) 294-4000
Information: inquire
Discount: up to 30%
Goods: Guild editions
Minimum Order: 4 books
within 2 years
Shipping, Handling: extra
Sales Tax: NY residents
Payment: check, MO
$$$

You can get $43 worth of books on gardening, plants, flowers, and related topics for $1 with your new membership in the American Garden Guild. You have to buy 4 more books, but you have 2 years in which to fulfill your commitment. These books are up to 30% less than the original publishers' editions, so your final savings are immense. This is a great way to get those books that should be on your reference shelf—*10,000 Garden Questions, The Gardener's Bug Book*—or stock up on gifts for your favorite horticulturists.

ANDERSON'S ROSE NURSERIES

Cults, Aberdeen,
Scotland
Catalog: free
Discount: 30% minimum
Goods: Scottish roses
Minimum Order: none
Shipping, Duty,

Anderson's believes that "a rose without fragrance is like a summer without sun," so all 149 varieties they export are scented. Their color catalog shows page after page of rich, beautiful roses, from miniature bushes with blooms the size of a wedding band to full-sized gems with flowers 5½ inches across and with as many as 70 petals per flower. The color range is outstanding: White Christmas (ice whites), Blue Moon (violet blue), Royal Highness (pale

110

ANDERSON'S ROSE NURSERIES

**Documentation, etc.:
$12 per dozen rose
bushes
Payment: check, postal
MO
$$$**

pink), Drambuie (deep amber—a child flower of gold Whiskey Mac), Rosy Cheeks (rose and yellow), Red Devil, Ernest H. Morse (crimson), and there are many more shades in between. There is even a luscious tiger striped variety called Harry Wheatcroft, in yellow and orange. The prices are low, mostly $1.40 to $1.65 per bush, with a few higher. The Andersons have consolidated all costs into a flat fee of $12 per dozen bushes, and tell you how to obtain an import permit from the Dept. of Agriculture. A hints booklet is available for $1 which details planting, pruning and care of all the Anderson roses.

CAPRILAND'S HERB FARM

**Silver St.
Coventry, CT 06238
(203) 742-7244**

Capriland's has over 300 varieties of herbs and flowers in their gardens. You can purchase them in 2-inch pots for $1 to $2. They offer all the standard culinary herbs and less common varieties like Egyptian onions, rue, wormwood, mugwort, monardas, artemisia, etc. For garden borders there are santolinas, germander, lambs ears, and nepetas, and for ground cover there are ajuga, camomile, woodruff, and thyme. There are also herb seeds at 50¢ per package, and a starter garden selection of 8 seed packets for $1.50. For the complete listing, see COSMETICS AND PERFUMES.

ALBERT CONSTANTINE AND SON, INC.

**2050 Eastchester Rd.
Bronx, NY 10461
(212) 792-1600**

For a mere $1.75, you can get a basswood birdfeeder that can be put together in a jiffy. For picky birds, you can get the elegant Swiss Inn or Alpine Chalet for $4.50 each. The feeders are made of durable mahogany plywood pieces that interlock, so no nails or glue are needed. They cost only half what other kits do, and even less than half of the cost of assembled feeders. For more information, see the main listing under CRAFTS AND HOBBIES.

DUTCH GARDENS, INC.

**P.O. Box 338
Montvale, NJ 07645
(201) 391-4366
Catalog: free
Discount: 30%
Goods: Dutch bulbs
Minimum Order: $40**

Dutch Gardens puts out one of the most beautiful color catalogs for tulips and other bulb flowers available anywhere. Every picture shows an exquisite flower in full bloom, and lists blooming time, bloom size, and height. There are many kinds of tulips, hyacinths, daffodils, narcissi, crocii, amaryllus, iris, and other exotic bulb flowers. The bulbs cost from 11¢ for crocus and other small bulbs to $5.35 for spectacular hybrid amaryllis, but most of the bulbs are

DUTCH GARDENS, INC.

Shipping, Handling, Duty, Inland Shipping Charges: included
Payment: check, bank draft
$$$

between 14¢ and 35¢ each. When you buy $40 or more in bulbs, the prices include shipping, customs charges, handling, and U.S. inland freight charges. The catalog is sent with a sheaf of order forms to enable you to collect orders from your friends and meet this minimum. If you order $70 or more, you get a 10% bonus of free bulbs of your choice, which makes the discount that much better. A set of planting instructions is included with each order.

ENVIRONMENTAL DYNAMICS

12615 La Cadena Dr.
Colton, CA 92324
(714) 783-1830
Brochure: free
Discount: 30%
Goods: house brand
Minimum Order: none
Shipping: FOB Riverside, CA
Sales Tax: CA residents
Warranty: by manufacturer
Payment: check, MO, MC, Visa, C.O.D.
$$$

Both hobbyists and commercial growers will find greenhouse kits here to suit their needs. There are 13 standard models, all constructed of nylon fiberglass and galvanized steel frames, and they have just added a line of aluminum and glass houses. Prices begin at $225. All the kits are complete, easily assembled, and accessories are also available from Environmental Dynamics, so you can build and outfit the greenhouse to suit your needs.

GOLDEN EARTH WHOLESALE

512 E. Lambert
Brea, CA 92621
(714) 990-0681
Catalog: membership $5
Discount: to 80%
Goods: house, brand names
Minimum Order: none
Shippng: FOB Brea, CA
Sales Tax: CA residents
Guarantee: unconditional, for all products
Payment: check, MO, MC, Visa
$$$$

Golden Earth is a wholesale club that offers great discounts on horticultural and nursery supplies. It costs $5.00 for membership which entitles you to discount rates and 6 product bulletins per year. Some of the bargains in the current catalog were: 3-tier wire baskets with chains and hook, $3.95 each or 3 for $10.95 (these are at least $8.95 each in New York), 2¼-inch peat pots at 2½¢ each, a "horn of plenty" special of 40 packs of vegetable and flower seeds for $3.95, etc. There are good selections of planters, pots, hangers, pruning tools, lamps, treatments, and other supplies. Golden Earth also offers equipment for serious gardening, like McGregor greenhouses at 25% below retail, fluorescent fixtures at about 45% off, compressed air sprayers, Titan heaters, and Arvin humidifiers. They also have a bookshelf. This club is a great idea for anyone who likes gardening, and membership would be a practical, inexpensive gift. For more information, see BOOKS AND RECORDS.

GREENLAND FLOWER SHOP

RD 1, Box 52
Port Matilda, PA 16870
(814) 692-8308
Catalog: 25¢
Discount: to 50%
Goods: live
Minimum Order: none
Shipping, Handling: 91¢
to $3.25
Sales Tax: PA residents
Guarantee: live delivery
Returns: within 5 days
Payment: check, MO
$$$$

You can get plants here for as little as 45¢ each, sent in 2¼-inch grow pots, guaranteed live upon delivery. Greenland Flower carries over 100 kinds of houseplants listed under their common and botanical names. There are jade plants, begonias, ivy, Boston fern, coleus, wandering jew, Irish moss, baby tears, and much more. They are all 50¢ each, but you can knock off 10% if you order in December or January for spring delivery. This is half the cost of plants in the florist shop, and the selection is stupendous. The Greenlands advise CA and AZ residents to check local restrictions regarding shipping certain plants.

HERBST BROTHERS SEEDSMEN, INC.

1000 N. Main St.
Brewster, NY 10509
(914) 279-2971
Catalog: free to WBMC
readers
Discount: to 93%
Goods: house, brand
names
Minimum Order: none
Shipping: prepaid, UPS
Sales Tax: NY State
residents
Payment: check, MO
$$$$

Herbst Brothers sell seeds for trees, shrubs, flowers and vegetables, plus brand name gardening supplies. The smallest amount you can order in seed is usually equivalent to several seed packets bought in the five and ten, but is much more inexpensive. Because Herbst Brothers is geared toward wholesale trade, they include many varieties of flowers and vegetables unavailable in a dimestore. There are 32 kinds of coleus, 23 types of gourds, 22 varieties of corn, etc. They give the estimated seeds per ounce count, so you know about what to expect from half an ounce or a pound. They offer excellent buys on Fertil pots, plant foods, treatments, and garden hardware. Some of the supplies are sold in only in large quantities, but you can store extras. Or get your friends together—you could even start a garden club!

HYDROCULTURE, INC.

P.O. Box 1655
Glendale, AZ 85311
(602) 934-3481
Catalog: $1
Discount: represented in
savings in water, time,
space, and high yields
Goods: exclusive
Minimum Order: none
Shipping: FOB Glendale
$$

Hydroponics is an old method of growing plants that is relatively new in practical applications. It involves cultivating plants in a solution of nutrients and water. Hydroculture, Inc., has developed "The Magic Garden," an almost totally automated greenhouse system that controls temperature, humidity, air circulation, and even feeding. Eight 26 x 128-foot greenhouses on 1 acre can produce the same amount of tomatoes that take 18 acres if field grown. The plants also require about 1/29th the water needed by field crops. Hydroculture sends an informative booklet describing hydroponics and the Magic Garden, plus copies of testimonials describing the merits of hydroponic feed: how animals get sick

HYDROCULTURE, INC.

less, are more fertile, have glossier coats, more stamina, and grow larger if fed hydroponically-grown feed from a young age. The systems start at $2,495 and run up to $21,000 for a "Magic Meadow." Hydroponics is a form of cultivation well worth investigating if you breed or raise livestock or vegetables—it is truly the farming method of the future.

KLINKEL'S AFRICAN VIOLETS

**Lucille Klinkel
1553 Harding St.
Enumclaw, WA 98022
(206) 825-4442
Miniatures Price List: 50¢
Mixed Price List: 50¢
Discount: 30% off florist
prices plus bonuses and
specials
Goods: rare and hard-to-
find
Miminum Order: $6
Shipping, Handling: 25¢
per plant plus $2 to
$2.50 per order
Sales Tax: WA residents
Returns: replacement of
mail damaged goods with
postman's verification
Payment: check
$$$**

Lucille Klinkel operates her store out of her home, which must be wall-to-wall plants. The 9-page price list she sends out lists over 300 kinds of African violets, miniatures, trailers, and foliage plants, and there are about 700 other varieties in her shop that aren't listed. She sells leaves from the plants, which will root in a vermiculite/perlite mix, at 75¢ and $1 each. Leaves are sent from May to November, and there are specials—20 leaves for $9 postpaid, 4 plants for $7, and bonuses with orders of $7 and $12.50. If you are a violet hobbyist, this shop should keep you in new varieties for quite some time. The leaves are labeled with common names and have one-line descriptions, so you should know violets or else be adventurous. If you're looking for a specific variety, write to Mrs. Klinkel with details and she'll most likely have what you want. Whether it's "baby roses," "dreamin," "Irish angel," "little rascal," "sassy lass," or "midget bonbon," you're sure to find what you need to begin a hobby or expand a collection. Order early in the spring for the best selection, and combine orders with your friends to get the bonus gifts.

J.E. MILLER NURSERIES, INC.

**5060 West Lake Rd.
Canandaigua, NY 14424
1-800-828-9630
NY orders: (716) 394-
0647
Catalog: free
Discount: 50% plus
Goods: house brand
Minimum Order: $10 on
charges**

You'll be ready to dig up your lawn and fill in the swimming pool to plant fruit trees and arbors when you see the luscious-looking offerings in Miller's nursery catalog. The problem will be choosing from the russet apples, golden plums, black grapes, red raspberries, indigo blueberries, ruby cherries, fat strawberries, and dozens of other fruit and nut trees. If it's shade you need, there are poplar, locust, maple, and ash trees, some of which grow house-high in just 3 years. Miller also carries asparagus, grapes, rhubarb, and some common flower bulbs. All the trees and shrubs come in plant form, and are guaranteed to grow or be replaced. Prices are

J.E. MILLER NURSERIES, INC.

**Shipping, Handling: 85¢
to 10% of the order value
Sales Tax: NY residents
Guarantee: against
failure
Payment: check, MO,
MC, Visa, AE
$$$**

guaranteed to win you over, too: 12 gladioli bulbs for $1.95, 4 foot apple trees for $11.45, 50 asparagus plants for $7.40, and concord grape vines at $1.85.

THREE OAKS WORM RANCH

**P.O. Box 26
Dresden, TN 38225
(901) 364-3755**

Three Oaks sells castings from worms that are excellent fertilizer in the garden. They also sell the worms, if you want to enrich the soil permanently. For the complete listing see SPORTS AND RECREATION.

U.S. GENERAL SUPPLY CORP.

**100 General Place
Jericho, NY 11753
(516) 333-6655**

U.S. General sells some garden equipment like sprinklers, lawnmower blades, and hoses in addition to its tools and hardware. For more information, see listing under TOOLS AND HARDWARE.

WESTON BOWL MILL

**Weston, VT 05161
(802) 824-6219**

There are 11 different bird houses and feeders here, plus an Audubon bird call to make sure they come. The feeders start at $2.95 for an apple-shaped feeder and go to $11.25 for a 22-inch-long seed and suet feeder made of pine and glass. One of the more unusual designs is a bowl feeder, made of 2 inverted bowls separated by a post, that costs only $3.25. There are also replicas of covered bridges in pine and glass for $6 and $9.50. For more information, see the listing under HOME.

FOOD and DRINK

Nice things to put in your belly shouldn't cost an arm and a leg. Here you'll find cheeses, lamb paté, "bee secretions," spices, foods from South America, molasses, great hams, and fox hunter's meal. Things you can get by mail are generally not perishable, so it may be wise to stock up in one order; you'll often get additional quantity discounts this way, too. For back-to-the-landers, down-to-earthers, and Mother Nature freaks, Pure Planet Products and Jaffe Bros. are interesting sources since they screen all products for suitability on the basis of purity, environmental protection, good health, and an all-around sense of morality.

AAA SCALE CO.

P.O. Box 496
Paramount, CA 90723

Triple A Scale sells a hand scale that is guaranteed 5 years to be accurate and is ideal for measuring small portions of food for cooking and calorie counting. See OFFICE SUPPLIES AND EQUIPMENT for complete listing.

CHEESELOVERS INTERNATIONAL

Cheeselovers
International Bldg.
Box 1200
Westbury, NY 11590
Information: inquire
Membership: $3 for 1 yr.;
$5 for 2 years
Discount: as low as 3 to
7¢ above wholesale
Goods: domestic,
imported
Minimum Order: none
Shipping, Handling: extra
Returns: membership can
be canceled and fee
refunded
Payment: check, MO,
MC, Visa
$$$

For a mere $3, the price of a pound of good cheddar, you get a year's membership in Cheeselovers and a certificate for $6 worth of free cheese. Members are sent a full color catalog every month that illustrates cheeses from all over the world—Germany, France, Norway, England, Portugal, Austria, Denmark, and the U.S.A. You can choose from cheddars, brie, jarlsberg, swiss, boursin, muenster, edam, camembert, port salut, provolone, and many other novel or unique cheeses. Some of the cheeses are priced as low as 3¢ to 7¢ above wholesale, which makes them much cheaper than comparable cheese found in gourmet cheese stores. Since you can cancel your membership and still get the $6.00 worth of free cheese, you can't lose. Gift memberships are half-price at this writing, and make wonderful presents for anyone who likes this versatile food.

DEER VALLEY FARM

RD 1
Guilford, NY 13780
(607) 764-8556
Catalog: 50¢, published
yearly, refundable
Discount: 30%
Goods: organic, natural
Minimum Order: $150
Shipping: FOB Guilford
Returns: authorized only
Payment: check, MO
$$$

Deer Valley sells whole grains, flours, cereals, baked goods, and nut butters. They also sell "organically grown" meats. Organically grown hamburger, which is $3.00 to $3.50 per pound in health food stores, costs $2.20 here. Deer Valley also makes raw milk cheese, and cheddar is only $2.00 to $2.30 per pound, which is actually less than overprocessed, chemical-filled supermarket cheeses. Show the catalog to your friends and combine orders to get the $150 minimum, and be prepared for an impromptu feast when the cartons arrive.

EREWHON

3 East St.
Cambridge, MA 02141
(617) 354-2001
Price List: free
Discount: 33%
Goods: house brand
Minimum Order: $200
Shipping: FOB
Cambridge
Guarantee: satisfaction,
or replacement or credit
Payment: certified check,
MO
Resale #: necessary
$$$

Erewhon is one of the best-known names in the health food business. They distribute all over the U.S., and virtually any natural foods store in the country will have at least a few of their products. If you or your co-op has a resale number, you can also buy from them at wholesale prices. Their huge range of goods includes nut butters, oil, grains, beans, seeds, nuts, Japanese products, pasta, granola, and flours. The minimum order is $200, which a co-op should have no trouble meeting.

ICEMART

P.O. Box 23
Keflavik International
Airport
Iceland

Icemart offers two "tempting food assortments" at $19.80 and $34.50 each. In the large assortment is smoked lamb, cheese spreads, lamb paté, lamb's liver paté, lamb's cheek, brook trout, shrimps, lumpfish caviar, herring tidbits in wine sauce, and kipper snacks. For the complete listing, see CLOTHING, FURS, AND ACCESSORIES.

JAFFE BROS.

P.O. Box 636-W
Valley Center, CA 92082
(714) 749-1133
Catalog: free
Discount: see text
Minimum Order: one unit
Shipping: extra, UPS or
FOB Valley Center
Sales Tax: CA residents
Returns: within 10 days;
authorized
Payment: check, MO
$$$$

Jaffe Bros. has been in business for 30 years, marketing their products under the label "Jaybee Natural Foods." Most of the foods are grown or dried organically so that no preservatives, chemicals, fumigants, sulphur, insecticides, weedkillers, sugar, salt, or additives are used. The people at Jaffe wanted to be listed as having "low prices," rather than claiming a specific percentage savings over health food store prices. This seems a little crazy, in view of the fact that it's possible to save over 50% here. For instance, shelled pecans, $6.66 per pound in the store, are $3.65 here; cornmeal that costs 55¢ per pound elsewhere is 32¢ here; Black Mission figs are as low as $1.31 here and $1.89 in the store; and honey comes out way ahead here at 67¢ to 79¢ per pound, compared to up to $2.20 in health food stores. Most of the food is available in 5 lb. units or larger. There are dried fruits, seeds, grains, oils, nuts, nut butters, soybeans, carob powder, lecithin, juice, and honey. The prices are so good that even when the cross-country postage is added, the savings are great.

CHARLES LOEB

615 Palmer Rd.
Yonkers, NY 10701
(914) 961-7776
Price List: free
Discount: to 96%
Goods: house, name
brand
Minimum Order: $10.00
Shipping: $1.31 to $7.00;
free on orders over $50
Returns: within 10 days
Payment: check, MO
$$$$

Charles Loeb supplies herbs and spices to restaurants, delis, fine food outlets, and to you, at astoundingly low prices. It is actually possible to save 96% over the cost of supermarket spices by buying in quantity from him. The average savings are 40 to 60%. The company carries over 25 different spices and seasonings, plus boullion, jerky sticks, Tic Tac candies, and Virginia Dere products. The spices are available in sizes from the small jars (supermarket sized and priced) to 1 pound canisters, 1- and 5-pound bags; of course, the 5-pound bags are cheapest per ounce. Mr. Loeb has written up a few tips for storing and using spices which he includes with the price list. Don't buy another overpriced jar of oregano or tin of cinnamon from the supermarket again—get your friends together to split up large amounts of spices and combine orders, because amounts over $50 are sent postpaid.

MILAN LABORATORY, INC.

57 Spring St.
New York, NY 10012

Milan sells all kinds of supplies and equipment for home beer and wine making. They also sell 50 different flavors for cordials, 13 flavors for liqueurs, and 9 flavors for brandies and whiskeys. You can take half an ounce of cordial flavoring which costs only 60¢, combine it with one pint of vodka and one pint of Karo corn syrup and have one quart of instant cordial. It's much easier to have several small bottles of extract on hand and make up liqueurs

MILAN LABORATORY, INC.

to order than jam your liquor cabinet with umpteen different large bottles, and it's also cheaper. Two flavors that may interest you are "Roman Punch" and "The Kiss"—at 60¢ a bottle you can afford to experiment. Even if you are a teetotaler, you'll want Milan's catalog for their listings of herbs, spices, and baking flavorings. You can save over 60% on some of these, and the minimum order is only four ounces. For more on Milan Lab, see CRAFTS AND HOBBIES.

MONEO AND SON, INC.

210 W. 14th St.
New York, NY 10011
(212) 929-1644
Catalog: $1.50
Discount: 15 to 20% quantity discount on low prices
Goods: house, name brands
Minimum Order: $25.00
Shipping, Insurance: extra
Payment: check, MO
$$$

Moneo sells food from Mexico, Spain, South America, Portugal, and other countries. There are hundreds of things, dried, fresh and canned from which to choose, from Spanish squid to sweets. Since the store is operated in a low rent area, they don't pass on a high overhead and your prices are low. They also offer a case discount, so stock up and save money.

GROCER.

PURE PLANET PRODUCTS

1025 N. 48th St.
Phoenix, AZ 85008
(602) 267-1000
Catalog: 20¢
Discount: 30% WBMC
Goods: house, brand name
Minimum Order: $30 for discount
Shipping: extra
Sales Tax: AZ residents
Returns: within 10 days
Payment: check, MO
$$$

DISCOUNT

This company sends a lovely little catalog with the Milky Way, a ginseng root, and tiger balm pictured on the cover. They carry a full line of several kinds of ginseng, and offer Royal Jelly and empty capsules. They include a guide to the ginseng root which tells the grading system. Pure Planet sells bulk herbs, honey, tiger balm, incense, and even ginseng cigarettes. There are natural hairbrushes, Chinese wood combs, and a porcupine brush from Germany; for the kitchen, stainless steel utensils, and for the bath, a full line of Dr. Bronner's products (the famous peppermint and almond castile liquid soaps), aloe-vera soap, Chinese sandalwood soap, and a 12-inch bar of castile. There are also books on natural cooking. Note: the WBMC discount is *not* available to residents of Arizona.

S & C HUBER ACCOUTREMENTS

82 Plants Dam Rd.
East Lyme, CT 06333

S & C Huber sells a plethora of articles devoted to crafts and country living in Early America, and have seen fit to include 21 herbs and spices among them. These are the regular standard spices like curry, coriander, allspice, ginger root, oregano, savory, and others. Some of the prices are half of what you pay in the grocery store, and all the herbs and spices are packed in 2 oz. bags. For the complete listing, see CRAFTS AND HOBBIES.

SIMPSON AND VAIL, INC.

53 Park Place
New York, NY 10007
(212) 344-6377
Catalog: free
Discount: 10% WBMC
Goods: connoisseur
grade
Minimum Order: none
Shipping: extra, UPS
Guarantee: total
satisfaction
Payment: check, MO,
MC, Visa ($15 min.
order)
$$$

Simpson and Vail sells gourmet coffees at prices from 10 to 15% lower than other coffee stores in New York City, to which they add another discount of 10% to readers of the WBMC. They have the standard American, French, and Italian roasts, fancy Spanish, Mocha-Java, decaffeinated, Kenyan coffees, and many more. They also sell connoisseur teas—jasmine, Earl Grey, lapsang souchong, oolong, etc. Be sure to mention WBMC when you request the catalog and when you order so that you get the 10% reader discount.

DISCOUNT

THE E.M. TODD CO.

and subsidiary Byrd Mills
Hermitage Rd. and Leigh
St.
P.O. Box 5167
Richmond, VA 23220
(804) 359-5051
Price List, Recipes: free
Discount: 10% over
discount prices to WBMC
readers
Goods: house name
Minimum Order: none for
E.M. Todd; 15 lb.
minimum for Byrd Mills
Shipping: included
Sales Tax: VA residents
Payment: check, MO,
C.O.D.
$$$

DISCOUNT

The E.M. Todd Co., founded in 1779 by Capt. Mallory Todd, sells old-Virginia-style hams, bacon, and "hermitage country-hams." These meats are salt cured for several weeks, smoke cured for several more, then coated with black pepper and molasses and set to age. Capt. Mallory began the business with razor-back hogs, and with close to 200 years experience they have perfected the process (though they don't use the razorbacks anymore). Prices are very good for these gourmet-quality meats: $2.06/lb. for slab bacon, $2.15/lb. for uncooked picnic shoulder, and up to $4.94/lb. for fully cooked boneless Virginia hams. Byrd Mills, the subsidiary, sells stone ground flours and things like brown rice, griddle cake mixes, and maple syrup. A history of the meats, description of the curing process, and a brochure of bread and cake recipes is included. Remember to mention the WBMC when ordering.

GENERAL

As a group, the general mail order merchandisers offer lower discounts than our other sources (although Unity Buying Service is a clear-cut exception). On the other hand, they provide "one stop" mail order shopping and their sale catalogs often offer terrific bargains. It's always handy to have one or more of these catalogs around. If you need a new plastic garbage can, or a birthday toy, or a nylon slip, why not get it cheaper from a catalog?

One caveat: you may want to comparison-shop a bit. We found that the manufacturers' list prices stated by these "generals" are sometimes rather high, thereby increasing the percentage discount the store claims to give.

ALDENS

5000 Roosevelt Rd.
Chicago, IL 60607
(312) 854-4141
Catalog: free
Savings: up to 44% on sales mdse.
Goods: house, brand name
Shipping Cost: by UPS rate chart or FOB Chicago
Sales Tax: IL residents
Warranty: by manufacturer
Guarantee: Aldens cust. satisfaction policy
Payment: check, MO, C.O.D., Aldens charge
$$$

Aldens is a mail order house built along the lines of Sears and Roebuck—general merchandise, sale flyer price cuts of 10 to 20%, and some items discounted 30 to 40%. Aldens also offers many name brands, especially in appliances, tools, tires, and luggage, which means you can comparison-shop. They have credit terms and their own charge system; but at an annual rate of 21% interest, you can cancel out your savings if you use it. When you order or price goods, be sure to include shipping charges in your final cost.

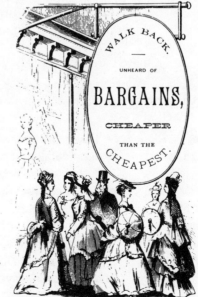

MADISON SQUARE PARK DISTRIBUTORS

19 East 26th St.
New York, NY 10010
(212) 889-7700
Catalog: free
Discount: 30 to 65%
Goods: name brand
Minimum Order: none
Shipping: extra; UPS or
FOB NYC
Sales Tax: NY residents
Guarantee: by
manufacturer
Returns: credit,
exchange, refund;
original cartons with
receipt within 7 days
Payment: check, MO,
MC, Visa
$$$$

Madison Square Distributors is one of New York City's many discount sources that carry several kinds of goods, all at discount prices. They sell appliances, cameras, jewelry, and luggage. There are appliances made by every major manufacturer, cameras by top names, and watches by Omega, Seiko, Benrus, Waltham, and Hamilton. The luggage manufacturers include Samsonite, Imperial, and American Tourister. Their catalog is free, and you can also call for price quotes.

MONTGOMERY WARDS

150 N. Broadway
Albany, NY 12201
(518) 447-2000
Catalog: $2 deposit for
shipping and handling

Montgomery Wards is a large, well-known mail order house with outlets all over the U.S. Their sale catalogs, published every 3 weeks or so, often have goods discounted 30% or more. To get a catalog, send a $2 deposit fee for shipping and handling to their Albany address. They will send you a catalog plus a gift certificate for $2.00. Note that some of the things they sell, especially appliances, are sold under the Montgomery Wards label but are often made by leading manufacturers, so quality is identical.

NATIONAL BUYERS EXCHANGE

968 Parkway Ave.
Trenton, NJ 08618
(609) 883-2702
Catalog: $1
Discounts: up to 50%
Goods: name brand
Shipping, Insurance:
extra, UPS, PP, FOB
warehouse

There are over 400 pages of name brand goods in the Exchange catalog at discounts of up to 50%. A sampling of the goods includes dinnerware sets, crystal, personal appliances, leather goods, clocks, kitchenware, phones, bathroom accessories, vacuum cleaners, tools, audio equipment, office goods, and sports supplies. Some of the manufacturers are J & G Meakin, Elgin, Texas Instruments, International Silver, Gorham, Towle, Norelco, Schick, Croos, Amity, Clairol, Regina, Revereware, Panasonic, and Spalding. Everything you buy from the Exchange is fully

NATIONAL BUYERS EXCHANGE

**Guarantee: by manufacturer
Returns: on resaleable goods only; authorized
Payment: check, MO
$$**

guaranteed and can be returned for refund, exchange, or credit. If you like to pore over catalogs, this is one to get lost in.

SERVICE MERCHANDISE CO., INC.

**P.O. Box 40818
Nashville, TN 37204
(800) 251-1212 (orders)
(800) 342-8398 (TN orders)
Catalog: free
Discounts: up to 40%
Goods: name brand
Minimum Order: $10
Shipping: UPS from Nashville
Sales Tax: NY, OH, TN, PA, AR, GA, AL, CT, IL, IN, TX, MA, ME, MI, MO, MS, NC, NH, NJ, OK, VT
Payment: check, MO, MC, Visa
$$$**

Service Merchandise is a great source for all kinds of merchandise such as cameras, audio equipment, tools and hardware, jewelry, leather goods, silver, appliances, TVs, and camping goods. The discounts average 20% to 40%, but some are higher. There are a lot of name brand goods—Murray bikes, Bancroft and Wilson racquets, Coleman camping equipment, Black and Decker tools, Panasonic and RCA TVs, Elgin watches, and appliances by Hoover, Eureka, Oster, Sunbeam, and Rival. Service Merchandise also runs catalog showrooms in several states, so you can see the goods on display.

SHAKLEE DISTRIBUTORS-RULAND

**1132 North Oakleaf Drive
Phoenix, AZ 85008
(606) 267-1878
Catalog: free (introductory offer form)
Discount: 33% on above offer
Goods: house name
Minimum Order: $10, intro. offer
Shipping: included
Sales Tax: AZ residents
Guarantee: money back
Payment: check, MO
$**

Al and Rose Ruland, Shaklee Supervisors in Phoenix, are offering a "get acquainted" special of assorted Shaklee products valued at $15 for $10. Some of their household cleaning products are real bargains—1 quart of Basic H, their all-purpose cleaner concentrate, makes 64 gallons of solution and costs $3.20. Basic G, their germicide, yields 64 gallons of disinfectant per quart, and costs $6.60 (prices are suggested retail). They also sell their own line of vitamins, beauty products, and fragrances.

UNITY BUYING SERVICE CO., INC.

**810 South Broadway
Hicksville, NY 11802
(516) 433-9100 x80
Membership: $6 per year
$10 for 2 years, $14 for 3
years; trial membership 3
mo./$3
Discount: up to 50%
Goods: name brand
Mininum Order: none
Service Charge: 8%
Shipping: extra; UPS, PP,
FOB warehouse
Sales Tax: NY residents
Payment: check, MO
Guarantee: satisfaction
$$$**

Unity Buying Service boasts over 1,200,000 card holding members who can order name brand merchandise directly through Unity at savings of up to 50%. They have all kinds of goods: clothing, home furnishings, kitchenware, appliances of every kind, sports equipment, jewelry and watches, musical instruments, TV and audio equipment, luggage, toys, furs, and more. Some of the manufacturers include Farberware, Rubbermaid, GE, Samsonite, Hitachi, MacGregor, Lenox, Superscope, Waring, GAF, Oneida, Hoover, Scovill, and Ideal. Membership includes a full-color Unity Buying catalog, a factory price selection, special closeout bulletins, and a free subscription to *Consumer Life* quarterly which gives practical advice on how to save money and "beat the system." If you aren't totally satisfied, you can return your card and catalog within 30 days for a full refund.

HANDICRAFTS and NATIVE PRODUCTS

There is simply no way to resist the astounding bargains in what are commonly called "imported" goods, or the handicrafts of a region or country. You can buy baskets from Ecuador, small olivewood camel caravans from Israel, lava ceramics from Iceland, filigree statues from Nepal, camelbone letter openers from India, princess rings from Thailand, hickory dolls from the Ozark Mountains, and much more. We fell in love with the catalog from the Tibetan Refugee Self Help Center, which sells beautiful rugs and other articles at incredibly low prices.

Because most of the goods are handmade, there may be delays in shipment if stock has run out, especially if you order during the holiday rush. So send for the catalogs as soon as possible, order early, and above all, be patient.

ANDEAN PRODUCTS

Apartado 472
Cuenca, Ecuador
South America
Catalog: $1.00
Discount: 50% minimum
Goods: handcrafted
Minimum Order: none;
$20 charge on orders
under $200.00
Shipping: air freight,
collect FOB Cuenca,
Ecuador
Payment: L/C or 50%
prepaid with check, MO
Letterhead: necessary on
orders under $200.00
$$$

"Productos Andinos" is an artisan-owned organization of many craft cooperatives. They sell clothing, jewelry, tapestries, rugs, furniture, dolls, linens, and decorative accessories. The prices are very low: tapestries starting at $6.00, handspun, handknit sweaters around $22, charming straw figures that would be good as Christmas tree ornaments, about $1 each, and many other items. They have a selection of lovely silver filigree jewelry in many styles, and no piece is over $25. There are gift pieces of handpainted wood in beautiful bright colors on white, red, and black backgrounds—candlesticks, bookends, spoons, and more. They also have baskets of duda reed that are white rather than the standard yellow, which are very cheap: a set of 3 wastepaper baskets is $5.40; a set of 6 nesting baskets with tops is $4.15; and a picnic hamper is $5.40. There are native dolls in the dress of the native Indian groups of Ecuador—Saraguro, Cuenca, Shauara, Oravalo—and a llama for the dolls to ride. Since this company deals primarily with wholesalers, they don't spell out duty procedures and shipping charges; you must contact the carrier of your choice to find rates. For more listings, see CLOTHING AND ACCESSORIES; and HOME.

CAPRILAND'S HERB FARM

Silver St.
Coventry, CT 06238
(203) 742-7244

If you are in the habit of buying an undistinguished pine bough wreath every year about December 10th and discarding it by the 31st amid a shower of pine needles, consider investing the same amount of money in a fragrant herb wreath from Caprilands which should last years. The St. Barbara's wreath is of wheat and rosebuds; the herb and flower wreath is made of artemisia, tansy, yarrow, and everlastings; and there is a kitchen wreath, Victorian wreath, and others with incense, wild herbs, and "witch" charm and rite materials. They also make herb and spice necklaces, doorway baskets, catnip mice, herb pillows, hot pads, and more. Wreaths cost from $10.95 to $18.00 which is much less than "city prices" on the same items. For more information see COSMETICS AND PERFUMES.

DEEPACK'S ROKJEMPERL PRODUCTS

61, 10th Khetwandi
Bombay 400 004, India

Deepack's sells all kinds of rough and cut stones, plus Indian handicrafts like ivory and bone jewelry and gift items, rosewood, buffalo horn, sandalwood, etc. See JEWELRY for main listing.

EILEEN'S HANDKNITS

Ardara, Donegal,
Ireland

Eileen's Handknits sells handknitted sweaters and accessories made by women in the cottages of Ireland. Each sweater is knitted in a pattern that has been handed down from generation to generation, so each is different. For more information, see listing under CLOTHING, FURS, AND ACCESSORIES.

GOOD SHEPHERD'S STORE

George T. Abu Aita and
Brothers
Mother-of-Pearl and Olive
Wood
Bethlehem, P.O. Box 96
Israel
Catalog: $1.00
Discount: minimum of
30%
Goods: handmade
Minimum Order: none

For $1.00 the Good Shepherd Store sends you a catalog full of religious and gift articles made of olivewood and mother-of-pearl. There are carvings of Moses, Mary, the flight to Egypt, the Saviour, and beautiful nativity sets, all in olivewood. Prices go from $3.75 for a face of the virgin to $78 for a beautifully detailed nativity set. They carry olivewood camels, connected with little chains to make a caravan, which cost from 60¢ to $12.75. There are also lovely vases, candlesticks, egg cups, salad sets, jewelry boxes, and Bibles, all made from olivewood. About twice as expensive and quite striking are the jewelry boxes, Bibles, crosses, crucifixes, and jewelry done in mother-of-pearl. At the

GOOD SHEPHERD'S STORE

**Shipping Cost: 15 to
20% of order
Payment: check, L/C,
C.O.D.
$$$$**

back of the catalog are 4 dolls, dressed in Bedouin, Arab, and national costumes, one on a camel, at $1.20 and $3.20. There are also chess sets in olivewood with boxes.

ICEMART

**P.O. Box 23
Keflavik International
Airport
Iceland**

Icemart sells Glit Lava-Ceramics, which are decorative pieces crafted from the lava of Iceland's active volcanoes. There are 2 vases, a planter, an ashtray, and a candleholder, all in a deep orange-red colored ceramic with craggy, glistening lava-rock adorning it. The designs are simple and attractive. The prices run from $16.50 to $99.00. For a complete listing, see CLOTHING AND ACCESSORIES.

KLOD HANS

**34 Hans Jensensstraede
DK-5000 Odense,
Denmark
Catalog: $1.00
Discount: to 50%
Goods: brand name,
handmade
Minimum Order: $20
Shipping: extra
Insurance: extra
Guarantee: satisfaction
Payment: certified check,
IMO, bank draft
$$**

This company sells Christmas decorations in simple, brightly colored designs: little elves made of wood, angels, and stars, as well as Easter decorations and gift items. They also sell Royal Copenhagen figurines.

D. MacGILLIVRAY AND COY.

**Muir of Aird
Benbecula
Western Isles, Scotland
PA88 5NA**

MacGillivray carries Highland dress accessories, including Tartan jackets, bonnets, caps, waistcoats, crests, jewelled dirks, skean dhus, bagpipes, drums, sashes, and more. Information is available on request. See CRAFTS AND HOBBIES for complete listing.

THE NEPAL CRAFT EMPORIUM

**G.P.O. Box 1443
Kathmandu, Nepal
Catalog: $3.00
Discount: to 90%
Goods: handcrafted
Minimum Order: inquire
Shipping: FOB
Kathmandu
Insurance: extra
Payment: bank draft or
irrevocable L/C
$$$$**

The Nepal Craft Emporium sends a 30-page catalog with black-and-white photos illustrating their beautiful selection of "metal images" (statues), studded filigree works, wood carvings, rugs, clothing, shoulderbags, and tantric icons and paintings. The metal statues are done in the "lost wax process," which they say is prehistoric. A wax model is made, covered with a mixture of hay, mud, and cow dung, and set to dry in the sun. The metal is cast, then chased and polished. The artisans also make gilded statues, which are quite beautiful. Nepal Craft has a selection of filigree articles that are studded with stones or glass and gilded with silver, then gold. There are boxes, ashtrays, water jars, a footed candlestand, and 2 striking dancing masks. There is also a group of 16 studded animals that would make delightful gifts. They include horses, rhinos, bulls, elephants, lions, seagulls, mice, owls, rabbits, peacocks, birds, deer, roosters, and a dragon. These statues are very handsome and true to detail, and cost from $1 to $18. The quality and level of craftsmanship place the things Nepal Craft carries far above run-of-the-mill export goods, and the prices are exceptionally low. For more listings, see ART AND ANTIQUES; CLOTHING AND ACCESSORIES; HOME; JEWELRY; and RELIGIOUS.

ORIENTAL HANDICRAFTS

**Capt. Sham Lai Rd.
Civil Lines
Ludhiana 141001
Punjab, India**

Oriental Handicrafts makes beautiful jewelry and articles for the home from camelbone. They also make gift items—bookmarks carved with elephants for 96¢ a dozen and letter openers in elephant and fish designs for up to $6.00 a dozen. There are carved cigarette holders 6 inches long for $9 a dozen, and the famous trio of wise monkeys who "see, hear and speak no evil" at 70¢ to $2.00 each. For the complete listing, see JEWELRY.

A.W.G. OTTEN AND SON

**Albert Cuypstraat 102-104-106
Amsterdam, Holland
Price List: free
Discount: 30% on orders
of 25 pairs or more
Goods: handmade,
exclusive
Minimum Order: none
Shipping: FOB**

Wooden shoes, or "klompen," are still worn in Holland by gardeners, fishermen, butchers, and dairy workers. A.W.G. Otten makes seven models, including souvenir shoes with windmills carved on the fronts. Most of the shoes are painted lively colors, and there is a low-cut model that is easier to walk in than the traditional style. Otten and Son sends a charming brochure on the history and manufacture of wooden shoes. In one part of Holland, a boy courting a girl would give her carved wooden shoes decorated with her initials. The "klompen" have even affected the language—there are several words in Dutch that are derived from

A.W.G. OTTEN AND SON

Amsterdam (rate chart included)
Insurance: incuded
Payment: check, bank draft, postal MO, Visa
$$$

the sound made by walking in wooden shoes. Prices for the decorative and functional shoes begin at $5.43 for white shoes in a child's size 4, and go up to $13.11 for souvenir shoes in a man's size 14. If you get carried away and buy 25 pairs or more, you can deduct 30% from the prices. Don't overlook the uses for these shoes—the large sizes can be used as doll beds, letter holders, planters, lamp bases, or even in the office to hold pencils.

OZARK OPPORTUNITIES, INC.

P.O. Box CC4
Harrison, AR 72601
(501) 743-2021

From the nimble fingers of mountain artisans come the charming crafts that button-pushing city folk love so much, and at prices everyone adores. A fat gingham hen doorstop is only $3.75; a large cedar-handled fabric purse is $3.75; and handshaped potholders are 75¢ and $1.25. Patchwork pillows, 15x15 inches, are a steal at $1.75 each, as are the quilts at $30 to $100. There is a whole collection of handmade white-oak baskets in every size and remarkably cheap, none priced over $6.00. It's nice to know that when you buy from Ozark Opportunities, all the money goes directly to the artisans so that they can ply their trades and keep the mountain crafts alive. For the complete listing, see TOYS AND GAMES.

RAMA JEWELRY

P.O. Box 858
987 Silom Rd.
Bangkok, Thailand

Rama Jewelry sells the pretty princess rings that Thailand is famous for, plus things like Thai silk and silk clothing, silver and bronze ware, leather goods, and teakwood carvings. For the complete listing, see JEWELRY.

SAXKJAERS

53 Købmagergade
1150 Copenhagen K, Denmark
Catalog: (complete) $2.00
Brochure: for collectors' plates, free
Discount: 40% minimum
Goods: name brand
Minimum Order: none
Shipping, Insurance: included
Payment: check, IMO
$$$

Saxkjaers sells the Christmas and Mother's Day plates issued each year by Royal Copenhagen, Bing & Grøndahl, Svend Jensen, and Porsgrund. All the plates are blue and white, and inscribed with the year. Saxkjaiers also sells Royal Copenhagen year mugs, Lladro figurines, and Bing & Grøndahl year bells and thimbles. The prices are much lower than U.S. prices, and the value of the plates increases steadily—an 1895 Bing & Grøndahl Christmas plate is worth $2,700 today!

SICANGU ARTS AND CRAFTS CO-OPERATIVE

c/o Chris Horvath
General Delivery Mission
Mission, SD 57555
Price List: SASE and 25¢

This organization is owned and operated by members of the Rosebud Sioux tribe and sells the handiwork of Indian artisans to the public, distributing the profits among the co-op members. You must write and inquire about specific items and their shipping policy. They carry beadwork, quillwork, quilts, and more.

SOUTHERN ILLINOIS QUILTERS ASSN.

Bonnie Krause
Rte. 1, Box 76
Alto Pass, IL 62905

The Southern Illinois Quilters get together and make quilts to order in traditional American patchwork patterns, much the way women long ago gathered to have quilting bees. They also do appliqué work and special orders. See HOME for the complete listing.

THE TIBETAN REFUGEE SELF HELP CENTER

Havelock Villa
65 Ghandi Rd.
Darjeeling, India
Catalog: $1
Discount: to 80%
Goods: handmade,
custom made
Minimum Order: none
Shipping, Packing: extra
Payment: bank draft,
send via registered mail
$$$$

The Tibetan Self Help Center was established in 1959 when Tibet was taken over by Communist China. Today over 650 refugees make it their home, and the handicrafts they produce are their main source of income. The small catalog they send is in black and white, but you can get an idea of the craftsmanship and design of the goods, if not the color. Their specialty is carpet making. They illustrate 23 rugs, all of which are 6x3 feet and cost $119 and $129. The designs are striking and unusual. There are several dragon patterns, a crane bird, lotus and bat, 8 lucky signs, and several more. The rugs are handwoven, and for 5% more you can have the rug woven in your own design. The Refugee Center also sells chair cushions in similar designs, woven fabrics, coats, shawls, and bags. There are Tibetan hats with fur trim, and exotic-looking boots, all costing from $9 to $20. For the home, there are candlestands, a brass stove, and carved tables. Even with packing and shipping the prices are extraordinarily low. Write to the Center for shipping information as it is not very clear in the catalog. Additional trade discounts are available for very large orders.

HOME

This section includes many different listings, since there are so many products designed for use in the home. There are 4 subdivisions here: *Bed and Bath, China, Glass, and Metal, Furniture and Accessories,* and *Maintenance and Building.* It seems to us that things for the home are the least commonly discounted items in ordinary retail stores, particularly the quality names in china, glassware, and furniture. The more you save on each item, though, the more you can put into your home.

There are many beautiful things for your home that are simply unavailable in the states. Check the foreign listings for these. There are also 'high tech'' items—industrial products that will transform well into home furnishings—that you should consider. Their prices are low and they're built to last.

Buy your plastic garbage bags in bulk. If you stop for a moment and think about how much you spend in a year on these "modern necessities," you'll write to Able Plastics fast and order a case. With your savings you can buy something that never has to be thrown away (or a new trashcan to hold the bags).

BED and BATH

DOWN HOME COMFORTS

P.O. Box 281
West Brattleboro, VT
05301
(802) 348-7944
**Catalog: retail brochure,
40¢; inquire about pillow
prices
Discount: 30% on small
pillows
Goods: made to order
Minimum Order: $40.00
Shipping: UPS, C.O.D.
Returns: none unless
they make an error
Payment: check, MO
$$**

Down Home Comforts makes small "occasional" pillows at 30% below retail in almost any size or shape. They use cream colored cotton ticking, cotton thread, and 50% duck down/50% small-feather mix. A 12x12-inch pillow with 8 oz. of fill is $15; 10 oz. fill is $18.00. Down Home guarantees that all materials are new and no substitutions are made without consulting the customer. They ask that you write to them and include specific measurements, or send a paper pattern (with seam allowances marked) for the pillow you want, and they will write back with the price. Note: the pillow ordered should be one inch bigger than the desired size, so it fits snugly in the cover.

ICEMART

**P.O. Box 23
Keflavik International
Airport
Iceland**

Icemart recommends that you keep one of its beautiful wool blankets in the car because its "cosseting warmth" can "help settle fractious children." The pure wool blankets are all 58x74 inches or 59x79 inches and are woven or knitted in white and black. Each blanket bears a symbol or design of Icelandic origin as part of the pattern—one is a volcano motif, another a sun and snowflake design; one has a stylized Viking boat pattern, and 2 have the word "Iceland" woven into them. They cost $35.90 to $43.50 each. There are also wool blend blankets in stripes and plaids at $29.90 each. For the floor, Icemart sells lush rugs of longhaired sheepskin in white and black, and cushions to match. The rugs are $33 for 5 to 6 square feet, up to $159 for 24 square feet, and the cushions are $29.70 each. See CLOTHING, FURS, AND ACCESSORIES for complete listing.

D. MacGILLIVRAY AND COY.

**Muir of Aird
Benbecula
Western Isles, Scotland
PA88 5NA**

MacGillivray sells "tartan travel rugs," 34x56 inches, at a very low $8 each, which are available in 9 tartans. A larger and heavier rug, 60x72 inches, is sold for $20. There are also Highland bedspreads in stripes, 70x90 inches, for $20, and Shetland bedspreads/rugs, 58x76 inches, for $22. For the floor, they offer "real Shetland sheepskin floor rugs," cured, combed, clipped, and washable, for $26 and $30. See CRAFTS AND HOBBIES for the complete listing.

RUBIN & GREEN

**290 Grand St.
New York, NY 10002
(212) 226-0313
Information: price quote
Discount: 30 to 40%
Goods: name brand
Minimum Order: $50
Shipping, Handling: extra
Returns: within 90 days
on resaleable, unopened
merchandise, credits on
returns
Payment: checks, MO
$$$**

Rubin & Green carries a wide selection of bath and table linens made by Wamsutta, Burlington, Martex, and Springmaid at discounts of up to 40%. They sell bath carpeting, shower curtains, pillows, blankets, sheets, comforters, napkins, table linens, and everything else the mills manufacture. Just write or call for a price quote.

J. SCHACHTER CORP.

115 Allen St.
New York, NY 10022
(212) 533-1150
Information: price quote
Discount: 20 to 30%
Goods: name brand
Minimum Order: none
Shipping: extra, UPS
Sales Tax: NY residents
Payment: check, MC,
Visa
$$$

For over 60 years, J. Schachter has been making comforters for the bedding industry and recovering old comforters for private customers. They will use your fabric, or their own sheets, to make a comforter and quilt it in the design of your choice. In addition to custom services, they sell readymade comforters, pillows, linens, and towels by Spring Mills, Wamsutta, Burlington Mills, West Point Pepperill, and Cannon. For prices on the quilting services and linens, send specific information (size of quilted piece, design of quilting, sheets to be used for fabric, special details, or the manufacturer and style number of the linens) for a price quote.

SOUTHERN ILLINOIS QUILTERS ASSN.

Bonnie Krause
Rte. 1, Box 76
Alto Pass, IL 62905
(618) 893-2014
Price List: free
Discount: varies
Goods: handmade,
custom made
Minimum Order: none
Shipping: UPS, Parcel
Post, extra
Sales Tax: IL sales tax
applied to every order
Payment: check, MO
$$$

This Association is a group of women who get together and quilt. All the work is done by hand. They make entire quilts: cutting, piecing, sewing, designing the quilting, stitching, etc. They also do appliqué and embroidery. Some of the quilt patterns listed are "Nine Patch," "Postage Stamp," "Mexican Star," "Log Cabin," "Rising Star," and "Tumbling Block." Prices go from $80 for a twin-sized quilt to $250 for a king size. They also do quilting (sewing the quilt top, batting, and backing together). Prices for quilting alone run from $50 to $100. If you want a special design, write to them for prices.

UNIVERSAL SUPPLIERS

P.O. Box 14803
Hong Kong
Price List: free

This is a large mail order house with several departments. They sell linen and china; the prices are Hong Kong cheap. When you request the catalog, specify "china and linens." See AUDIO for complete listing.

CHINA, GLASS, and METAL

A. BENJAMIN AND CO., INC.

82 Bowery
New York, NY 10013
(212) 226-6013, 6014
Information: price quote
Discount: 25 to 50%
Goods: brand name
Minimum Order: $25.00
Shipping: extra
Guarantee: by
manufacturer
Sales Tax: NY residents
Payment: certified check,
bank check
$$$

Benjamin sells top brand names in china, glass, silverware, jewelry, and giftware. They also sell diamonds. Some of the silver companies they carry are Reed and Barton, Gorham, Towle, Wallace, and International. All sales and pricing are done on a price quote basis, and they say that *you must mention WBMC when you call or write to them.* Since they carry so much merchandise, you should send them a list of anything you are pricing in the way of stemware, china, silver, or giftware, and see if they have it. Don't forget model or style numbers, pattern and piece names, and colors.

WALTER DRAKE SILVER EXCHANGE

5902 Drake Building
Colorado Springs, CO
80940
(303) 596-3140
Price List: free
Discount: 40 to 75%
Goods: name brand
Minimum Order: none
Sales Tax: CO residents
Guarantee: satisfaction
Payment: check, MO
$$$

If you've just mangled a spoon from your new set of silver in the garbage disposal and want to replace it or if you'd just like to complete grandma's silver service, you can do it through Walter Drake's Silver Exchange. They carry active, inactive, and obsolete patterns. All you have to do is write to them with the pattern name and manufacturer, and if you're not sure of it, write for the free pattern identification booklet. It's possible to save up to 75% over retail prices, so now there's no excuse for an incomplete set.

MICHAEL C. FINA

580 5th Ave.
New York, NY 10036
(212) 757-2530
Catalog: inquire
Discount: 10 to 40%, plus

Fina has been in business for 45 years, and claim that they are the largest jewelers in New York City. They have a 250-page catalog of watches, clocks, radios, china, and jewelry, all by top manufacturers. In china, they have Royal Doulton, Lenox, Georg Jensen, Haviland, etc. In silverware, they carry Gorham, Interna-

MICHAEL C. FINA

Goods: name brand
Minimum Order: none
Shipping: extra, UPS
Sales Tax: NY residents
Guarantee: "We stand by
everything we sell."
Payment: check, MO,
MC, Visa, AE
$$$

tional Silver, Wallace, Stieff, Lunt, Towle, and just about every line of hollowware that is made. For more information, see JEWELRY, GEMS, AND WATCHES.

PARIS BREAD PANS

Clyde Brooks
500 Independence Ave.
S.E.
Washington, DC 20003
(202) 544-6858
Price List, Recipe: free
Discount: 30 to 50%
Goods: house brand
Minimum Order: none
Shipping: included
Sales tax: DC residents
Guarantee: satisfaction
Payment: check, MO
$$$$

These French bread pans are a great buy. They were designed by Clyde Brooks so that he could duplicate the bread he had eaten in France. They have become very popular, and are recommended in *The Cooks Catalogue*. They are made of quilted aluminum, and Mr. Brooks (and a flock of customers) assures us that there is "nothing as good" as these for making this bread. One set of pans makes 2 loaves, and costs $8.95 (compared to up to $20 for bread pans in gourmet stores). Mr. Brooks has also come up with a milk-less, shortening-less recipe, worthy of the pans, that sounds terribly easy and dangerously good.

RAMA JEWELRY LTD.

P.O. Box 858
987 Silom Rd.
Bangkok, Thailand

Rama Jewelry specializes in jewelry of semiprecious stones, but also sells silverware and metalware for the table, teakwood carvings (salad bowl sets, cups, trays, etc.), and bronzeware. For the complete listing, see JEWELRY.

STECHERS LTD.

62 Independence Square
Port-of-Spain, Trinidad,
W.I.
Information: by price
quote

Stechers is an incredible source for top quality jewelry, china, crystal, silver, leather goods, perfume, and ceramics. They carry china by Wedgwood, Royal Doulton, Aynsley, Royal Copenhagen, Beleek, Haviland-Limoges, Royal Delft, and Spode. There is crystal by Daum, Kosta, Boda, Waterford, Lalique, and Orrefors,

STECHERS LTD.

Discounts: 30 to 50%
Goods: name brand
Minimum Order: inquire
Shipping: inquire
Payment: inquire
$$$$

and watches by Piaget, Piguet, Seiko, Vulcain, and many other companies. In addition, Stechers sells Dunhill and Dupont lighters, jewels (an 87 carat aquamarine priced at $8,000), trifles by Cartier, Silver by Georg Jensen, hairbrushes by Kent, Lanvin and Ballenciaga perfume, and dozens of other things. The people who run Stechers ask that you send them pictures from catalogs of the things you want, and they will attempt to locate them and give you a price. Try to include as much information as possible about what you want to aid them. You can save up to 50% on these luxury goods, which makes them much more affordable.

TREASURE TRADERS LTD.

P.O. Box N-635
Nassau, Bahamas
General Price List: free;
specific brochures upon
request
Discount: 25 to 40% off
Goods: brand name
Minimum Order: $100;
Georg Jensen, $400
Shipping, Insurance:
included
Payment: check, MO
$$$$

Treasure Traders Ltd. deserves its name: they sell the highly coveted and very expensive sterling flatware, china, and crystal of the best companies. In silver, they offer Towle, Gorham, Wallace, Reed & Barton, Tuttle, Oneida, Lunt, and International. They also sell the sleek designs of Georg Jensen, which are so costly here, at 30% off the usual U.S. retail price. In china, they carry Royal Worcester, Coalport, Rosenthal, Richard Giorni, and Wedgewood at 30 to 40% off. They carry the lines of Stuart, Royal Brierley, St. Louis, Kosta, Boda, Daum, and Baccarat crystal at prices 40% below the U.S. list price. A few photos of brochure covers are pictured in the price list, but you must request specific brochures to get them. There is absolutely no excuse for buying flatware, china or crystal in the U.S., at least from a department or jewelry store, with prices this low by mail. You can get sterling flatware for the same price you'd pay for silverplate here. There is one catch—the delivery time runs from 6 weeks to 12 months, so be patient. When your dinnerware finally arrives, you'll have saved a bundle and bought the best.

FURNITURE and ACCESSORIES

ANDEAN PRODUCTS

Apartado 472
Cuenca, Ecuador
South America

In addition to a large selection of handmade handicrafts and clothing, Andean makes some beautiful and unusual articles for the home. They have a selection of wrought iron mirrors, candleholders, and decorations that are quite striking and very cheap. There are several candle sconces that hold 1, 2 and 3

ANDEAN PRODUCTS

candles, from $3.40 to $8.25 each. There are two handsome chandeliers, one electric for $55 and one designed to hold four candles for $5.65. The design of the ironwork is best described as modified scrollwork and looks like a cross between Mexican and Early American artistry. Andean also makes wood and leather furniture in a heavy, simple, modern design that looks like overweight Danish modern. The wood can be either blonde or walnut, and the most expensive piece is the 2-seater sofa at $93. The furniture all looks terrifically solid and sturdy and would be great in a den. There are also richly embroidered table linens in bright colors, and tapestries for the wall done in different designs. For complete listing, see HANDICRAFTS AND NATIVE PRODUCTS.

ASHLEY FURNITURE WORKSHOPS

3a Dawson Place
London W2, England
Catalog: free, $2 airmail
Discount: 30 to 50%
Goods: made to order
Minimum Order: none
Shipping: FOB U.S. port
Insurance,
Documentation, Packing:
included
Payment: bank draft
$$$

Ashley Furniture Workshops makes reproductions of classic sofas and chairs for about half of what you'd expect to pay here—that is, if you could find them. They are all made to order, using the finest materials, and the work is done by hand. The furniture is upholstered in hand pleated and buttoned leather in your choice of colors and grades. Prices begin at $205 for a Chippendale stool with a plain or buttoned top, and peak at $1,775 for a sedan chair which boasts glass windows, nearly 5,000 brass stud nails, and rails for carrying. More practical is the luxurious Chesterfield sofa in cushion or button seats and made in 2, 3, and 4-person models, priced from $1,375 to $1,725. A matching Chesterfield chair is $895 and the ottoman is $240. There are straight-line, untufted Cromwellian pieces from $320 to $1,765 that are more understated, and four handsome swivel chairs on wheels, suitable for an office, from $550 to $870. There are several club, wing, and slipper chairs, each beautifully designed and true to tradition, and one modern-looking rocking chair in curving steel and leather for only $365. These prices may seem high, but custom-made furniture ordered through a decorator in New York City would cost at least twice as much.

THE BEDPOST

5921 N. High St.
Worthington OH 43085
(614) 885-5172
Catalog: $1.95

The Bedpost sell two waterbed kits for much less than it costs to buy them readymade. The $120 kit has a box lap seam mattress with a 10-year limited warranty, a fitted liner, and a solid state heater with a 4-year warranty. The "motionless mattress" has a

THE BEDPOST

Discount: up to 30%
Goods: house, name
brand
Shipping: extra
Sales Tax: OH residents
Payment: check, MO
$$$

10-year limited warranty, liner, and heater, for $199.95. Write to the Bedpost for information on these and other models, or if you're shopping for a hot tub—they've just added a line straight from California at great prices.

BLOOM & KRUP

206 First Ave.
New York, NY 10009
(212) OR3-2760

Bloom & Krup sells all kinds of furniture and home products at discount prices. They have bedding by Sealy, Simmons, and Therapedic, La-Z-Boy chairs, Childcraft cribs, Kirsch drapery rods, Yorktown wooden kitchen cabinets, El-Kay sinks, Perrego baby strollers, paint by Red Devil and Pentagon, and furniture by Bassett, Lane, Singer, and Kemp. For the main listing, see APPLIANCES, TELEVISION, AND VIDEO.

CAMBRIDGE WOOLS, LTD.

P.O. Box 2572
16-22 Anzac Ave.
Auckland 1, New Zealand

Cambridge Wools sells sheepskins dyed in a spectrum of colors—pink, white, moss, marigold, apricot, blue, etc. The nap is 1½ inches long, the skins average 30x25 inches, and they cost only $22. See CRAFTS AND HOBBIES for complete listing.

DRAPERIES DIRECT, INC.

112 Lincoln Ave.
Bronx, NY 10454
(212) 993-5668
Catalog: $1
Discount: 30 to 50%
Goods: services
Minimum Order: none
Shipping: FOB Bronx
Sales Tax: NY residents
Payment: certified check,
MO, C.O.D., MC and
Visa: add 5%
$$$

Draperies Direct will quilt your bedspreads, slipcovers, draperies, and accessories for greater durability and body. The goods are quilted with handguided machines on looms, and the prices are much, much lower than what department stores charge for the same service—and they are very prompt.

FIDELITY PRODUCTS CO.

**705 Pennsylvania Ave.
Minneapolis, MN 55426**

Fidelity specializes in office supplies, but they also carry items that are useful in a home: plastic garbage bags, rubber door mats, vinyl hall runners that are good in muddy weather, an air purifier, and more. Be innovative—a swing top garbage pail would be a great clothes hamper for kids and is easily cleaned; the smoking urns are very sleek in chrome and you just dump the butts into the receptacle below the tray instead of forever emptying ashtrays and replacing them; and the antifatigue mats work just as well in the kitchen as they do in the factory. For the complete listing, see OFFICE SUPPLIES AND EQUIPMENT.

GOLDBERGS' MARINE

**202 Market St.
Philadelphia, PA 19106**

Goldbergs' Marine carries equipment and supplies for boats and yachts, including small refrigerators, teakwood accessories for the bathroom, and some other good-looking galley utensils that would work well in a home. For the complete listing, see AUTOMOTIVE AND MARINE SUPPLIES.

LAMP WAREHOUSE

**1073 39th St.
Brooklyn, NY 11219
Information: price quote
by mail only
Discounts: up to 30%
Goods: name brand
Minimum Order: none
Shipping: extra, UPS or
FOB Brooklyn
Sales Tax: NY residents
Payment: check, MO,
certified check
$$**

Write to the Lamp Warehouse for a price quote on any lamp you want by Stiffel, Fine Art, Westward, or Nathan Lagan. They also carry other brands and all kinds of lamps—desk, table, swag, hanging, wall—and will even special order lamps for you that they don't stock.

MATERIAL FLOW, INC.

**835 North Wood St.
Chicago, IL 60622
(312) 421-7111**

Material Flow sells supplies and equipment to industry at low prices. You should write on business letterhead if possible. The goods are heavy duty and made to stand up under hard use. There are 6 kinds of aluminum or fiberglass ladders from $42 up

MATERIAL FLOW, INC.

to several hundred dollars for heavy 16-foot ladders. If you want a functional look in your home, consider using their basic work benches, in 60, 72, or 96-inch lengths, for a kitchen worktable. A 60-inch-long, 32-inch-high, 30-inch-wide steelframe table with a solid 1¾-inch-thick maple top is $179. Add some of their industrial-look stools, and you have a dining table that will endure all kinds of abuse. You can organize a workroom or sewingroom with their steel bins or shelving units and use them in lieu of closets if you like an open look. Material Flow also sells runners, scraper mats, and fatigue mats, which are invaluable in halls, doorways, and kitchens. There is a "kik-step" stepstool that moves across the floor on wheels yet stays put when you step on it, and trash can liners for as little as 7¢ each. For more information, see TOOLS AND HARDWARE.

NATIONAL FURNITURE AND FABRICS SALES

1949A W. Green Drive
P.O. Box 2314
High Point, NC 27261
(800) 334-2509
(919) 888-4084 NC
Catalog: $2 (National's furniture); $5 (brand name furniture), $5 both
Discount: to 40%
Goods: brand, house name
Minimum Order: none
Shipping Cost: FOB High Point, NC
Sales Tax: NC residents
Returns: on defective goods
Payment: check, MO
$$$

National sells two kinds of furniture. One is the upholstered line they make themselves, and the other is a collection of furniture from over 300 manufacturers at 30 to 40% off normal list price. Some of the brand names are White, Singer, Century, Stiffel, and Barcalounger. Both catalogs are in color and are very informative and attractive. National stresses the craftsmanship and quality of goods that go into its own furniture, and the catalog includes pictures of the construction process. The styles are traditional classics: Chesterfield, Lawson, and Tuxedo-style sofas and loveseats, handsome leather pieces, sleepers, wing chairs, easychairs, and ottomans. Prices run from $121 for an ottoman to $1,270 for a long tuxedo sofa in the finest fabric (there are 14 grades). There are many styles among the brand names: Chippendale, Early American, French Provincial, Hepplewhite, contemporary, and some strikingly modern pieces in a soft, upholstered-to-the-floor look. Prices are available by phone or mail, and National's decorators are happy to help with your decorating problems. The catalog price is refundable with first purchase.

THE NEPAL CRAFT EMPORIUM

G.P.O. Box 1443
Kathmandu, Nepal

In addition to statues of Buddhist deities and studded animal figures, the Emporium sells articles for the home. Among the filigree works, studded with coral or turquoise stones, are many small boxes including a powder box, heartshaped box, 8-sided Pali box, and very ornate studded Bajara boxes. These cost from 85¢ to $3.75. There are several ashtrays, dancing masks for wall decoration, and waterjars. The Emporium makes "thekies," which are wooden butter or oil pots studded with bone figures. These cost from $5.75 to $10. There is a striking lamp with a carved temple-lion crouched beneath the lantern for $20, and lamp bases in graceful, carved column shapes for $5 and $8. For $60 you can buy a "tika jhya," which is a magnificently carved frame encasing two small carved doors. The Emporium also sells carpets, which they say are known as Tibetan rugs, in designs of dragons and flowers—3x6 feet at $75 each. It is not clear whether these are genuine Tibetan rugs or copies; if you want to buy one, don't order before you see the catalog from the Tibetan Self Help Refugee Center which makes the real thing. For more information, see listing under HANDICRAFTS AND NATIVE PRODUCTS.

ORIENTAL HANDICRAFTS

Capt. Sham Lai Rd.
Civil Lines
Ludhiana 141001
Punjab, India

Oriental Handicrafts sells a wonderful assortment of jewelry and gift items made of polished camelbone. They also sell things for the home at extraordinarily low prices. There are salt spoons at 96¢ a dozen, fork and spoon sets, napkin rings and cocktail picks. There are also carved table lamps, complete with fittings, at $10.50 each. For the complete listing, see JEWELRY.

PLEXI-CRAFT QUALITY PRODUCTS CORP.

195 Chrystie St.
New York, NY 10002
(212) 673-4550
Catalog: $1
Discount: over 50%
Goods: house brand
Minimum Order: none
Shipping: extra, UPS or
FOB NYC
Sales Tax: NY residents
Payment: check
$$$

Plexi-craft manufactures their own line of acrylic goods including pedestals, cubes, shelving units, magazine racks, towel holders, chairs, record holders, etc. These goods all cost up to 50% less than they do when bought in department stores and elsewhere, and Plexi-craft can even do special orders if you give them a picture and dimensions of the item you want made.

JAMES ROY, INC.

15 East 32nd St.
New York, NY 10016
(212) 679-2565
List of Brands: free
Pricing: by price quote
Discount: at least
33 1/3%
Goods: brand name
Minimum Order: none
Shipping: FOB
manufacturer or
warehouse
Sales Tax: NY residents
Guarantee: by
manufacturer
Payment: check, MO,
MC, Visa
$$$$

James Roy guarantees at least one third off manufacturers' suggested retail prices on an impressive list of 66 nationally known furniture lines, plus *all* brand name carpeting. They carry Drexel, Henredon, Heritage, Broyhill, Lane, Stiffel, Thayer Coggin, Sealy, Thomasville, Simmons, Pennsylvania House, and Stanley, to name a few. They have no catalog—you must write or call with the style, model, and color numbers or codes to get a price quote and arrange for purchasing. Furniture is delivered from the manufacturer or warehouses, and shipping charges depend on the mile per pound rate. James Roy's furniture is on display in their New York City showroom, but you can use furniture in anyone's showroom to get the model and style numbers you need for a price quote—just tell the salesman that you're comparison-shopping.

S & C HUBER, ACCOUTREMENTS

82 Plants Dam Rd.
East Lyme, CT 06333

In addition to crafts supplies, S & C Huber also sells finished pieces such as candles made of bayberry, beeswax, and tallow. These candles contain no stearic acid or paraffin, and burn just as the originals would have. (The tallow candles are slightly smoky and smell like steak, they say.) They carry stoneware in several colors, with a starter set of 16 pieces at $40, and Bennington pottery is available on request. There are also tin lighting devices, made to look like old tinware, in several sconce and chandelier styles. The prices are very good on these, running from $13 per pair of candle sconces to $126.50 for a 6-arm electric chandelier. See CRAFTS AND HOBBIES for complete listing.

SION FUK ENTERPRISES

125-2 Wu-Fu 2nd Rd.
Kaohsiung, Taiwan
Republic of China
Catalog: $5.00
Discount: 30 to 70%
Minimum Order: $5,000
Payment: bank draft
$

Sion Fuk sends a small catalog full of exotic, well-designed pieces of furniture in rosewood, teak, and camphorwood. They sell shelf units in rosewood, carved coffee tables, nesting table sets, screens, liquor cabinets, chests, dining room table and chair sets, and more typical household furniture. There is a truly handsome Spanish desk with 7 drawers for $200.00, 2 china cabinets over 6 feet long for $350 and $400, a magnificent gun rack and cabinet for $200, and a lovely roll top desk for $200. Prices range from $45 for chess sets to $750 for an elegant dining room set, and

SION FUK ENTERPRISES

everything is worth much, much more. The minimum U.S. order is $5,000, so if you want to order, start calling your friends and neighbors. You might also try writing to Sion Fuk to see if they would lower their minimum, or whether by paying the shipping charges beforehand you should have the minimum waived.

THE TIBETAN REFUGEE SELF HELP CENTER

Havelock Villa
65 Ghandi Rd.
Darjeeling, India

The Center sells beautiful handwoven rugs of several kinds and will do custom orders. They also sell carved wooden tables, picture frames of carved wood, and chair cushions. See HANDICRAFTS AND NATIVE PRODUCTS for a complete listing.

TRADE EXCHANGE CEYLON, LTD.

72 Chatham St.
Colombo 1, Sri Lanka

Trade Exchange sells "Lakloom" batik bed linens, coverlets, fabrics, lampshades, and wall hangings. The hangings, beautiful examples of Indian art, are done in striking colors and depict scenes from India's past. The lampshades are cylinders of fabric stretched over a frame, and look like stained glass when lit from within. For more on what they carry, see CLOTHING AND ACCESSORIES.

WESTON BOWL MILL

Weston, VT 05161
(802) 824-6219
Catalog: 35¢
Discount: up to 30% over NYC prices; more on seconds; 30 to 50% wholesale discount for teachers and decorators
Minimum Order: $3
Shipping: included on some items; on others, extra, via UPS
Sales Tax: VT residents
Guarantee: satisfaction
Payment: check, MO
$$$

The Weston Bowl Mill makes bowls and hundreds of other things made of wood. The salad and chopping bowls run from 6 inches to 20 inches in diameter and can be used for many purposes as long as you keep them oiled. Weston sells seconds of these bowls that have minute flaws, but that function and last just as well as first quality, for up to 35% less. Weston also sells salad servers, bowl stands, chopping boards, carbon-steel knives, knife racks, birch plates, candlesticks, pepper mills, Vermont stoneware mugs, wine racks, wall shelf units, towel and tissue holders, boxes, wooden spoons and utensils, bowl choppers, nut crackers, wall pegs, and much more. There are fireplace bellows of wood, brass, and leather for $12.35 to $20.25, napkin rings at 50¢ each, a lapboard, duck weather vanes for $7.95 and $9.95, and cribbage boards. Don't miss the stools and quiltstands. For more on what they carry, see COSMETICS AND PERFUMES; FARM AND GARDEN; and TOYS AND GAMES.

RICHARD B. ZARBIN AND ASSOCIATES

225 W. Hubbard St.
Chicago, IL 60610
(312) 644-2997
Information: price quote
Discount: up to 40%
Goods: name brand
Minimum Order: none
Shipping: FOB factory
Sales Tax: IL residents
Guarantee: by
manufacturer
Payment: check, MO,
MC, Visa
$$$

Zarbin's sells name brand furniture at discounts of up to 40%. They carry all the top manufacturers: Directional, Kroehler, Broyhill, Thomasville, Lane, Hardin, Drexel, Flexsteel, La-Z-Boy, Charleton, Stieffel, Barcalounger, Flair, Selig, Burlington, and Sealy. They also have carpeting by Burlington, Salem, Galaxy Monticello, and Karastan. To get a price quote and a shipping estimate, just write to Zarbin's with the model number and manufacturer of the furniture or carpet you're interested in.

HOME MAINTENANCE and BUILDING

ABLE PLASTICS CO.

38-15 98th St.
Flushing, NY 11368
(212) 458-0975
Price List: free
Discount: 50% and more
Goods: house brand
Minimum Order: $15
Shipping: included
Sales Tax: NY residents
Guarantee: satisfaction
or replacement, or
money back
Payment: check, MO
$$$

Able Plastics sells garbage bags and can save you half of what you're probably paying for them now in the supermarket. They are sold in lots of 100, 200, or 250 bags, depending on the size. Able carries many sizes unavailable in stores, and can also have bags made in custom sizes. The delivery is free within 300 miles of New York City, and 95¢ for each additional 300 miles. The man who runs Able Plastics says that many of his customers have been doing business with him for 5 and 6 years, and they are so pleased with the bags that they refer their friends. If you aren't satisfied, you can get replacement bags or your money back. This is a great way to save money on something you use every day, and still get good quality.

B.B. PLASTICS

2015 Blake St.
Berkely, CA 94704
(415) 845-6527
Catalog: $1, refundable
Discount: 30% minimum
Goods: house name
Minimum Order: none
Shipping: FOB Berkely,
CA

The people at B.B. Plastics say that installing a skylight is as easy as building a wooden box frame on your roof, sealing it, cutting out the roof, dropping the skylight into place, and nailing the sides. They sell only plexiglas bubble skylights, which they say are 10 times more impact resistant than flat skylights. There are 3 kinds: clear (total light and heat), white (translucent and private), and solar bronze (transparent, minimized heat gain). There are also ventilating bubbles which can be cranked open to 30 degrees, and insulated bubbles. Prices run from $60 for a 16x32-

B.B. PLASTICS

Sales Tax: CA residents
Guarantee: 5 years
Payment: check, Visa,
MC
$$$

inch clear bubble to $175 for a 48x74-inch solar bronze. Special bubbles cost more. There are larger sizes, and pole cranks and plexi cleaners are available. The bubbles are guaranteed to be watertight and free of defects for 5 years.

MILVAN

7799 Enterprise
Newark, CA 94560
(415) 793-7918
Price List: 25¢
Discount: up to 50%
Goods: house brand
Minimum Order: $10
Shipping: included
Sales Tax: CA residents
Warranty: limited;
replacement or refund
only
Payment: check, MO
$$$$

You can save up to 50% over the cost of garbage and food bags by buying from Milvan, and they even pay shipping. The have over 350 sizes, from 2x2-inch to 55 gallon. They also have pallet covers, bag ties, cling film, sheeting, tubing, heat-sealers, and press-to-seal bags. Their food bags are FDA approved and of "virgin" polyethylene (large garbage bags can contain reused plastics). Most of the bags are sold in lots of 100, or about a year's supply, although the prices on 25,000 (enough for a neighborhood) are much lower. Don't miss this chance to save on a necessity.

RAIN JET CORP.

301 South Flower St.
Burbank, CA 91503
(213) 849-2251
Brochure: free
Discount: to 35%
Goods: house name
Minimum Order: one
Shipping: included
Sales Tax: CA residents
Returns: satisfaction or
money back
Payment: check, MO
$$$

This company has three sleek rotary showerheads, ranging in price from $19.95 to $29.95 (regularly $19.95 to $39.95). There are two in "mother-of-pearl" finish, one in silver chrome, and all give rotary massage action. The brochure gives complete installation instructions, and also describes exactly how the showerheads are constructed, what they're made of, and what you can use them for. The showerheads are also guaranteed for 1 year against faulty materials or workmanship.

ROBINSON'S WALLCOVERINGS

Dept. WBMC
225 West Spring St.
Titusville, PA 16354
(814) 827-1893
Catalog: 50¢, pub. in Jan.
Discount: to 50%
Goods: brand name
Minimum Order: $10 for charges
Shipping Cost: 75¢ to $4.00
Sales Tax: PA residents
Returns: 30 days
Guarantee: money back
Payment: check, MO, MC, Visa
$$$

Robinson's Wallcoverings went into mail order business in 1919, and the catalog prices look as if they haven't risen in 60 years. They begin at $1.15 a roll for "Susie" a pretty *orangey flower* print, and top at $4.95 a roll for flocked wallpaper in 5 luscious colors. Almost all the prints are conservative and old fashioned, but there are some very handsome patterns that would blend with many kinds of decor: pastel powder-room prints, designs for children, vegetables and fruits for the kitchen, and a den pattern called "Rustic Signfare" that reproduces old-time shop signs. All the papers are pretrimmed and most are prepasted. Robinson's includes a guide to rolls needed per room, and they sell all the tools and supplies that you'll need to hang the paper. Matching fabrics are available for some patterns at $4.50 per yard, by special order.

SARGENT-SOWELL, INC.

1185 108th St.
Grand Prairie, TX 75050
(214) 647-1525
Catalog: $5, published twice a year
Savings: up to 30%
Goods: name, house brand
Minimum Order: $15.00
Shipping: extra, UPS or FOB point of manufacturer
Sales Tax: TX residents
Payment: check, MO, MC, Visa
$$

SA-SO puts out an enormous 400-page catalog that will keep you entertained for hours. Whether it's a snakebite kit you need, lanterns, trashcans, plastic office plants, watchman's clocks, state flags, traffic cones, stop signs, or even a small firetruck, it's all here. Their line of safety equipment—flashlights, first aid kits, hard hats, goggles, and respirators—is also very complete. They carry uniforms, a full line of office furniture, playground supplies, stretchers—anything and everything for municipal use. Chances are you'll find scores of items that would function very well in the house.

JEWELRY, GEMS, and WATCHES

If you know anyone whose business is selling jewelry and watches at retail prices, ask him or her for a loan. Retailers must be doing well, because there are fantastic savings available and our discounters are *still* able to make a profit.

These sources are perfect places to buy gifts—your recipient will think you were willing to spring for much more than you actually did. (Gee, and all this time they thought you were a skinflint bargain nut!) They are also good for those of you who want to collect or invest in something of beauty and lasting value that can keep you ahead of inflation. Rennie Ellen will actually give you a good and reliable deal on diamonds, the most hustled stone in the world. When buying precious or semiprecious gems from overseas, bear in mind that those ridiculously low prices probably reflect a quality that is not exactly first rate. Still, comparable items are bound to cost much more here.

ANKA CO., INC.

95 Washington St. Dept. WW
West Warwick, RI 02893
(401) 826-0564
Catalog: $1.00, refundable
Discount: up to 79%
Goods: house name
Minimum Order: $50
Shipping, Handling: $2.00
Payment: check, MO, certified check
$$$

Anka sells all kinds of jewelry, mainly rings and pendants. They send you an attractive 28-page color brochure illustrating "tailored and baroque rings to suit milady's fancy," "handsome, rugged rings for men," and wedding bands, professional rings, dinner rings, etc. Most of the rings are set in 18kt. heavy gold electroplate, 10kt. gold-filled, or sterling silver bands. All the semiprecious gems are manmade, but they use genuine tiger eye, jade, pearls, star sapphires, and opals. There are four Masonic rings for men, plus professional rings for truckdrivers, policemen, and firemen. Prices on these are listed as $54 retail, and $12 to you. A pretty ring with 2 cultured pearls was $27 retail, $5.25 here. There are also display sets of kiddie rings, "Indian" rings, and fashion rings that look like the kind in the five and dime stores. Some of these would be suitable for party favors and gifts, and are very cheap.

BHAVANI GEMS

**Post Box No. 2731
Bombay-400002 India
Price List: free
Discount: minimum of
30%
Shipping: FOB Bombay;
forwarding charges extra
Insurance: included
Payment: check,
cashier's check, bank
draft
Resale #, Letterhead:
either one must be used
to get price list
$**

Bhavani Gems is a new firm that has just been started by Mr. C. Zaveri. He sells cut and rough precious and semiprecious stones, wooden cobra stands, and a variety of wooden meditation beads. A price list is being prepared at the moment, but to obtain it you must write to Mr. Zaveri on business letterhead or send your resale number. The prices are low, and since Mr. Zaveri is a former associate of another gem company that disbanded to form several new ones, he is already very experienced in mail order gems.

T.M. CHAN & CO.

**P.O. Box 33881
Sheung Wan Post Office
Hong Kong**

Chan has a lovey selection of Seiko, Rolex, and Omega watches in a large variety of styles for men and women. There are chronographs, digitals, quartz, and even alarm watches. For more information, see CAMERAS.

THE CROWN CULTURED PEARL CORP.

**580 Eighth Ave.
New York, NY 10018
(212) 947-0540
Leaflet: free
Discount: 20 to 40%
Goods: house brand
Minimum Order: $15
Shipping, Handling:
$1.50
Sales Tax: NY residents
Guarantee: satisfaction
Payment: check, MO
$$$**

Crown Pearl sells all kinds of loose and strung pearls for the jeweler and the hobbyist. They also have jade, ivory, and coral. The pearls are cultured, and there are the familiar white ones, as well as blue and cream pearls. The discounts are great, especially for a U.S. firm, and if you need something that isn't listed in the leaflet, just write—they have a tremendous stock.

DEEPACK'S ROKJEMPERL PRODUCTS

**61, 10th Khetwandi
Bombay 400 004, India**

Deepack's sells precious and semiprecious rough, cut and polished gemstones from amethysts to zircons. The prices are aston-

DEEPACK'S ROKJEMPERL PRODUCTS

Catalog: free
Photo Catalog: 2 IRC's
Discount: to 80%
Minimum Order: $25
Shipping: included
Insurance: included
Returns: authorized only
Payment: cashier's
check, bank MO, U.S.
postal MO, bank draft,
certified check
$$$$

ishing: medium quality Mysore rubies for 50¢ a carat, garnets at 30¢ a carat, emeralds for $2.00, etc. In addition, they offer silver jewelry, genuine ivory and bone jewelry and decorations, sandalwood meditation necklaces and gift items, buffalo horn carvings, rosewood carvings, glass beads, brass artware and chains, jewelry tools, leather goods, and clothing. Ivory bracelets are $2 to $13, ivory elephant towers with 3 to 8 elephants are $2.50 to $6.50, and the same items in bone are about half as much. There are carved and inlaid sandalwood boxes from $7.50 to $12.25, ivory magic balls, silk shirts for $6, rosewood elephant bookends, and even a carved elephant lamp. Some of the goods are typical India export fare, but others are unusual and quite beautiful. It's a good idea to send the 2 IRC's and get the catalog with the photographs, so you have a better idea of what you're ordering.

DIAMONDS BY RENNIE ELLEN

15 W. 47th St. Room 401
New York, NY 10036
(212) 246-3930
Catalog: $1
Discount: 50 to 75%
Goods: ready made,
custom made
Minimum Order: none
Shipping, Handling:
minimum $5.00
Sales Tax: NY residents
Returns: within 5
working days, less
mountings and labor
Guarantee: money back
Payment: bank teller's
check, personal check
(15 day wait)
$$$$

It's hard to believe that you can buy diamond engagement rings wholesale, but that is Rennie Ellen's business. She claims to sell at 50 to 75% below retail, which makes you wonder what the retail markup on diamonds is. Rennie Ellen is one of the few female diamond cutters in the industry, and will personally cut and set diamonds of any shape, size, and quality to order, in platinum or gold. She also buys diamonds, and you can call her (person-to-person) for price quotes. Rennie Ellen is part of a vigilance effort to keep New York's diamond district free from disreputable dealers, and from everyone's good words about her, she seems a paragon of integrity as well as a good jeweler.

FAR EAST CO.

K.P.O. Box TST 7335
Kowloon, Hong Kong

Far East has a large selection of Seiko watches for men and women. They have digital quartz watches, chronographs, and very nice dress watches for women. There are photos of every watch, plus short descriptions, and most of the watches are available in stainless steel or gold plate. Prices run from $40 to $175, or 30 to 50% off U.S. list. For the complete listing, see CAMERAS.

MICHAEL C. FINA

580 5th Ave.
New York, NY 10036
(212) 757-2530

Fina is one of the best sources for jewelry in NYC. They buy diamonds straight from the mines, have them set, and sell them to you at savings of 10 to 40% off comparable retail prices. They also have gold jewelry and good quality costume jewelry. Their watch lines include Bulova, Longines, and Seiko, and they will special-order a watch for you if they don't have it in stock. For more on what they carry, see HOME.

GOLD 'N' STONES

Mel and Reita Anderson
P.O. Box 636
Sterling, Alaska 99672
Catalog: 50¢
Discount: 30% WBMC
Goods: house name
Minimum Order: $25 for discount
Shipping: postage paid
Sales Tax: AL residents
Returns: within 15 days
Payment: check, MO
$$$$

Gold 'n' Stones sells mainly jade and gold nugget jewelry, but has a good variety of other things—gifts, specimens, slab rock, etc. They carry a large selection of jade jewelry for men and women, ranging in price from 56¢ for jade baby charm earrings to $84 for an ivory and jade nugget necklace. There are jade fidget stones, bookends, slabs, "bug brooches," and even clocks. They also carry jewelry of flame agate, jaspar, rhodondite, ivory, and gold. They sell gold nuggets at prices starting at $3. Since gold nuggets begin at $130 at Tiffany's, this seems very cheap. There are specimens of quartz, marble, copper ore, garnet, tin, lead, malachite, caribou horn, soapstone, and Brazilian agate. The prices are very low after the WBMC discount—where else can you buy your own "Little Jade Mountain" for only $4.20 a pound?

THE GOOD SHEPHERD'S STORE

Bethlehem, P.O. Box 96
Israel

Along with lovely articles in olivewood, this store sells mother-of-pearl jewelry at very low prices. See HANDICRAFTS AND NATIVE PRODUCTS for main listing.

ICEMART

P.O. Box 23
Keflavik International
Airport
Iceland

Icemart sells jewelry and spoons of Icelandic design, made of sterling silver and semiprecious stones. The designs are modern and striking, especially the snowflakes, runic letters, and charms for good luck, victory in war, love, and good health. The charms are available in small and large sizes, with chains, at $11 and $23.60 each. There is also a pendant replica of Thor's hammer, a necklace with the figure of Mjolnir, the pagan good luck symbol, and other pendants for $32 to $35. Icemart's three souvenir spoons are of simple, beautiful design and cost $28 to $32. All prices include insurance. For more information, see listing under CLOTHING, FURS, AND ACCESSORIES.

INTERNATIONAL IMPORT CO.

P.O. Box 747
Stone Mountain, GA
30086
(404) 938-0173
Catalog: free
Discount: courtesy to
dealers
Goods: cut and polished
stones
Minimum Order: $6.00
Shipping: extra
Sales Tax: GA residents
Insurance: extra
Returns: on approval
items only
Payment: check, MO,
IMO
Resale #, Letterhead:
necessary for discount
$$$

International lists 2,622 different cut precious and semiprecious gems and stones in their catalog. To get the dealer "courtesy discount," you must write on company letterhead, stating your resale number. All the gems are cut, and specifications of weight, size, shape, and color are included. There are no illustrations, and all gems are sent on approval. You must send a deposit of 50%, and you have 5 days to decide before keeping or returning them. If you have a good idea of what you want, this is an excellent source for cut stones.

INTERNATIONAL SOLGO, INC.

77 W. 23rd St.
New York, NY 10010
(212) 895-6996

Solgo carries a full line of name brand jewelry and watches, which are discounted up to 40%. See APPLIANCES, TELEVISION, AND VIDEO for the main listing.

KEN LANGE

6031 N. 7th St.
Phoenix, AZ 85014
(602) 266-5637
Catalog: $4
Discount: 40%
Goods: genuine Indian
jewelry
Minimum Order: $100
initial order
Shipping: Handling,
Insurance: 25¢ per item
Guarantee: complete
satisfaction
Returns: within 14 days
Payment: cashier's
check, MO, MC, Visa (5%
surcharge on charges)
$$$

The fad for Indian jewelry that swept the nation a few years ago created a huge demand for the beautiful pieces made by the Navajo, Hopi, and Zuni tribes. It also drove the prices sky high and brought on hordes of imitation jewelry. Ken Lange warns about the simulated turquoise being sold as genuine, and stands behind the authenticity of his pieces. He sells handcrafted Navajo, Hopi, and Zuni jewelry, which is sterling silver set with turquoise and coral, at prices from $3 to $2,500. There is a cheaper line of equally lovely sandcast jewelry which is set with coral, turquoise, shell, and red rock. The pieces are illustrated in a lovely color catalog and are done in Indian motifs and symbols. There are earrings, rings, keyholders, tietacks, chokers, watchbands, moneyclips, bolo ties, and some beautiful charms, at prices starting at $1.75. For more on Lange's other lines, see ART AND ANTIQUES; BOOKS AND RECORDS; and LEATHER GOODS.

D. MacGILLIVRAY AND COY.

Muir of Aird
Benbecula
Western Isles, Scotland
PA88 5NA

MacGillivray sells "Scottish Grouse Claw Brooches," using real claws mounted on sterling silver, for $9 each. See CRAFTS AND HOBBIES for complete listing.

M/S. SHREE MUKTANAND EXPORTERS

16-A
Dr. Kashibai N. Marg
New Gamdevi
Bombay 400 007, India
Information: inquire
Discount: 30% minimum

This firm is an associate of Samarth Gemstones (see listing), so when you write to them for information, be sure to refer to Samarth and WBMC. Shree Exporters sells pure silver filigree jewelry from 50¢ to $25—very cheap.

THE NEPAL CRAFT EMPORIUM

G.P.O. Box 1443
Kathmandu, Nepal

The Craft Emporium makes handsome jewelry in gilded metal studded with stone and glass. They have a "Gocha" design necklace of large beads alternated with small ones, with a matching ring, bracelet, and earrings. There is a necklace set with medallions similar to Navajo styles, one reminiscent of the medieval gem-studded necklaces with jewel pendants, and a pretty Tayo (wedding) necklace. All of them cost from $3.25 to $6.50. They sell pendants with gods and goddesses, striking filigree stars, all from $1.75 to $2.75. Lovely rings to match in a myriad of designs are available for 75¢ each, plus god and goddess brooches for 80¢ and 90¢. There are many other pieces, all stunning and individual, and very cheap. For more information, see HANDICRAFTS AND NATIVE PRODUCTS.

ORIENTAL HANDICRAFTS

Capt. Sham Lai Rd.
Civil Lines
Ludhiana 141001
Punjab, India
Price List, Photos: $1
Discount: to 95%
Goods: handcarved
Minimum Order: $50

Oriental Handicrafts sells handcarved camelbone jewelry, which they say is a "shimmering ivory color." It's very likely that this is palmed off by shady importers as ivory, but here they call a bone a bone and sell it at skeletal prices. Oriental enclosed a photo of a necklace with 12 elephant beads and one large elephant pendant which was charming. There were elephant earrings and an elephant pin to match. They sell pendants, necklaces, pins and earrings made of beads that are carved as roses, camels, pea-

ORIENTAL HANDICRAFTS

Shipping: included; add 25% for air mail
Payment: bank check, MO
$$$$

cocks, and lions. There are also plain and fretwork beads if the animals are too exotic for you. The prices are phenomenally low; the necklaces of beads and pendants run from 85¢ for a 12-elephant necklace to $8.00 for what they describe as fretwork beads "extra thick—something really charming and unusual." Matching bracelets are 20¢ and 40¢ each. The minimum order is $50, which should be easy to meet since the jewelry is so appealing, attractive, and suitable for gifts. For more listings, see HOME; and HANDICRAFTS AND NATIVE PRODUCTS.

RAMA JEWELRY LTD.

P.O. Box 858
987 Silom Rd.
Bangkok, Thailand
Catalog: free
Discount: 33% and up, including 10% WBMC reader discount
Goods: house brand
Minimum Order: none
Shipping: included
Insurance: included
Guarantee: satisfaction
Payment: certified check, IMO, bank draft
$$$

DISCOUNT

Rama Jewelry is compiling a new catalog with new prices which should be available in 1979. Their brochure shows lovely color photos of 404 pieces of jewelry, mainly rings. There are many styles, but one of the most fetching is the princess ring which is traditionally made of opals, rubies, sapphires, pearls and onyx. There are 18 men's rings, and several kinds of bracelets, earrings, and brooches. Rama Jewelry also sells Thai silk clothing, teakwood carvings, silverware, bronzeware, and leather goods. When writing for the catalog and ordering, be sure to mention WBMC for the 10% discount.

SAMARTH GEM STONES

P.O. Box 6057
Colaba, Bombay 400 005
India
Catalog: free
Discount: to 80%
Goods: hand and machine finished
Minimum Order: $50.00
Shipping: $3.00 to $30.00
Insurance: 1.75% cost of goods
Returns: authorized only
Payment: check, certified check, bank draft, transfer, L/C
$$

Faceted rubies for $1 a carat? Sapphire cabochons at $5 a carat? Emerald necklaces at 25¢ per carat? Samarth has these and many more unbelievable bargains on tiger eye, agate, garnet, amethyst, moon stone, jasper, turquoise, and lapis lazuli. They have no middlemen or salesmen, which they say accounts for their low prices. The minimum order is $50, and you can get gems on an approval basis. There is also a sliding quantity discount of 5% on orders over $500 up to 20% on orders over $2,000. Samarth understands that you may have some doubts about buying gems through the mail and encourage you to write if you have questions. They say: "Considering our past 15 years experience we feel that people are still afraid to import gemstones because they think that there will be lot of paper works as well as the brain tension. But, dear friend . . . we shall give the best of care to meet your requirements as close as possible."

STECHERS LTD.

62 Independence Square
Port-of-Spain, Trinidad,
W.I.

Stechers sells watches by Patek Phillippe, Piaget, Audemars Piguet, Borel, Cartier, International, and many other firms. They offer discounts of 30 to 50% on the watches and on all the goods they carry. For more information, see HOME.

UNIVERSAL SUPPLIERS

P.O. Box 14803
Hong Kong
Price Lists: free, $1.80 by
air

Universal sells Rolex and Seiko watches at a good savings over U.S. prices. The prices include insurance. See AUDIO for a complete listing.

A. VAN MOPPES AND SON

Albert Cuypstraat 2-6
Amsterdam, Holland
Catalog: $2.00
Discount: 10% to WBMC
readers
Shipping: included
Handling: $1.00 on
orders under $100
Customs: Van Moppes
refunds 50% of the duty
Insurance: included
Guarantee: against
defects in materials and
workmanship
Warranty: trade-ins
accepted for full
purchase price
Returns: within 10 days
Payment: check, MO,
bank draft, cable or mail
transfer, MC, Visa, AE,
DC, Carte Blanche
$$$

Van Moppes has won several awards for jewelry design, including the Diamonds International Award for a stunning brooch of diamonds, gold, and onyx. The color catalog is full of beautiful pieces, mostly diamonds and gold, but also pieces with rubies, sapphires, pearls, coral ivory, turquoise, amethyst, and other semiprecious stones. Even the costume jewelry is well designed, and there is a selection of pretty charms in Dutch motifs that are available in gold and silver. The prices range from $2.00 for a silver anchor charm to $4,345.00 for a diamond marquise cluster ring of 1.86 carats (that's without the WBMC discount). Van Moppes used only blue-white, flawless diamonds, and gives you a written guarantee that states the exact quality and weight of the piece. (Never buy a diamond without a detailed bill of sale that states color, cut, color, and carat weight—the "4 c's.") You can trade in your jewelry at any time with this guarantee and receive the original purchase price applied against another piece. Van Moppes will provide an official appraisal certificate for your diamonds for $10. They do engraving, and will design jewelry to order at no extra charge. Remember the WBMC discount of 10% when ordering.

LEATHER GOODS

There's something odd about the luggage industry. We wouldn't dare to explain what it is, nor make any allegations, but if you go looking for discount luggage sources you'll see what we mean. Name brand suitcases just don't come at a discount, unless you're a reader of *The Wholesale-By-Mail Catalog* and know about our precious finds. We were not permitted to mention brand names in many cases. Investigate. It will be worth it.

ACE LEATHER PRODUCTS

2211 Ave. U
Brooklyn, NY 11229
(212) 891-9713
Catalog: inquire
Discount: "we'll beat anyone-else's price"
Goods: brand name
Minimum Order: none
Shipping: by UPS, extra
Sales Tax: NY residents
Returns: 5 days
Payment: check, MO
$$$

The man who answered the phone at Ace Leather said that he had been working there since the age of 12, and that one of the other workers had been there for 66 years. He told us that there are 5 full stockrooms. He was unable to fix an exact figure on the amount of discount, but said that Ace will beat anyone else's prices—which is a sweet-sounding guarantee in the overpriced world of luggage and small leather goods. Because his suppliers wouldn't like it, the name brands can't be mentioned, but they are all the top lines. The catalog is in preparation; you can get information in the meantime by sending the name, color, and style number of the luggage or article you want and requesting a price quote. If you are dealing with a discount line, send him the price to insure a lower one.

BONDY EXPORT CO.

40 Canal St.
New York, NY 10002

Bondy carries Samsonite luggage at a good discount, along with name brand appliances and audio components. For more information, see APPLIANCES, TELEVISION, AND VIDEO.

KUNST SALES

45 Canal St.
New York, NY 10013
(212) 966-1909

Kunst Sales is one of the few discount houses that authorizes the printing of the fact that they sell American Tourister and Samsonite luggage at a discount. For the main listing, see APPLIANCES, TELEVISION, AND VIDEO.

KEN LANGE

6031 N. 7th St.
Phoenix, AZ 85014
(602) 266-5637

Lange sells 12 handsome styles of western leather bags at 50% off retail. They are hand dyed, tooled and hand laced, and come in tan or brown. They have a small bag suitable for a girl, several shoulder styles, and two tote bags. Prices run from $7.43 to $33.72. For more information, see listing under JEWELRY.

RAMA JEWELRY LTD.

P.O. Box 858
987 Silom Rd.
Bangkok, Thailand

Rama Jewelry sells mainly jewelry and gems, but also carries a line of leather goods—hand bags, wallets, and belts. See JEWELRY for the complete listing.

MEDICAL
and
SCIENTIFIC

This section includes drugs, vitamins, health supplements, chemicals, hearing aids, eyeglasses, biological products, and supplies. You will find tremendous savings on vitamins, and if you take one or more every day you're just wasting money by buying them at your local health food or drug store.

We cannot vouch for the quality of the hearing aids, especially since the hearing aid industry has been fraught with fraud over the years. The companies we've listed seem reliable, though. Try to investigate the available products ahead of time, but beware of asking an audiologist—he *sells* the things. Our companies offer money back guarantees, so if the price is right, your risk is not too great.

When buying discount prescription drugs, remember that they take more time to arrive. Your savings will only be legitimate if you *have* the drugs when you need them. To order generic drug equivalents instead of the brand names, you must have your doctor mark the prescription—remember to ask him to do that.

The Watkins and Doncaster catalog of botany, zoology, oology, and geology is truly a marvel of breadth, fascination, and old-world quality. You might well find tools, etc. that could be put to other uses if you're not into science, and browsing through their material is a trip in any event.

AAA SCALE CO.

P.O. Box 496
Paramount, CA 90723
(213) 774-3320

Triple A Scale makes a hand scale that is very useful for measuring things in the lab. See OFFICE for complete listing.

ACE SCIENTIFIC SUPPLY CO., INC.

**P.O. Box 127
Linden, NJ 07036
(201) 925-3300
Catalog: $35, refundable
against $200 in
purchases
Discount: up to 40% in
quantity
Goods: name brand
Minimum Order: quantity
orders for discount; $25
for full retail price orders
Shipping: extra
Sales Tax: NJ, CT
residents
Payment: check, MO
$$**

Ace Scientific sells chemicals, supplies, and instruments to medical, educational and industrial laboratories, and will sell to you at retail prices if you order $25 or more from them, and at wholesale prices if you buy in quantity. Their catalog is a whopping 1,500 pages, which accounts for its $35 price tag (refundable when your order exceeds $200). It's worth considering the investment if you use large amounts of certain chemicals or products like rubber tubing in a hobby or profession.

AMERICEAR

**1411 Santa Rosa Ave.
Santa Barbara, CA 93109
Price List, Descriptions:
free
Discount: 50%
Goods: house name
Minimum Order: none
Shipping: included
Sales Tax: CA residents
Returns: within 14 days,
postpaid
Payment: check, MO
$$$**

This hearing aid company sells three models: a body style for severe losses and 2 very unobtrusive behind-the-ear devices. Each aid is illustrated by a line drawing and specifications—acoustic gain and output, harmonic distortion, frequency range, weight, etc.—are listed. The purchase policy is simple: you buy the aid, test it for 14 days, and return it if you don't like it. Mr. Cameron of Americear guarantees that his prices are half of retail, and will double the difference if you can find his hearing aid priced less. He guarantees parts and labor for one year, and will do repairs. The aids are moderately priced, and Mr. Cameron includes a few tips on borrowing money if you find it hard to meet the purchase price.

BUDGET UNIFORM CENTER, INC.

**941 Mill Road
Cornwells Heights, PA
19020
(212) 245-0300: main
line, PA orders
(800) 523-6582: medical
and individual orders
(800) 523-5750: group
orders**

Budget makes their own line of nurses' uniforms, labcoats, and other apparel related to the medical profession. They also have a featherweight stethoscope for $6.99, an electronic stethoscope for $130 ($200 elsewhere), and a blood pressure monitoring kit for $23. For the complete listing, see CLOTHING AND ACCESSORIES.

RIC CLARK

9530 Langdon Ave.
Sepulveda, CA 91343
(213) 892-6636
Catalog: free
Discount: 50% plus
Good: brand name
Minimum Order: none
Shipping: postpaid
Sales Tax: CA residents
Returns: 30-day trial
period
Guarantee: money back
within trial period
Warranty: 1 year
Payment: check, MO
$$$$

Ric Clark puts out a polished little catalog featuring the three models of hearing aids that he carries. They are photographed next to a pen or eyeglasses to give an idea of size. These aids are for mild, moderate, and severe hearing losses, and come with a month's supply of hearing aid batteries for your trial period. You can pay a deposit of $10 to try the aid, and if you buy it you can pay $20 a month (with a 10% finance charge) or the cash price. The aids cost from $179.49 to $219.49 without the interest charges. You must send them a note from your doctor saying you may need a hearing aid, or else sign a waiver form. Ric Clark says that his prices are half of what dealers charge, and all his repair work is guaranteed.

DUK KWONG OPTICAL CENTER

17A Cameron Rd. G/F
Kowloon, Hong Kong
Price List: free
Discount: 30 to 50%,
plus quantity discounts
Goods: house name
Minimum Order: none
Shipping, Handling:
$2.00 per pair
Payment: check
$$$

Duk Kwong sells very stylish eyeglass frames and sunglasses at incredibly low price—$8 to $30, including wire frames. The lenses cost 10 to 90% of the cost of the frames and are available in different colors in glass or plastic. Duk Kwong also sells hard and soft contact lenses which are made from your prescription or duplicated from your own lenses. Clear or tinted hard lenses are $38, and soft lenses are $90. Name brand soft lenses sell for $250 in U.S. optical shops, which gives you an idea of the savings. There are discounts of 10% for orders of 2 pairs, and 15% for orders of 3 pairs or more. The frame styles are wide-ranging and include designer-look and aviator styles in plastic. You're bound to find a frame to suit you, and the prices should please everyone. Be sure to send the most recent prescription you have available, and remember to request safety tempered lenses ($4 extra) which are required in all glasses made in the U.S.

GETZ PHARMACY

916 Walnut St.
Kansas City, MO 64199
(816) 471-5466
Catalog: free, pub. Feb.,
Sept.
Discount: up to 60%

Getz sells vitamins and dietary supplements, over-the-counter remedies, prescription drugs, beauty aids, etc. You can save up to 50% on vitamins and nonprescription drugs by buying their house brand, and up to 60% on prescription drugs by buying the generic equivalent. To prove that there is no difference in quality, they include the formulas for the vitamins and the nonprescription

GETZ PHARMACY

**Goods: house, brand
name vitamins; brand,
generic equivalent drugs
Minimum Order: $5.00
Shipping, Handling: UPS,
PP free; first class,
additional charge; orders
under $5.00 without Rx
charged 50¢ handling
Guarantee:
unconditional; returns
within 30 days
Payment: check, MO
$$**

remedies in the catalog, so you can see that the ingredients in the brand names and the house names are identical. The vitamins and supplements are things like Theragran, Unicap, Stresstabs, Super Plenamins, Myadec, Geritol, and other nationally known brands. The drugs are listed with their familiar names, Miltown, for example, and the equally familiar prices (200 mg. 100's for $5.70), along with the chemical name (meprobamate), and the lower price—$2.50, in this case. If you want to get the cheaper prescription drugs, ask your doctor to specify the generic name on the prescription; they suggest showing him the catalog.

LAURENCE CORNER

**62/64 Hampstead Rd.
London NW1 2NU
England**

Laurence Corner sells government surplus goods including resuscitators, tracheotomy tubes, oxygen tents, crutches, surgeons' needles (for veterinary and biological use), and many other items for lab and medical use. The prices are great, and if you need something in particular in the way of surplus medical equipment, you should write to them. For more information, *see* CLOTHING AND ACCESSORIES.

RITE-WAY HEARING AID CO.

**P.O. Box 59451
Chicago, IL 60659
(312) 539-6620
Information: free
Discount: 30% plus
Goods: house brand
Minimum Order: none
Shipping: extra on aids,
included on batteries
Sales Tax: IL residents
Guarantee: satisfaction
Warranty: 1 year, parts
and labor
Payment: check, MO
$$**

For a $10 deposit, you can try out a Rite-Way hearing aid for 30 days. If you decide to buy it, you can pay a third of the cost and the rest in $10 monthly installments with no finance charges. The aids are priced from $159.50 to $189.50. There are 3 over-the-ear models, one style for in-the-ear use, and a super power body model for severe hearing losses. The specifications for the frequency, range, battery type and life are included. Mercury, silver oxide, and penlight batteries are for sale, so you can stock up while buying your aid. Rite-Way's policy is especially convenient because of the small deposit and the 30-day trial period, and satisfaction is guaranteed.

SCHUBEL & SON

P.O. Box 214848
Sacramento, CA 95821
(916) 487-5722

Schubel sells basic scientific equipment and some supplies, including 72 chemicals and 45 rock and mineral specimens. They also have Pyrex beakers, Florence flasks, Erlenmeyer flasks, thistle tubes, gas collecting bottles, test tubes, tubing, burets, drying tubes, pipets, all kinds of equipment for burner experiments, petri dishes, slides, corks, and microscopes. The equipment can be used in chemistry experiments, geological identification, and some items can be "borrowed" from the lab for use in the home: corks for any bottle at 3¢ to 50¢ each, a mortar and pestle for kitchen use, all-purpose tubing, etc. For the serious scientist, there are several labware assortments at good savings over the individual prices. For more information, see TOYS AND GAMES.

STAR PROFESSIONAL PHARMACEUTICALS

11 Basin St.
Plainview, NY 11803
(516) 822-4621
Catalog: free
Discount: up to 60%
Goods: house, name
brand
Minimum Order: none
Shipping: included
Handling: 75¢ on orders
under $10
Sales Tax: NY residents
Returns: 30 days
Guarantee: satisfaction
Payment: check, MO
$$$

Star is one of several companies making formula equivalents of brand name vitamins and health aids for up to 60% less. They carry single and multi-vitamins, iron, calcium, yeast and protein products, and natural supplements—bran, kelp, alfalfa, etc. They also have a line of "natural" beauty treatments and makeup, and several catalog pages of standard brand name health aids. Their catalog winds up with typical drugstore miscellany like rubber gloves, batteries, film, and light bulbs. See ANIMAL for further listing.

SUNBURST BIORGANICS, INC.

838 Merrick Rd.
Baldwin, NY 11510
(516) 623-8478
Catalog: free
Discount: up to 60%
Goods: house name
Minimum Order: none
Shipping: included
Returns: within 30 days
Payment: check, MO
$$$

Sunburst manufactures its own vitamins, supplements, and beauty aids under the Sunburst label. The vitamins and supplements are formula equivalents of standard name brands and are priced around 40% less. There are also bonuses included with purchases of $10 up to $50, and specials at 60% off. Sunburst carries a unique and possibly exclusive selection of starch-and-sugar-free vitamins and minerals that should please every purist.

U.S. GENERAL SUPPLY CORP.

100 General Place
Jericho, NY 11753
(516) 333-6655

If rising inflation is making your blood boil, get hold of U.S. General's discount catalog where you can find a blood pressure kit and stethoscope cheap! See TOOLS AND HARDWARE for complete listing.

UNIVERSAL SUPPLIERS

P.O. Box 14803
Hong Kong
Price List: free, $1.80 by
air

Universal sells, among other things, glasses and contact lenses made by A.O. Company of America. These are prescription glasses only, and the prices are very low. For a complete listing, see AUDIO.

VITAMIN QUOTA, INC.

14 E. 38th St.
New York, NY 10016
(212) 685-7026
or:
1125 South Crenshaw
Blvd.
Los Angeles, CA 90019
(213) 936-7221
Catalog: free
Discount: 50% plus
Goods: house brand
Minimum Order: none
Shipping, Handling: 59¢
Sales Tax: CA, NJ, NY,
NV residents
Payment: check, MO,
MC, Visa, AE
$$$

Vitamin Quota sells vitamins, minerals, dietary supplements, health aids, and pet vitamins, all under their own label. They have duplicates of some name brand vitamins at half the cost or less. There are equivalents of One-A-Day, Stesstabs, Theragran, and Geritol, standard formula vitamins A through E, duplicates of Bayer aspirin, Excedrin, Nyquil, Allerest, Sominex, and Dristan, and things like chelated zinc and wheat germ oil. Most of the products are available in bottles of 100 to 1,000 and there are further discounts on the large sizes. Vitamin Quota also carries pet vitamins—see the listing under ANIMAL.

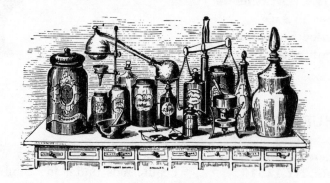

WATKINS AND DONCASTER

Four Throws
Hawkhurst, Kent,
England
Catalog: free
Discount: 30% minimum
Goods: house, brand
name

This firm was founded in 1874 by William Watkins and Arthur Doncaster. Doncaster was deaf and dumb, and communicated with customers via a slate hung around his neck. They started the business with butterflies, developed the taxidermy department in response to the craze for stuffed animals, added oology (the study of birds' eggs) because an assistant was an expert on it, and so on. In addition, they now carry supplies and equipment for aquaria,

WATKINS AND DONCASTER

Minimum Order: none
Shipping Cost: by quotation
Insurance: by request
Returns: defective articles replaced
Payment: check, MO, credit transfer, letter of credit
$$$

botany, zoology, general entomology, and geology. There are glass eyes for all kinds of animals, stereoscopic microscopes, fossils, geological hammers, moth traps, killing bottles, beating trays, many kinds of dissecting tools, and fine-looking educational charts of different species of animals and trees. The people who run this company are very conscious of the conservation measures that must be taken to ensure the survival of insects, birds, and butterflies, and include a list of 35 guidelines to follow in collecting.

WESTERN NATURAL PRODUCTS

P.O. Box 284-W
South Pasadena, CA 91030
(213) 441-1458
Catalog: free
Discount: 30 to 50% plus
Goods: house name
Minimum Order: $10
Shipping: free on orders over $10
Sales Tax: CA residents
Guarantee: satisfaction or full refund
$$$$

This company makes health supplements that are duplicates of name brands, but sell at 30 to 50% less. They are also "natural," meaning that synthetic vitamins are not used, and when the chewable vitamins are sweetened, it's with honey—not sugar or saccharin. A quick comparison with brand name Theragran vitamins showed that Western's "Plan I" multi-vitamin had twice as much vitamin E and B-6 as Theragran, more B-12, and included folic acid, which Theragran lacked. It was $2.95 per 100, compared to $6.80 for Theragran 100's. In addition to general vitamins, minerals, enzymes, and other supplements, Western sells kelp, ginseng, and pet vitamins. Their no-questions-asked money-back guarantee should convince those hesitant about abandoning Myadec and One-A-Day that they have nothing to lose and money to gain.

MUSIC

You can bet that most professional musicians don't pay full price for their fine instruments, and there's a good chance that they bought them at a great discount from one of the sources we have included. Our listees sell top-quality musical products. While they often came into being to serve the needs of the knowledgeable, they are perfectly happy to deal with you even if you don't know the difference between an eighth note and a G clef. If you're buying something good, your savings can run into hundreds of dollars. If you're equipping a band, you might be able to save enough to buy a van to haul all that good stuff from gig to gig. Go for quality when buying a musical instrument—it can last a lifetime and the resale market value of many products is often very high. Old Fender electric guitars from the 50s and 60s, for example, are worth more than new ones.

ACCORDION-O-RAMA

Alas Accordion Co.
16 W. 19th St.
New York, NY 10011
(212) 777-4780
Catalog: free
Discount: 30% minimum
Goods: brand, house name
Minimum Order: none
Shipping: extra, UPS or truck
Insurance: included
Sales Tax: NY residents
Guarantee: all accordions covered by a "long time" guarantee
Payment: check, MO
$$$

Accordion-O-Rama carries all the top names in accordions: Avanti, Arpeggio, Excelsior, Hohner, Sonart, Sonola, Serenelli, and more. Their catalog consists of several pages of special offers and several cards highlighting individual models. These cards come with color photos attached which give you an idea of how beautiful the instruments are. Prices for these deluxe models run from $125 to $1,200, while normal list is $340 to $3,000. Accordion-O-Rama also sells accordion synthesizers, accordion speakers, organ-accordions, and an accordion stand and invisible accordion strap by Bandoleer, both of which are exclusives. They are authorized Cordovox dealers, and give you the strap or the stand free with any Cordovox purchase. They sell reconditioned models, do trade-ins, overhauls, and repair work.

SAM ASH MAIL ORDER SERVICE

301 Peninsula Blvd.
Hempstead, NY 11550
(800) 645-3518
(212) 347-7757
Catalog: free, purchasing
done through price
quotes
Discount: 30 to 40% plus
Goods: brand name
Minimum Order: $15.00
Shipping Cost: UPS
collect
Warranty: by
manufacturer
Payment: bank check,
MO, MC, Visa
$$$

Sam Ash is one of the big stores that supplies all kinds of professional musical equipment from hundreds of manufacturers at discounts from 30% up. Their mail order service is available only to those living 30 miles or more from a Sam Ash store. They publish sale bulletins from time to time, but you must write or call with brand name and model number for price quotes and shipping information. All merchandise is covered by Sam Ash and/or manufacturers' warranties. At any given moment, the store will be having a "half off" sale on good equipment, so be sure to call them before you buy elsewhere.

CARROLL SOUND, INC.

895 Broadway
New York, NY 10003
(212) 533-6230
Catalog: free
Discount: 20%
Goods: house, brand
name
Minimum Order: none
Shipping: extra
Sales Tax: NY residents
Warranty: by
manufacturer
Payment: MO
$

This company sells what it calls esoteric percussion instruments (African pianos, Dōmbecks, congas) in both their own brand and name brands. They also have all the standard percussion equipment: steel drums, bell trees, gongs, and much more. There was no catalog at this writing, but the man at Carroll Sound said that it would be available in 1979, free. All the instruments are backed by manufacturers' guarantees.

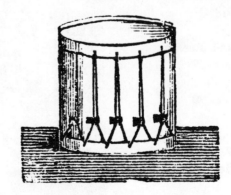

JAMES C. BOYCE, GUITARMAKER

**Box 608
North Falmouth, MA
02556
(617) 563-9494
Catalog: 50¢
Discount: about 50% on strings
Goods: house name strings, custom made guitars
Minimum Order: none
Shipping: included for U.S. orders; Canada, $3.00 extra for over 3 string sets
Returns: refunds on unused goods
Payment: check, MO
$$**

James Boyce sells guitar, mandolin and banjo strings in lots of 1, 3, 6, and 12. The 50% discount applies to 12 set lots. There are 4 different gauges, and they are wound in silk and steel, bronze, and silverplate. Prices go from $5.50 per set of bronze-wound strings for guitar to $2.75 a set if you order 12 sets. The 12-string sets go from $9.00 if you order 1 set to $4.50 per set if you order 12. Boyce includes a description of the strings and how they are made. He also makes custom guitars which are featured in an elegant little booklet and guaranteed to last the life of the owner.

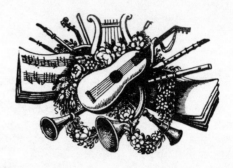

CARVIN

**Dept. 79W
1155 Industrial Ave.
Escondido, CA 92025
(714) 747-1710
Catalog: free
Discount: minimum 30% over comparable brand names
Goods: house name
Minimum Order: $10
Shipping Cost: FOB Escondido, CA
Sales Tax: CA residents
Insurance: included
Returns: 10 days
Warranty: guitars, 5 years
amps, mixers, etc., 2 years
meters and tubes, 90 days
speaker systems, 1 year
JBL speakers, 2 years
Payment: certified check only
$$$**

Carvin makes good electronic music equipment—mixers, amps, mikes, monitor systems, and electric guitars. Most of the guitars are look-alikes for classics like Les Pauls, but cost much less. Carvin gives you a 10-day free trial period, and if you are not 100% satisfied you can return the equipment for an immediate refund. This guarantee covers all the Carvin products. They list all the specifications, features, and specific guarantees with the description of each item. After looking at the beautiful color catalog, one musician remarked that "any company that can promise no buzz on an action 1/16 inch from the neck is making a really *fine* guitar." In other words, they guarantee a superior product. All servicing and performance testing under the warranty is done free of charge.

FREEPORT MUSIC

114K Mahan St.
W. Babylon, NY 11704
(516) 643-8081
Catalog: $1
Discount: 30 to 60%
Goods: name brand
Minimum Order: $25 on
charges
Shipping: extra
Sales Tax: NY residents
Guarantee: defective
goods replaced or
refunded
Payment: check, MO,
MC, Visa, AE, CB, DC
$$$$

Freeport has been in business since 1921 and will probably be here in 2021 because you can't beat great prices and a good selection. There are Ludwig drums at 40%-off list, drums by Pearl, Slinger Land, Earth amps and mixers, electronic equipment made by Fender, Marshall, Kingston, Marlboro, Morley, and Shadow, Shure mikes, Seth Thomas and Franz metronomes, etc. There are also guitars and accessories by Martin, Fender, Gibson, Guild, Ovation, and Yamaha. Freeport carries Olds brass instruments, Leigh woodwind accessories. Benge brass, Armstrong flutes, Arp electronics, Hohner harmonicas, and disco lighting and stage effects for rock groups. They also have good buys on used instruments and coupon "specials"—don't buy an instrument or another set of strings before you get this catalog.

D. MacGILLIVRAY AND COY.

Muir of Aird
Benbecula
Western Isles, Scotland
PA88 5NA

MacGillivray's sells bagpipes and drums and other Scottish instruments. See CRAFTS AND HOBBIES for complete listing. Write for more information on the instruments.

SILVER AND HORLAND

170 W. 48th St.
New York, NY 10036
(212) 869-3870
Information: price quote
Discount: 30 to 50%
Goods: name, house
brand
Shipping: extra, UPS
Sales Tax: NY residents
Guarantee: by
manufacturer
Payment: certified check,
C.O.D.
$$$$

Silver and Horland has it all in music equipment and supplies. They sell both new and used instruments, and carry all the top names: Yamaha, Takamine, Gibson, Fender, Guild, Martin, Selmer, Armstrong, etc. They carry Moogs, guitars, brass instruments, percussion, and accessories such as reeds, picks, mouthpieces, strings, straps, drumsticks, and stands. Call Silver and Horland with the model number or brand and description of whatever you need and they will give you a price quote. If you want to sell your old equipment, call them, too; they buy all kinds.

OFFICE SUPPLIES and EQUIPMENT

Whether you are interested in refurbishing an office or just need a box of envelopes, you can save time and money by ordering from an office supply house. Discounts usually run up to 50% off list price on brand name goods, many of which you use every day—pens, pencils, tape, paper, etc.

Most of the companies offer complete lines of desk products, files, envelopes, shelving systems, storage bins, lockers, coat racks, mats, security equipment, wastecans, office machines, phones and accessories, murals, plastic plants, printing services, directory boards, office furniture, and even "instant offices"—divider systems that create fully functioning cubicles.

The office supplies are designed for long years of constant use, and most would function well in the home as the new so-called "High Tech" decor. Be sure to remember these sources when shopping for back-to-school goods.

A & B BEACON

36 West 33rd St.
New York, NY 10001
(212) 736-1440
Information: price quote
Discount: 20% plus
Goods: name brand
Minimum Order: none
Shipping: UPS collect
Sales Tax: NY residents
Guarantee: 90 days, most models
Payment: check, MO, MC, Visa
$$

A & B Beacon specializes in office machines such as typewriters, calculators, word processors, and they also carry an extensive line of typewriter ribbons. The machines available are manufactured by Sperry, Sanyo, Olympia, IBM (reconditioned), Remington, Adler, SCM, Olivetti, Hermes, Norelco, and Casio. Their initial prices may not be as low as other discount stores, but they have a shop on the premises and will service what they sell. They honor both their own guarantee and manufaturers' warranties on almost all the products.

AAA SCALE CO. DISCOUNT

P.O. Box 496
Paramount, CA 90723
(213) 774-3320
Catalog: free
Discount: 30% to WBMC
readers
Goods: house brand
Minimum Order: none
Shipping: included
Sales Tax: CA residents
Warranty: 5 years
Payment: check, MO
$$$$

The handy little scale these people sell is sent in a pocket-size case that includes a chart of postal rates and a copy of the 5-year guarantee. It usually sells for $3.00, but is $2.10 for readers of WBMC. AAA Scale also sells brass test weights. The smallest is one gram, the largest 4 ounces, and they run from 75¢ to $3.00 each. The scale is guaranteed for 5 years to perform "accurately and properly." Several functions are suggested: postage rate determination, food measurement, lab use, and weighing herbs. When ordering the scale, be sure to mention WBMC in order to get the discount of 30%. (The weights are not discounted.)

ADIRONDACK DIRECT

Dept. WMP
219 E. 42nd St.
New York, NY 10017
(800) 221-2444
(212) 687-8555: NY State
residents
Catalog: free, pub. Jan.,
May, Sept.
Discount: up to 43%
Goods: brand name
Minimum Order: varies
Shipping Cost: FOB
factory
Guarantee: free
replacement
Payment: check, MO,
MC, AE, DC, Visa
$$$

Adirondack Direct sells office equipment and supplies and has a full line of modern office furniture (wood-grained formica-topped desks, naugahyde upholstered chairs) at good prices. They also sell room dividers, calculators, and other goods such as park benches, stacking fiberglass chairs, lecterns, announcement boards, display cases, and cafeteria tables. To get the biggest discount, you usually have to buy 3 or more of the same item, but even the higher prices are competitive. Remember to add shipping costs when pricing any item, since all the merchandise is FOB factory.

BUY DIRECT, INC.

216 W. 18th St.
New York, NY 10011
(212) 255-4424
Catalog: free
Discount: up to 30%
Goods: house brand
Minimum Order: varies
Shipping: included
Sales Tax: NY residents
Payment: check, MO
$$

Buy Direct sells business forms, envelopes, and letterhead and printing services at a savings of about 30% over normal printers' prices.

COPEN PRESS

100 Berriman St.
Brooklyn, NY 11208
(212) 235-4270

Copen Press is a complete offset service that does sheet runs, books, booklets, and leaflets. The prices are low and the service is fast. For complete listing, see BOOKS AND RECORDS.

FRANK EASTERN CO.

625 Broadway
New York, NY 10012
(212) 677-9100
Catalog: free
Discounts: 10 to 60%
Goods: name, house
brand
Minimum Order: $30
Shipping: extra; UPS or
FOB NYC
Guarantee: by
manufacturer
Payment: check, MO
$$$

Frank Eastern carries everything you need for your business or home office at discounts of up to 60%. You can stock up on BIC pens, Flair markers, tape, files, envelopes, corrective typing aids, and other supplies, and save by buying by the dozen. Eastern has an excellent selection of "tidi" files which are perfect for storing magazines, and also sells transfer, inactive, and sturdy standard files. There are shelf units, chalkboards, calculators, checkwriters, copiers, lamps, mirrors, coat racks, IBM Selectric typing elements, Lexan mats, etc. They also have a good selection of handsome, functional office furniture in many styles—anything from an all-purpose stool to an executive desk and chair set. For peace, quiet, and privacy, try their "instant offices"—they start at $399. If you run an office or are just trying to get organized, this catalogue should prove helpful.

FIDELITY PRODUCTS CO.

705 Pennsylvania Ave.
So.
Minneapolis, MN 55426
(800) 328-0624
(612) 540-9700: MN
residents
Catalog: free, pub. Sept.,
Jan.

Fidelity is "the nation's largest supplier of corrugated storage and general business products." They sell all kinds of heavy duty file units in corrugated cardboard, which is much cheaper than metal, plus shipping supplies, parts bins in 23 sizes, industrial shelving, ladders, dollies, lockers, office furniture, and other accessories. There are office supplies, machines, stationery, and even photo-murals to liven up the walls. Most items are cheaper when bought in quantity, and some can only be ordered in multiples of

FIDELITY PRODUCTS CO.

Discount: to 40%
Goods: brand name
Minimum Order: none
Shipping: FOB point of manufacture, collect or billed
Sales Tax: MN residents
Returns: 30 days, authorized
Fidelity's Guarantee: satisfaction or money back
Manufacturers' Warranties: standard
Payment: check, MO
$$

3 or 6 (or 500, for pencils). Consider individual price on items you use constantly—they have plastic trash can liners that are as low as 2¢ each, while at supermarkets they average 10¢ apiece. Remember to figure in the cost of freight for your true price. For more listings, see HOME; SAFETY; and TOOLS AND HARDWARE.

JILOR DISCOUNT

1178 Broadway
New York, NY 10001
(212) 683-1590
Information: price quote
Discount: 5 to 50%
Goods: name brand
Minimum Order: none
Shipping: extra; UPS or FOB NYC
Payment: check, MO, certified check
$$$

Jilor has office equipment, calculators, phone answering machines, TVs, and something called a fuzz buster radar detector, which retails at $130 and sells for $90 here. In office machines they carry lines by Sanyo, Olivetti, SCM, Olympia, Hewlitt Packard, Sharp, Texas Instruments, Casio, Victor, Toshiba, Unitrex, Electrosan, Record-A-Call, and Phonemate. They say that they "discount anything and everything we can sell," so even special orders should be well-priced. For more on what they carry, see APPLIANCES, TELEVISION, AND VIDEO.

LINCOLN TYPEWRITERS AND MICRO MACHINES

1989 Broadway
New York, NY 10023
(212) 787-9397
Information: price quote
Discount: 30 to 40%
Goods: name brand
Minimum Order: none
Shipping: extra
Sales Tax: NY residents
Warranties: by
manufacturer, some
extended by Lincoln
Payment: check, MO,
C.O.D.
$$$

Lincoln has all kinds of office machines in addition to typewriter ribbons, cartridges, etc. The machines are by IBM, SCM, Olivetti, Royal, Olympia, and Hermes, and some have warranties extended by Lincoln Typewriter. The discounts are substantial—write or call for a price quote.

LONGACRE OFFICE MACHINES CO., INC.

20 East 40th St.
New York, NY 10016
(212) 684-2471
Information: price quote
Discount: 10 to 30%
Goods: name brand
Minimum Order: none
Shipping, Insurance:
$2.50 minimum
Sales Tax: NY residents
Warranty: by
manufacturer
Guarantee: parts and
labor
Payment: certified check,
MC, Visa
$$

Longacre sells office machines by IBM (used), SCM, Hewlit Packard, Texas Instruments, Sharp, and several other firms. They have their own service department and will guarantee parts and labor on all the used IBM typewriters and checkwriters. They also have adding machines, hand-held calculators, and scientific calculators. Write or call for a price quote.

METROPOLITAN TELETRONICS

35 W. 35th St.
New York, NY 10001
(212) 594-4030
Catalog: $2.00
Discount: 25 to 35%
Goods: house, name brand
Minimum Order: none
Shipping, Insurance: $2.50 to $3.00 per phone
Guarantee: 1 year
Payment: check, MO, AE, DC
$$$

If you're sick of "renting" the telephone you're using and paying a monthly charge, why not do what businesses are doing and buy your own? Metro Teletronics has all kinds of phones, including some very old styles. Not only do you stop paying extra money when you buy your own phone, but you can choose from a huge assortment and get exactly what you want, whether it's a French Provincial reproduction or a Mickey Mouse phone for the kids.

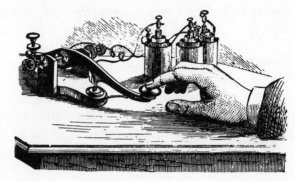

PHONE CONTROL SYSTEMS

92 Marcus Ave.
Garden City Park, NY 11040
(516) 248-3636
Information: price quote
Brochure: free
Goods: name brand
Shipping: extra
Sales Tax: NY residents
Payment: check, MO
$$$

This company sells phone and office machines. They have brand name answering machines, cordless extension phones, dictating and transcribing machines, a printing calculator, and various devices for the phone such as WATS line extenders, instant memory redialing, "music on hold," and more. They have a 10-day money-back guarantee and steep discounts.

STATIONER.

TELEPHONES UNLIMITED

Box 1147
San Diego, CA 92112
(714) 563-5555
Catalog: 50¢
Discount: 20 to 30%
Good: name brand
Minimum Order: $10
Shipping: extra, UPS
Payment: check, MO,
MC, Visa, C.O.D.
$

One of the best ways to beat the high cost of phone alterations and rentals is to buy your phone and hardware and make the changes yourself. You can install a high-voltage buzzer, bell chime, tone ringer, change a regular phone junction box into a jack outlet, make any phone portable with a portable plug, etc., for less than the phone company charges to do the same thing, and without incurring additional monthly fees. (These practices may be outlawed in some areas, so you should check the phone company's rules before you make changes.) All the phones and equipment Telephones Unlimited sells are brand new. They have phones in almost every style—standard wall and desk phones, a gumball machine phone, a periscope model, Mickey Mouse, French cradle phones, folding phones, cordless phones, and many modern and old-fashioned styles. Prices run from $17.50 to $450 for a cordless telephone, but standard phones are usually under $30. If you're considering changing your service or phone at all, see this catalog first—it could save you hundreds of dollars.

VENUS OFFICE SUPPLY CORP.

396 Broadway
New York, NY 10013
(212) 966-6900
Catalog: $3.50;
refundable
Discount: 20 to 33%
Goods: name, house
brand
Minimum Order: $25
Shipping: included
Sales Tax: NY residents
Returns: within 7 days
Payment: check, MO
$$

Venus puts out a 342-page catalog with thousands of office supplies and equipment listed. The prices given are generally list prices, so you must write or call for a *price quote* on goods in which you are interested. In addition to pens, pencils, files, envelopes, binders, calendars, scissors, reference books, sharpeners, corrective typing aids, rulers, templates, clips, wastebaskets, and numerous other items, they do printing, make rubber stamps, sell office furniture, and data processing supplies. A sampling of the manufacturers they carry includes Oxford, Vernon, Boorum & Pease, National, Acco, Duotang, Rolodex, Wesco, X-Acto, Sanford, Liquid Paper, Faber-Castell, Dennison, Swingline, Dixon, Eaton, Papermate, BIC, Sheaffer, Pentel, Lindy, etc. Although the discounts here are less than other office supply firms, the selection is one of the best. This will be your source for all those hard-to-find items.

WALDNER'S

222 Old Country Rd.
Mineola, NY 11501
(212) 895-1621

Waldner's has a whole array of office supplies and equipment that it sells in closeouts for up to 50% off list price. You can call or write to them with requests for specific items, which may or may

WALDNER'S

Information: inquire
Discount: up to 50%
Goods: name brand
Minimum Order: $10
Shipping: extra, UPS, or
FOB Mineola
Sales Tax: NY residents
Warranty: by
manufacturer
Payment: check, MO,
MC, Visa, AE, DC
$$$

not be available. At this writing, they had an executive armchair by Steelmaster at $63 from $105, Lexan chair mats at half off, and accounting pads, handing folders, transfer cases, and wastebaskets at similar discounts. All the goods are brand name and can be found on sale in stores at twice the price they are here. All merchandise is shipped freight collect from Mineola.

WOLFF OFFICE EQUIPMENT

1841 Broadway
New York, NY 10023
(212) 581-9080
Price List: free
Discount: 20 to 50%
Goods: name brand
Minimum Order: none
Shipping, Handling,
Insurance: extra, UPS or
FOB New York City
Guarantee: by
manufacturer
Payment: MO, MC, Visa
$$$$

Wolff backs up the goods they sell with a 15-man service department that does complete repairs. They sell typewriters, calculators, dictating machines, telephone answering machines, and office furniture. Some of the brands they carry include SCM, Olivetti, Olympia, Royal-Adler, Remington, IBM (rebuilt), Sharp, Hewlitt-Packard, Texas Instruments, Victor, Phillips-Norelco, Sanyo, and Phone Mate. They have a large selection of office furniture by Steelmaster, Cole, and other leading manufacturers. They do price quotes, and also have a free price list—just write or call.

RELIGIOUS

Just as you can buy handicrafts much more cheaply from the countries where they're made, you can get great buys on religious articles that can be very expensive when they are bought in the United States. You can buy beautiful olivewood and mother-of-pearl crucifixes from Israel, meditation beads and Buddhist embroidered scrolls from India, and exquisite statues of Hindu gods and goddesses from Nepal. Catalogs from foreign countries inevitably have a section of goods associated with religion, if only china Christmas plates, creches, or handcarved nativity scenes—check the "gift" and "holiday" sections of other catalogs for these goods.

BHAVANI GEMS

Post Box No. 2731
Bombay-400002

Bhavani Gems sells precious and semiprecious stones, and also sells a variety of meditation beads. See JEWELRY for the complete listing.

THE GOOD SHEPHERD'S STORE

P.O. Box 96
Bethlehem, Israel

This store sells all kinds of religious statues and carvings in olivewood, and beautiful crosses, crucifixes and rosaries. See HANDICRAFTS AND NATIVE PRODUCTS for complete listing.

THE NEPAL CRAFT EMPORIUM

G.P.O. Box 1443
Kathmandu, Nepal

The Craft Emporium sells metal statues which are cast in bronze or copper, and some are finished in gold. The images are all of Buddhist gods and goddesses: solemn Dipankar, the Buddha of confession; squat and winged Garuda, spiritual vehicle of the Yogis; potbellied dragon-riding Kuber, the god of wealth; fierce sword-wielding Manjusri, creator of Nepal; and multi-armed Yamantaka, the destroyer of death. There are 36 statues in all, and one of the most exquisite is Tara, the goddess of protection, who is portrayed in several poses. The statues range in price from $2.90 for a 4-inch Buddha to $1,124.50 for a 36-inch tall "foo dog" which is probably gilded. There are Tibetan calendars and pictures of Buddha, Padmapani, and the thousand-armed god of mercy which are done on hammered copper sheets and cost from $5 to $12.50. The Craft Emporium also sells prayer wheels for $4 to $6 like those which Tibetan monks carry while they walk, and Nepalese tantric icons, meditation charts, tantras and chakra paintings, all available upon request. For more information, *see* HANDICRAFTS AND NATIVE PRODUCTS.

THE TIBETAN REFUGEE SELF HELP CENTER

Havelock Villa
65 Ghandi Rd.
Darjeeling, India

The Center sells lovely Tibetan religious scrolls for $110 and $165. These are brocade scrolls that sell for hundreds of dollars in the U.S. They also sell prayer wheels of several kinds. For a complete listing, *see* HANDICRAFTS AND NATIVE PRODUCTS.

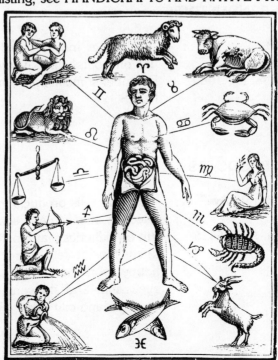

SAFETY
and
SECURITY

It's a sad fact of life in our society that we must live with threats from fire, chemicals, and intruders. These sources will help you deal with the problems.

You will often be able to save money twice. You'll purchase the items you need at a discount, and, further, many insurance companies will reduce your premiums if you have protection devices in your home or office. Beyond saving money, items like burglar and fire alarms are sensible ways of gaining extra peace of mind. There are also safety and security products in catalogs listed in the TOOLS AND HARDWARE and SURPLUS sections.

ALLIED ELECTRONICS

Dept. C-78
401 East 8th St.
Fort Worth, TX 76102

Allied sells components for alarm systems, mainly bells and signals. They also have an Archer photo-electric relay warning system which works on a light sensitive photo cell. For more information, see complete listing under TOOLS AND HARDWARE.

DEFENDER INDUSTRIES

255 Main St.
P.O. Box 820
New Rochelle, NY 10801

Defender Industries sells several kinds of fire extinguishers for use on boats which would be equally suitable for the home. See Defender's main listing in AUTOMOTIVE AND MARINE SUPPLIES.

FIDELITY PRODUCTS CO.

705 Pennsylvania Ave.
So.
Minneapolis, MN 55426

Fidelity sells products for the office, and they also have a good selection of safety and security equipment. There are several lights run on batteries that function in a power outage, fire extinguishers, safety tape, safety mirrors, and first aid kits. If you do a lot of hobby work that involves corrosives, consider their emergency eyewashes and showers. There are also safety cans in which to store gas and oily waste. For further listings, see OFFICE.

MATERIAL FLOW, INC.

835 North Wood St.
Chicago, IL 60602
(312) 421-7111

Material Flow has 36 pages of safety equipment in their catalog for use in factories and institutions, some of which would be useful in schools, workrooms, and homes. There is an emergency oxygen kit for heart attacks, a stretcher for $120, and fully stocked first aid kits for 25 to 100 people that cost from $15.39 to $101.35. Every home workshop should be equipped with safety glasses or goggles—there are 8 models here priced as low as $8.25 a dozen. If you store oil, benzene, naptha, kerosene, or flammable liquid waste at home, consider safety cans for accident proof storage, which run from $13.91 to $47.56. Material Flow sells CO' and dry chemical fire extinguishers in 3 sizes priced from $11.03 to $102.69. Their 5 lb. dry chemical model, good for all types of fires and ideal in a kitchen, costs only $20.45. For hand protection against dirt, abrasives, grease and chemicals, there are 11 different kinds of gloves priced as low as $3.04 per dozen. At these great savings, it makes more sense than ever to provide your home and workshop with equipment and supplies that could prevent accidents and injuries. For the complete listing, see TOOLS AND HARDWARE.

OLSON ELECTRONICS

260 S. Forge St.
Akron, OH 44327

These people sell burglar alarms of several kinds, closed circuit TV systems, and other security devices. See complete listing under AUDIO.

SARGENT-SOWELL, INC.

1185 108th St.
Grand Prairie, TX 75050

SA-SO carries a complete line of safety and security equipment for traffic, home, and industrial use. They have safety cans for all kinds of hazardous materials, emergency washes and showers, goggles, ear plugs, shields, dust guards, safety footwear, emergency lights, alarms, sirens, fire extinguishers, mirrors, first aid kits, inhalators, stretchers, and even a firetruck. For more information, see the main listing under TOOLS AND HARDWARE.

U.S. GENERAL SUPPLY CORP.

100 General Place
Jericho, NY 11753
(516) 333-6655

U.S. General carries some Medeco locks and cylinders at discount prices, plus some fire prevention equipment. For more information, see listing under TOOLS AND HARDWARE.

SPORTS and RECREATION

Hey-Ja! We bought judo *gis* from S&P Imports, and threw each other all over the living room. It was great fun, and at a 32% discount, yet. Then we skateboarded down the hall on an Ampul skateboard at 50% less than retail, and were pleased to see that it didn't scratch the floor.

One of the best sources for fishing tackle and hunting supplies is Robinson and Son, Ltd. They sell all kinds of brand name rods, reels, line, lures, traps, hooks, tackle boxes, books, Zeiss binoculars, clothing, shotguns, rifles, holsters, gunracks, belt buckles, knives, and more. Remember to consult your local laws when ordering any kind of firearm, and treat firearms catalogs as you would any piece of information that could be misused if it fell into the wrong hands.

For great buys on camping clothing and gear see the SURPLUS section listings.

Studies have shown that people who purchase sports and recreational equipment at a discount have more fun.

AMERICAN PULTRUDED PRODUCTS CORP.

**100 West Alameda Ave.
Burbank, CA 91502
(213) 841-0300
Manufacturer's
Brochures: free
Discount: 50% on some
models
Goods: house name
Minimum Order: none
Shipping: $3.00 per
board
Sales Tax: CA residents
Payment: check, MO
$$$**

American Pultruded (Ampul) has an exciting selection of skateboards and skateboard accessories. They sell the complete skateboard as well as the fiberglass deck, urethane wheels, trucks, aluminum and wood decks, and safety equipment: helmets, padded shorts, padded gloves, knee pads, elbow pads, etc. They also sell parts to repair your board. The skateboards are gorgeous colors—bubble gum pink, silver, bright yellow, Hawaiian print, and striped. The wheels are often each a different color, which must make watching whoever is flying by that much more interesting. The people at Ampul say the prices are a minimum of 30% below retail, and some are 50% off and more.

AMERICAN TROPHY AND AWARD CO.

823 Wabash Ave.
Chicago, IL 60605
(312) 939-3252
Catalog: free
Discounts: 50 to 70%
Goods: name, house brand
Minimum Order: $10 net
Shipping, Insurance: free on orders over $50
Sales Tax: IL residents
Guarantee: engraved as requested
Payment: check, MO, C.O.D.
$$$$

American Trophy sells trophies, plaques, and awards for almost any sport, game, or activity. They put out 2 color catalogs, one with goods that are discounted during certain time periods (up to 60%) and another larger one with 50% discounts. You can also get bonus discounts of 10% if you order specific groups of trophies. The trophies and plaques are made of Italian marble, wood, and metal, and are available in countless models to suit all tastes and functions. There are hundreds of different figures available to have mounted on the trophies, including the obligatory sports figures and symbols, plus a canary, an apple, cars, a bottle of beer, a caduceus, a microphone, dogs, a heart, religious symbols, an outhouse, a peanut, and many others. There are a mutitude of different plaques, disk accessories, medals, tiaras, loving cups, and a selection of silver-plated presentation pieces. Not only can you save up to 70%, but in the discount catalog, engraving is free!

BERMAN'S RACQUETS

17065 West Dixie Highway
North Miami Beach, FL 33166
(305) 949-2722
Catalog: free
Discount: up to 30%
Goods: name brand
Minimum Order: none
Shipping: $2.50 per racquet; other items UPS rates
Sales Tax: FL residents
Payment: check, MO, MC, Visa (3% extra for credit cards)
$$$

Berman's runs the largest tennis facility in the state of Florida, and advertises that it's "not to be undersold." They sell professional quality racquets by Aldila, Bancroft, Donnay, Yamaha, Yonex, Spalding, Wilson, Head, Groves, Kelco, Garcia, and many others. They have tennis balls by Penn, Spalding, and Dunlop, ball machines, clothing, and even Gatorade mix. You should get this catalog if you play tennis, if only to compare Berman's "unbeatable" prices with everyone else's "guaranteed lowest" to see who really gives you the best buy.

CUSTOM GOLF CLUBS, INC.

**10206 Interregional
Highway
Austin, TX 78753
(512) 837-4810
Golf Catalog: $1
Tennis Catalog: $1
Fishing Catalog: $1
Discount: 30 to 50%
Goods: house, name
brand
Minimum Order: $10
Shipping: extra, UPS, or
FOB Austin
Sales Tax: TX residents
Guarantee: satisfaction,
on house brand
merchandise
Payment: check, MO,
MC, Visa
$$$**

Custom Golf sells supplies and equipment for both golf and tennis. They carry their own line of golf equipment that is sold under the name "Golfsmith," in addition to every major manufacturer of pro line clubs. They have driving and range equipment, Jockey and Arrow shirts, Dexter and Bata shoes, all kinds of repair components, club materials, tees, spikes, sunsport caps, etc. In tennis goods, they carry nets, ball dispensers, stringing machines, and racquets and equipment by Wilson, Spalding, and Davis. If you play golf or tennis, you'll want to have this catalog before you buy another tee or ball. If you fish, you'll want their catalog for their new line of brand name tackle, also at full discount prices.

FUNCTIONAL CLOTHING LTD.

**20 Chepstow St.
Manchester MI 5JF,
England
061-236-2606
Catalog: $1
Discount: 30% less than
comparable clothing
Goods: house brand
Minimum Order: none
Shipping: $14 airmail on
orders under $100
Returns: on resaleable
items
Payment: bank draft
$$$**

Functional jackets and outerwear are protecting climbers and expeditions from the Himalayas to Mount McKinley with a maximum of warmth and a minimum of uncomfortable condensation. Functional's exclusive fabric construction uses layers of air between the waterproof outer shell, the sandwich foam, and the inner lining. This airflow is what insulates you and helps deter condensation so you stay comfortable. There are coats, jackets, and accessories, constructed with deep pockets, heavy nylon zippers, and Velcro closings. Some are suitable for work, casual wear, and others for camping and climbing. They come in navy blue, black, slate, pale olive, and orange, and are available in sizes for men and women, and a few in "junior" sizes (size charts are included in the catalog). Combine "airflow" garments with Functional cold-weather pile garments and you have protection against wind, water, and cold. Firms like Gulf Oil and Coca Cola use them for their workers, so you know they're trusted. What one customer called the Rolls-Royce of outdoor clothing comes at a Volkswagen price, with $52 for a coat the top price. This is the answer to a camper's prayer—something warmer, drier, and cheaper than down.

GOLF HAUS

700 N. Pennsylvania
Lansing, MI 48906
(517) 489-0707
Catalog: free
Discount: 20 to 60%
Goods: name brand
Minimum Order: $10
Shipping: included
Sales Tax: MI residents
Guarantee: a minimum
of 1 year
Payment: check, MO,
MC, Visa
$$$

Golf Haus has the "absolute lowest prices on pro golf clubs" anywhere. They carry every possible manufacturer including Titleist, Lynx, and Dunlop. They have Bag Boy carts, Dexter and Etonic shoes, and brand name clothing. Any company that claims an "absolute lowest price" on anything should be checked out, and especially for high-priced, pro-quality golf equipment.

LAS VEGAS DISCOUNT GOLF AND TENNIS

4813 Paradise Rd.
Las Vegas, NV 89109
1-800-634-6745
Brochure and Price List:
free
Discount: 25 to 60%
Goods: name brand
Minimum Order: none
Shipping: extra, $2.50
per order
Sales Tax: NV residents
Guarantee: by
manufacturer
Payment: cashier's
check, MC, Visa, AE, DC
$$$$

Las Vegas sells name brand golf and tennis gear. In golf equipment, they carry Wilson, Spalding, Ram, Lynx, Hogan, Powerbilt, Ping, Footjoy and Dexter. The tennis lines they offer include Wilson, Spalding, Kawasaki, Prince, MF Head, Yamaha, Yonex, Dunlop, Aldila, and Trabert. There are also socks by Izod and shoes by Puma, Bata, and Fred Perry. For price and selection, this source is hard to beat.

LAURENCE CORNER

62/64 Hampstead Rd.
London NW1 2NU
England

Laurence Corner carries all kinds of kit bags, haversacks, packs, sleeping bags, tents, lamps, mess equipment, and clothing for camping and hunting. Their prices are very good, and most of the goods are surplus and well made. For more information, see CLOTHING, FURS, AND ACCESSORIES.

PRO SHOP

4550 W. Oakton St.
Skokie, IL 60076
(312) 675-5286: IL
residents
(800) 323-4047: all
others
Catalog: free
Discount: 20 to 50%
Goods: name brand
Minimum Order: none
Shipping: included
Handling: $2.50
Sales Tax: IL residents
Payment: check, MO,
MC, Visa
$$$

This store has a huge stock of pro line golf equipment by manufacturers like Wilson, Spalding, MacGregor, Lynx, Ping, and others. They have club bags by Burton, Bag Boy carts, Foot Joy shoes, clothing by Izod (the famous Lacoste shirts), etc. Since shipping is included, you save even more than the 20 to 50% discount on the goods.

RAYCO

3917 Texas St.
P.O. Box 4034
San Diego, CA 92104
(714) 295-4777
Price List: free, pub.
quarterly
Discount: up to 50%,
plus quantity discounts
of up to 25%
Goods: house, brand
name
Minimum Order: $25
Shipping: free on prepaid
orders
Sales Tax: CA residents
Guarantee: satisfaction
Returns: within 15 days
Payment: check, MO,
Visa, MC, C.O.D.
$$$

Rayco specializes in tennis gear and accessories, and has great buys on closeouts and one-time specials. Their feature items are racquet stringing machines, designed for use by professional stringers or vigorous tennis players who want to save the cost of frequent restringing. Their $98 model is the cheapest in the industry, and comes with all the instructions you'll need to learn how to restring. They also have a combination pickup device/throwing machine, racquets, strings, jumpropes, and more. There are quantity discounts on top of the low prices-2% on prepaid orders of up to $100, 5% on orders over $100, and on up to 25% on orders of $1600 or more.

THOMAS D. ROBINSON & SON, LTD.

321 Central Ave.
White Plains, NY 10606
(914) 948-8488
Catalog: free, pub. Feb.
Discount: 25 to 50%
Goods: name brand
Minimum Order: none
Shipping: extra, UPS
Sales Tax: NY residents
Payment: check, MO,
MC, Visa
$$$

There are close to 200 manufacturers represented in the catalog of fishing and camping goods from Thomas Robinson and Son. There is fishing tackle for everyone from flyfishermen to big game fishers. Twenty pages are devoted to reels, 15 to rods, and 25 pages to sinkers, hooks, lures, flies, and accessories. There are nets, fly boxes, wading clothes, and even an eel spear. Their books are discounted 10 to 40%, and there are hundreds of titles like *Varmint Hunters Digest*, the *Angler's Bible*, and *Crow Shooting Secrets*. The last half of the catalog is filled with hunting clothes, boots, supplies, and equipment. There are almost 40 pages of shotguns and carbines by Remington, Browning, Marlin, Savage, Winchester, etc., plus replicas of old rifles and derringers, pistol kits, air rifles, and a whole section of gun and leather maintenance products. They sell anything associated with guns, from holsters to gunracks, and some goods like mink oil, compasses, hand warmers, and belts and buckles can be used by anyone. The catalog ends with an assortment of fishing and hunting knives, and 16 kinds of Swiss Army knives which should satisfy anyone's need for the ultimate in multi-purpose tools.

S & P OF NEW YORK BUDO, INC.

P.O. Box 2
Depew, NY 14043
(716) 681-7911
west of the Mississippi:
California S & P, Inc.
479 Ninth St.
San Francisco, CA 94103
Catalog: $1.00
Discount: 30 to 40%
Goods: name, house
brands
Minimum Order: $30; 4
uniforms for the discount
Shipping, Handling:
included
Sales Tax: NY, CA
residents
Returns: resaleable
goods only
Payment: certified check,
MO, C.O.D.
$$$

Anyone who practices martial arts will be interested in S & P's selection of uniforms, weaponry, plaques, awards, and books, which are mainly for judo, karate, aikido, kung-fu, kendo, and tae kwondo. There are gis for karate, kung-fu, and judo, in light and heavy cotton. Prices are more than 30% below retail when you buy 4 or more items from a group—a group being belts, uniforms, equipment, or books. The gis are all the Yamatosakura brand which are tailored and sized for Americans. They run from $6.25 to $53.50 a set, depending on the weight of the cotton and how many you buy. There is a full line of protective devices including guards for feet, knees, forearms, knuckles, hands, shins, instep, groin, chest, and face, which is also covered by the quantity discount. The catalog ends with several pages of lethal-looking weapons or pseudo-weapons which justify all the padding. The people who run S & P are all trained in martial arts and can answer questions and recommend the proper equipment. For information on their books, see the listing under BOOKS AND RECORDS.

THE SHOTGUN NEWS

Box 669
Hastings, NB 68901
(402) 463-4589
Order Form: free
Sample Copy: $2.00
Minimum Order: 1 year
subscription
Payment: check, MO
$$

The *Shotgun News* is a bimonthly publication with a circulation of 135,000 that offers "the finest gun buys and trades in the U.S." Sample copies are $2, and subscriptions of 24 issues per year are $7.50 for 1 year, $14 for 2, and $20 for 3 years. The *News* sounds like a good way to beat the high cost of firearms purchased new, and it has a much better selection than the typical secondhand store.

STUYVESANT BICYCLE

349 W. 14th St.
New York, NY 10014
(212) 254-5200: sales
(212) 675-2160: parts
Catalog: inquire
Discount: 10 to 30%
Goods: name brand
Shipping: extra, FOB
NYC
Minimum Order: $5
Guarantee: for life on the
frame, 90 days on parts
Payment: certified check,
MC, Visa
$$$

Stuyvesant has been in business for 35 years selling bicycles and equipment. They carry bikes for children and adults, tandems, specials and closeouts, and accessories like helmets, jerseys, shoes, cleats, clips, pumps, water bottles, etc. They specialize in racing equipment. The brands they carry are Cinelli, Atala, Bottecchia, Columbia, Ross, and Raleigh. These people are very helpful and good to deal with, and can answer just about any question you have about bicycles.

THREE OAKS WORM RANCH

P.O. Box 26
Dresden, TN 38225
(901) 364-3755
Price List: free
Discount: 80%
Goods: homegrown
worms
Minimum Order: varies
from type to type
Shipping: postpaid,
except CA, OR, WA, ID,
UT, CO, NE (these states
add 10%)
Sales Tax: TN residents
Payment: MO
$$$

Three Oaks sends you a price list and an enthusiastic write-up in worm-colored print about their "hybrid Tennessee browns" and "super gray hulas super worms." These are worms for fishers, worm breeders, gardeners, and people who like worms. They also sell worm castings to gardeners for enriching the soil. Along with the worms, they send a method of raising them on a soilless formula. The worms come in breathing bait bags, 1,000 to a bag. $12.50 buys 1,000, on up to $50 for 5,000. Since 12 often retail for $1.00, or 120 for $10.00, this represents a huge savings.

SURPLUS

Surplus is absolutely the best way to save money. In the case of U.S. Government surplus, you also get a chance to recoup some of the money you paid to Uncle Sam this year (if he was better at spending it, you'd pay less tax and there wouldn't *be* any surplus). The goods are not always high fashion, but they're functional and durable, and often made to tolerate more strenuous use and abuse than ordinary consumer items.

ADIRONDACK DIRECT

Dept. WMP
219 E. 42nd St.
New York, NY 10017
(212) 477-2020

Adirondack sells all kinds of furniture, equipment, and supplies for the office, as well as items for the library and school: park benches, picnic tables, bike racks, litter receptacles, lockers, literature and magazine racks, book trucks, and all kinds of chairs and tables that would be suitable for an auditorium, lunchroom, or cafeteria. For complete listing, see OFFICE.

THE AIRBORNE SALES CO.

P.O. Box 2727
Culver City, CA 90230
(213) 870-4687
Catalog: 50¢
Discount: up to 90%
Goods: surplus
Minimum Order: $10
Shipping: extra, UPS or
FOB Culver City
Sales Tax: CA residents
Payment: check, MO,
MC, Visa
$$$$

The Airborne Sales Company has been in business for 35 years and is still going strong, selling all kinds of government surplus at tremendous discounts. Their goods are described by them as "hobbyist and do-it-yourself materials," and include generators, starters, and motors for airplane and marine use, and model cars, boats, planes, and trains. They also have an extensive line of hydraulics, hardware, tools, and strange and unique items only found in surplus catalogs.

LAURENCE CORNER

62/64 Hampstead Rd.
London NW1 2NU
England

Laurence Corner is a surplus store that deals mainly in clothing, but also stocks art materials, camping gear, lab equipment, and some hardware. The prices are very good, and they have some of the bizarre and wonderful items that surplus sources are famous for. For more information, see CLOTHING, FURS, AND ACCESSORIES.

MESHNA

P.O. Box 62
East Lynn, MA 01904
(617) 595-2275
Catalog: 25¢
Discount: up to 90%
Goods: surplus
Minimum Order: $5 cash,
$10 charge
Shipping, Insurance:
extra, UPS or FOB E.
Lynn
Handling: 25¢
Sales Tax: MA residents
Payment: check, MO,
MC, Visa
$$$$

Electronics buffs will have a field day with Meshna's catalog of components, equipment, and hard-to-find surplus items. They have huge amounts of small parts like photo-resistive cells, lamps, capacitors, thermistors, transistors, ceramic disc cups, LEDs, and numerous other items. There are many components for use in computers—digit displays, keyboards, cases, control data power supplies, terminals, heat sinks, memory stacks, etc. And there are pages and pages of true surplus goods, useful and strange, at incredible prices: stereo cabinets and chassis hardware, speakers, a stereo-to-quadraphonic converter for $6, 2-inch magnifying lenses for 75¢, magnets, alarms, a U.S. Navy geiger counter for $35, underwater sonar, mikes, organ keyboards for $13.25, aerial camera lenses for $35, and a giant solar cell for $8.50, to mention just a few. There is even a giant memory drum, sold to the U.S. Air Force for $6,400, at a mere $100—a bargain hard to beat.

RUVEL

3037 North Clark
Chicago, IL 60657
(312) 248-1922
Catalog: $1
Discount: up to 70%
Goods: surplus
Minimum Order: none
Shipping: extra
Sales Tax: IL residents
Payment: MO
$$$

Ruvel specializes in U.S. Army and Navy surplus goods: GI issue duffle bags at $12.75, high-powered binoculars that sell for $250 elsewhere, only $128.75 here, a leather flyer's jacket selling in clothing stores for $200, $125 here, Justrite carbide and electric lamps at wholesale prices, strobe lights that were $85, now $28.50, etc. The armed forces always bought the best, and now you can, too, at savings of up to 70%. Be sure to list second choices, as stock is almost always limited and bargains like these move fast.

TOOLS, HARDWARE, ELECTRONICS, and ENERGY

Our favorite listing in this section is Paul Morris' ingenious heat lamp—perfect for the bathroom or warming yourself while reading on a chilly night. He says it will even heat 3 rooms. Another is Maryland Magnet. Browsing through their catalog, you find yourself dreaming up all kinds of uses for magnets. They have some magnets that are so powerful they need personal information about your use before they will sell you one. Hmmm.

If you fix anything, or make anything, or have a home or boat, you're naked without the U.S. General Supply catalog.

Are you an abrasive person? If not, try World Abrasives. They have products at super discounts that will do the job for you.

ALLIED ELECTRONICS

Dept. WBMC
401 East 8th St.
Fort Worth, TX 76102
(817) 336-5401
Catalog: $1
Discount: to 50%
Goods: brand, house name

Allied sells industrial electronics parts, components, supplies, and equipment. They say their main customers are engineers, teachers, hobbyists, and technicians, but this may be the only place you can readily find knobs that would fit an old gas stove or some strange piece of hardware that holds the vacuum cleaner together. They have wire cable, solid state devices, resistors, transformers, switches, CB test equipment, connectors, relays, capacitors, and even a micro-computer system for under $600. There

189

ALLIED ELECTRONICS

Minimum Order: $15
Shipping Cost: FOB
shipping point
Sales Tax: where
applicable
Returns: 30 days,
authorized only
Warranty: by
manufacturer
Payment: check, MO,
C.O.D., MC, Visa
Resale: necessary for
sales tax exemption
$$$

are also solar kits, solar cells and panels, a solar flashlight, and components for building a whole home solar system. Allied also has a good selection of utility cabinets at good prices, some shop equipment, and a whole section of books on electronics.

BAILEY'S

P.O. Box 550
Laytonville, CA 95454
(707) 984-6133
Catalog: free
Discount: up to 50%
Goods: house brand,
name brand
Minimum Order: none
Shipping: FOB
Laytonville, CA
Sales Tax: CA residents
Warranty: by
manufacturer
Payment: check, MO
$$$$

From suspenders to chain saws, Bailey's carries everything a logger could need. At this writing, they are selling a 100-foot length of Oregon chain for a chain saw for $269 compared to the $500 list price. They have climbing gear, all kinds of loggers' clothing and caulk boots, and books. Their safety equipment includes 3 or 4 kinds of stretchers, and a first aid kit that they say is a hot item—it tells how to treat emergency situations directly, and is magnetized to stick in a truck or car. The logging supplies include sharpening implements, chain saws, specialty equipment, and tree jacks, which cost from $259 to $1,500. And for loggers who move around a lot, there is a portable chain saw with accessories. All orders are shipped the same day they are received. The Baileys are very friendly people and will do their best to help you.

ALBERT CONSTANTINE AND SON, INC.

2050 Eastchester Rd.
Bronx, NY 10461
(212) 792-1600

Constantine's sells woodworking tools and related products: carbide saw blades, finishing brushes, wire strippers, power tool brake switches, safety goggles, machinist's jacks, and fine rules and gauges. In addition to the standard tools, there are also large selections of period hardware for furniture and cabinetry. For more information see CRAFTS AND HOBBIES.

FIDELITY PRODUCTS CO.

705 Pennsylvania Ave.
So.
Minneapolis, MN 55426

Fidelity carries shelving, workbenches, tool cabinets, and parts cabinets, in addition to its office supplies. For more information, see OFFICE.

GILLIOM MFG., INC.

1109 North Second St.
St. Charles, MO 63301
(314) 724-1812
Brochure: 50¢
Discount: to 75%
Goods: house name kits
Minimum Order: none
Shipping: FOB St.
Charles, MO
Handling: 65¢ on orders
under $6.50
Sales Tax: MO residents
Guarantee: satisfaction
guaranteed; metal parts
guaranteed 5 years
against mechanical
failure
Payment: check, MO,
bank draft, C.O.D.
$$$$

Lyle Gilliom began his business in 1946 with plans and parts for one tilt/table bench saw. He now makes 7 basic machines, all based on the original concept of "combining a plywood and wood frame which the customer builds for himself with machined mechanical parts provided in kits." These kits have several advantages over factory-made goods: they are much cheaper, and since you make them yourself you can alter, adjust, and add to the basic features, building a machine for the functions your work requires. The 7 machines Gilliom makes are 9-inch and 10-inch tilt/table saws, 12-inch and 18-inch band saws, a drill press lathe, 6-inch belt sander, and a wood shaper. The kits cost from $46 (sander) to $120 (18-inch band saw), excluding the motor and table assembly. The motors cost from $36 to $68. All parts and the plans themselves are available individually, so you can buy just one piece if you need it. Saw blades, sanding belts, shaper cutters, and home workshop accessories are also available. A reprint of a *Mechanix Illustrated* article is enclosed with the brochure in which the author notes tips on assembling the tools and how to strengthen the tables, so you end up with a tool that's cheap but very well made.

GOLDBERGS' MARINE

202 Market St.
Philadelphia, PA 19106

Goldbergs' has all kinds of things for boat and yacht, including beautiful brass hardware and some fine tools. The brass hardware, which would look fine in a home, is very low priced. There are also porthole mirrors you can install if you get carried away and want a nautical feeling all through the house. For a complete listing, see AUTOMOTIVE AND MARINE SUPPLIES.

GOLDBLATT TOOL CO.

511 Osage
Kansas City, KS 66110
(913) 621-3010

Goldblatt has been in business for almost a century, making and selling "specialty products for the trowel trades and related industries." While many of the goods are at list or comparable

GOLDBLATT TOOL CO.

Catalog: free
Discount: up to 30% on some items
Goods: name brand
Minimum Order: $5
Shipping, Handling: 10% on orders up to $50; 5% on orders over $50
Sales Tax: KS residents
Guarantee: satisfaction
Payment: check, MO
$$

retail prices, there are quite a few products priced the same or less than discount tool and hardware supply sources. There are knee pads from $5.85 to $10 a pair, rugged vinyl boots at $11.95 a pair, trowels at the same prices as the discount houses, levels that are cheaper, neoprene gloves, wallpaper brush kits at $5, etc. Goldblatt also sells several items that can be used for very nonutilitarian purposes. They have ceiling glitter that's just the same as craft glitter in 1 lb. units for $3.60 and $4.15. You can choose from silver, gold, baby blue, red, fuscia, green, royal and multi-colored. For cheap, snappy looking luggage, try their roomy tool bags. They're made of heavy canvas, finished with leather handles and bottoms, and cost from $8.80 to $32.80. You can even use their soft orange leather nail bags as stash bags or purses—they attach to your belt and cost under $10, which is cheaper than most "disco bags."

KARL HEIDTMANN

563 Hemscheid 14
Postfach 140 309
West Germany

Mr. Heidtmann sells fine woodcarving tools at good low prices. He has many sizes and blades to choose from, and the tools are set in hornbeam handles. For more information, see CRAFTS AND HOBBIES.

INTERNATIONAL ELECTRONICS UNLIMITED

225 Broadway
Jackson, CA 95642
(209) 223-3870
Catalog: free
Discount: 30% plus
Goods: house, name brand
Minimum Order: $10
Shipping: 75¢
Sales Tax: CA residents
Payment: check, MO, MC, Visa
$$$

If you know what breadboards, schottkys, common anodes, and tantalum capacitors have in common, you can use this catalog. IEU sells amps, capacitors, diodes, LED's, resistors, sockets, and a host of other electronic components. They have resistor and capacitor kits, IC assortments, projects bezels, soldering equipment, diode handbooks, and much more. They also offer quantity discounts of 10 to 15% on IC's, LED's, and transistors.

MANUFACTURER'S SUPPLY

Box 157-W
Dorchester, WI 54425
(715) 654-5821
Catalog: free
Discount: 20 to 40%
Goods: name, house
brands
Minimum Order: none
Shipping, Insurance:
extra; UPS, PP, or FOB
Dorchester
Sales Tax: WI residents
Guarantee: satisfaction
Warranty: by
manufacturer
Payment: check, MO
$$$

One of the unwritten laws of mechanics is that anything that works will break down sooner or later. Because your chain saw, lawnmower, motorcycle, and snowmobile are not immune, there are companies like Manufacturer's Supply, where you can buy the saw chain, condenser, engine, bearings, sprocket, or whatever it is your machine needs. They also sell service manuals and a good selection of specialized tools to make the job easier. They offer several pages of chain saws, grinders, and sharpeners, plus repair parts. You can save money in the house too by installing a "Magic Heat" circulator on your furnace, stove, or fireplace, which reclaims the heat usually lost up the flue. For more on what Manufacturer's carries, see AUTOMOTIVE AND MARINE SUPPLIES.

BLACKSMITH.

MARYLAND MAGNET CO.

8825 Allenswood Rd.
Randallstown, MD 21133
(301) 922-2272
Brochure: free
Discount: 30% plus
Goods: house, name
brand
Minimum Order: none
Shipping, Handling:
$1.00 to $4.70
Sales Tax: MD residents
Payment: check, MO
$$$

Maryland Magnet sells every kind of magnet you could ever imagine needing or using. There are all shapes and sizes of permanent magnets which cost from 6¢ to $15. There are round magnets, flat and bar magnets, stick magnets that "reach where you can't," and rubber magnets that can be cut by a knife. For $2.25, there is a "job master" bar magnet that can pick up 60 pounds of hot greasy metal. If you have peculiar cattle, you may find their cow magnet useful in getting the herd together, and their magnetic bracelets might become next year's big novelty item (and pull the hands off your watch). Every kitchen and shoproom can use the $2 magnetic tool holder which is identical to knife holders priced at $7 and $8. If you are messy with pins or nails, or want to clear a beach or driveway of hazardous bits of scrap metal, their 3-foot-long magnetic sweepers will make the job a breeze. There are a multitude of uses for magnets, and one for every purpose at Maryland Magnet.

MASTER MECHANICS

P.O. Box A
Burlington, WI 53105
(414) 763-3282
Catalog: 25¢
Discount: 10 to 40%
Goods: house, name
brand
Minimum Order: $5
Shipping: extra, UPS or
FOB Burlington
Sales Tax: WI residents,
4%
Returns: within 10 days
Payment: check, C.O.D.
$$$

Master Mechanics sells generator sets, winches, jacks, pumps, motors, welders, and all kinds of hand and power tools. They manufacture their own generators and can save you up to 40% over comparative retail prices.

TURNER.

MATERIAL FLOW, INC.

835 North Wood St.
Chicago, IL 60622
(312) 421-7111
Catalog: free
Discount: to 40%
Goods: house name
brand
Minimum Order: varies,
but reasonable
Shipping: FOB point of
origin
Guarantee: unconditional
Payment: check
$$

Material Flow sells equipment for warehouses, institutions, and industry. They have everything from 3-inch wheels to relocatable plant offices which can be set up within a matter of hours. Their catalog illustrates stockroom ladders, workbenches, cabinets, parts bins, shelves, mercury vapor bulbs, handtrucks, drum racks, safety equipment, line striping machines, dust collectors, air guns, conveyors, boom cranes, storage cabinets, wheels and casters, tarps, folding gates, wastecans, and lockers. Prices are low, and even lower after the quantity discounts. There are workbenches starting at $31.40, hydraulic jacks for $35.35, wheel chocks at $11.00, a spotlight for $15, lockers for $40.30, and 32-gallon wastecan liners as low as 7¢ each. Many of the items can be used in the home, and some in schools and institutions (lockers, lunchroom tables, etc.). For further listings, see HOME and SAFETY.

MORRIS WELDING SERVICE

1070 Inner Drive
Schenectady, NY 12303
Information: by inquiry
Savings: 150 gallons of
heating oil per year

Paul Morris is an inventor who gained fame for his energy efficient welder, but has turned to heat production—driven, most likely, by the high cost of heating oil. He has come up with a heat lamp that can save about 150 gallons of heating oil a season at a cost of less than $9.00 a month to operate. The lamp costs

MORRIS WELDING SERVICE

(@$.50 per gal., this is
$100.00 a season)
Goods: exclusive,
original
Minimum Order: none
Shipping: inquire
Handling, Insurance,
Sales Tax, Payment:
inquire
$$$

$26.50, is 14½ inches high, and uses 2 ordinary light bulbs inside a tube. If you are interested in the heat lamp, write to him for information and specifications.

PYRAMID PRODUCTS

3736 South 7th Ave.
Phoenix, AZ 85041
(602) 276-5365
Brochure: free
Discount: 30% plus over
cost of foundry services
Goods: house brand
Minimum Order: none
Shipping: FOB Phoenix
Sales Tax: AZ residents
Payment: check, MO
$$$

Any hobbyst, artisan, or mechanic who works with metal or metal parts and has occasion to use the services of a commercial foundry should consider buying a small foundry and doing it himself at a fraction of the cost. Pyramid foundries use sand molds and can be run on natural, manufactured propane or butane gas. They come in 5 sizes, from a 3 lb. metal capacity to 53 lbs., and cost $140 to $255. Each foundry set includes the furnace chamber and lid, electric motor, a blower-mixer, blower tube, flexible hose, crucible tongs, flask, sand, flour silica, a high-grade silicon carbide crucible, and an instruction booklet. Replacement parts, extra sand and silico, pouring shanks to use with the crucibles when pouring metals, and pyrometers that gauge the temperature of the molten (nonferrous) metals are also available. In addition to duplicating tools, models, and parts, the foundries can be used by artists, sculptors, and jewelers to cast their work.

SARGENT-SOWELL, INC.

1185 108th St.
Grand Prairie, TX 75050
(800) 527-2450: all states
except AL, HA, TX
(800) 492-4200: TX
residents
(214) 647-1525: others,
collect
Catalog: $5, published
twice a year
Discount: up to 30%
Goods: name, house
brand

SA-SO's 400-page catalog has a little of everything for municipal, commercial, and industrial use. They have over 60 pages of every kind of sign you could ever need or want, and they will also make signs up for you. They have die-cut letters, stencils, building letters, traffic signs, safety cones, barricades, line markers, voting booths, clocks, padlocks, files, office furniture, globes, fake grass matting, ceiling fans, instant offices, fountains, etc. They also have a large selection of goods for law enforcement officers (many of which can't be sold to unqualified customers). Among the more interesting items are the training targets at 15¢ each, "Instant Drunk" tests for $2.10 (see if you're sober enough to drive), and a 2-foot plastic marijuana plant, for the rare law enforcement agent who has never seen a live one, for $10.95. SA-SO has more

SARGENT-SOWELL, INC.

Minimum Order: none
Shipping: extra, UPS or
FOB Point of
manufacture
Sales Tax: TX residents
Payment: check, MO,
MC, Visa
$$$

things than it would ever be possible to list here, but let it suffice to say that the catalog is definitely worth $5. For information on their safety equipment, see SAFETY.

U.S. GENERAL SUPPLY CORP.

100 General Place
Jericho, NY 11753
(516) 333-6655
Catalog: $1.00,
refundable additional
catalogs 50¢ each
Discount: to 37%
Goods: brand, house
name
Minimum Order: None
Shipping: extra
Sales Tax: NY State
residents
Returns: within 30 days
on unused merchandise
only
Guarantee: unconditional
Payment: check, MO,
MC, Visa
$$$

This company has 6,246 items at "rock bottom prices," mainly tools, machinery, and hardware, but also things like used telephones, car maintenance supplies, filing cabinets, scales, binoculars, lawn and garden care supplies, 12 kinds of scissors, a blood pressure kit, and BB guns. Most of the tools and hardware are name brands: Black and Decker, Stanley, Unibraze, Skil, Rockwell, Arco, Milwaukee, Wen, Electro, Dremel, Toolkraft, and more. Almost every item is illustrated by a line drawing, and all vital information and specifications are included. Both the suggested retail price and their discount price are listed, so you can figure your savings. For futher listings of what U.S. General sells, see AUTOMOTIVE AND MARINE SUPPLIES; FARM AND GARDEN; SAFETY; CRAFTS AND HOBBIES; and MEDICAL AND SCIENTIFIC.